Entrepreneurship, Investment and Spatial Dynamics

NEW HORIZONS IN REGIONAL SCIENCE

Series Editor: Philip McCann, *Professor of Economics, University of Waikato, New Zealand and Professor of Urban and Regional Economics, University of Reading, UK*

Regional science analyses important issues surrounding the growth and development of urban and regional systems and is emerging as a major social science discipline. This series provides an invaluable forum for the publication of high quality scholarly work on urban and regional studies, industrial location economics, transport systems, economic geography and networks.

New Horizons in Regional Science aims to publish the best work by economists, geographers, urban and regional planners and other researchers from throughout the world. It is intended to serve a wide readership including academics, students and policymakers.

Titles in the series include:

Entrepreneurship, Investment and Spatial Dynamics

Lessons and Implications for an Enlarged EU

Edited by

Peter Nijkamp
Department of Spatial Economics, Free University Amsterdam, The Netherlands

Ronald L. Moomaw
Spears School of Business, College of Business Administration, Oklahoma State University, USA

Iulia Traistaru-Siedschlag
Economic and Social Research Institute (ESRI), Dublin, and Center for European Integration Studies (ZEI), University of Bonn, Germany

NEW HORIZONS IN REGIONAL SCIENCE

Edward Elgar
Cheltenham, UK • Northampton, MA, USA

Published by
Edward Elgar Publishing Limited
Glensanda House
Montpellier Parade
Cheltenham
Glos GL50 1UA
UK

Edward Elgar Publishing, Inc.
136 West Street
Suite 202
Northampton
Massachusetts 01060
USA

A catalogue record for this book
is available from the British Library

Library of Congress Cataloguing in Publication Data

Entrepreneurship, investment and spatial dynamics : lessons and
Implications for an enlarged EU / edited by Peter Nijkamp, Ronald L.
Moomaw, and Iulia Traistaru-Siedschlag.
        p. cm. – (New horizons in regional science series)
    Includes bibliographical references.
1. Entrepreneurship–European Union countries. 2. Investments–European
Union countries. 3. European Union countries–Economic conditions–Regional
Disparities. 4. European Union countries–Economic Integration. I.
Nijkamp, Peter. II. Moomaw, Ronald L. III. Traistaru-Siedschlag, Iulia. IV. Series: New
horizons in regional science.
    HB615.E6344 2006
    330.94–dc22

                                                        2006040019

ISBN-13: 978 1 84542 451 0
ISBN-10: 1 84542 451 4

Printed and bound in Great Britain by MPG Books Ltd, Bodmin, Cornwall

Contents

Editors

Peter Nijkamp is Professor in regional and urban economics and in economic geography at the Free University, Amsterdam. His main research interests cover plan evaluation, multicriteria analysis, regional and urban planning, transport systems analysis, mathematical modelling, technological innovation and resource management. In the past years he has focused his research in particular on quantitative methods for policy analysis, as well as on behavioural analysis of economic agents. He has a broad expertise in the area of public policy, services planning, infrastructure management and environmental protection. In all these fields he has published many books and numerous articles. He is member of editorial boards of more than 20 journals. He has been visiting professor in many universities all over the world. He is past president of the European Regional Science Association and of the Regional Science Association International. He is also fellow of the Royal Netherlands Academy of Sciences, and is immediate past vice-president of this organisation. Since June 2002 he has served as president of the governing board of the Netherlands Research Council (NWO). Also, he is president of the European Heads of Research Councils (EuroHORCs) as from 2005.

Ronald L. Moomaw is the Associate Professor of Business Administration and Professor and Head, Department of Economics and Legal Studies in Business in the Spears School of Business, Oklahoma State University. His main research interests are in the spatial dimensions of productivity, the effects of economic freedom on economic performance, and regional economic development. He is an editor of the *Review of Regional Studies* and on the editorial board of the *Journal of Regional Science*. He has published in the *Quarterly Journal of Economics*, the *Journal of Urban Economics*, the *Journal of Regional Science*, *Regional Science and Urban Economics*, and the *Southern Economic Journal*, among others. He has served on the faculty of the University of Virginia, visited at the University of British Columbia and been a senior research associate at the Urban Institute and Center for European Integration Studies (ZEI) of the University of Bonn.

Iulia Traistaru-Siedschlag is Head of Centre for International Macroeconomic Analysis, The Economic and Social Research Institute (ESRI), Dublin, and Senior Researcher at the Center for European Integration Studies (ZEI) of the University of Bonn. Her key areas of expertise include the economics of European integration, international trade, open economy macroeconomics, intra-national macroeconomics and applied econometrics. She is currently scientific co-ordinator of the research program at ZEI on 'European Integration, Structural Change and Adjustment to Shocks' which includes research projects, policy advice and the co-ordination of a European network of researchers and policy makers. She has been a consultant to the European Commission, European Central Bank, World Bank, Inter-American Development Bank and the World Economic Forum.

Contributors

Udo Brixy, Institute for Employment Research, Nürnberg

Victoria Burke, University of Kentucky

Andrzej Cieślik, Warsaw University

Daniela Luminita Constantin, Academy of Economic Studies of Bucharest

Ronald A. Fleming, University of Kentucky

Seyit Köse, Abant Ýzzet Baysal University

Maira Lescevica, Latvia University of Agriculture (LUA) and Vidzeme University College (VUC)

Ronald L. Moomaw, Oklahoma State University

Michael Niese

Peter Nijkamp, Free University Amsterdam

Fazia Pusterla, ISLA, University 'Luigi Bocconi', Milan

Michael Ryan, Western Michigan University

Eric A. Scorsone, Michigan State University

Margarita Somov, University of Kentucky

Balint Toth, Free University Amsterdam

Iulia Traistaru-Siedschlag, ESRI, Dublin and ZEI, University of Bonn

Marina van Geenhuizen, Delft University of Technology

Hasan Vergil, Zonguldak Karaelmas University

Preface

In our present world we witness an intense interest in economic growth, innovation and knowledge usage. The concept of a knowledge society can become very much 'en vogue'.

This book offers new empirical evidence regarding the spatial dimension of investment, entrepreneurship and knowledge spillovers with the aim to draw lessons and policy implications for growth prospects in the recently enlarged European Union (EU). These subjects are addressed in both individual and cross-country analyses using innovative methodologies and novel modelling efforts.

The eleven chapters included in this book are the result of recent research undertaken by a research network initiated and coordinated by the Center for European Integration Studies (ZEI) of the University of Bonn in Germany on regional production structures, growth and convergence in the context of European integration. A number of these chapters were presented at a conference on 'European integration, regional convergence, location of industrial activity and labour market adjustment', hosted by the Center for European Studies of the University 'Alexandru Ioan Cuza' of Iasi in Romania. We gratefully acknowledge the financial support from the 5th Research and Technological Development Framework Programme of the European Community and from the Center for European Integration Studies of the University of Bonn. This conference brought together established and young researchers as well as policy makers who discussed issues that have recently attracted heightened interest, such as regional growth and patterns and convergence/divergence, regional specialization and concentration of industrial activity, foreign direct investment and regional development, monetary integration and fiscal transfers, local culture and the labour markets, local networks of small and medium size enterprises, and regional policy experiences.

The novelty of this book consists of its focus on the interaction of investment, entrepreneurship and knowledge spillovers for understanding the spatial dimension of growth. In addition, this book provides new empirical evidence on these issues using unique data sets, in particular from the EU accession countries.

We wish to thank the contributing authors for their efforts in following our editorial deadlines and guidelines. We are also grateful to many colleagues for stimulating discussions during various seminars, workshops, conferences, and informal meetings. In particular, we thank Jürgen von Hagen, Director of the Center for European Integration Studies of the University of Bonn, for his constant encouragement and support for this book project. Finally, we wish to thank Hadya Eisfeld for her excellent editorial assistance.

Peter Nijkamp, Department of Spatial Economics, Free University
Amsterdam
Ronald L. Moomaw, College of Business Administration, Oklahoma State
University
Iulia Traistaru-Siedschlag, The Economic and Social Research Institute,
(ESRI), Dublin, and Center for European Integration Studies (ZEI),
University of Bonn

PART I

OVERVIEW

1. Spatial Patterns of Entrepreneurship and Investment: Lessons and Implications for the Enlarged European Union

Peter Nijkamp, Ronald L. Moomaw and Iulia Traistaru-Siedschlag

1.1 INTRODUCTION

Enlargement of the European Union *ipso facto* increases economic diversity and more particularly inequality among countries and regions of the union, making cohesion among countries and regions more difficult. Attempts to reduce this inequality through economic growth require a proper understanding of the interaction of investment, knowledge spillovers and entrepreneurship. The collection of studies in this volume provides information relevant for understanding this interaction. In this introductory chapter, we provide background information pertinent to these economic and policy issues and an overview of the chapters in the present volume.

1.2 ENTREPRENEURS AND REGIONAL CLUSTERS

The standard economic wisdom on regional economic convergence is rather straightforward. A neoclassical growth model applied to regions or states within the EU would imply that low-wage areas would attract capital from and export labor to the high-wage areas. As this process continues, the wage rate would rise in the former and fall in the latter, and the return to capital would do the opposite, leading to a convergence in wages and returns to capital. European spatial economies have experienced and are experiencing greater economic integration. This greater integration, implying greater mobility of labor and capital, would in the neoclassical view facilitate the predicted convergence.

This model, however, relies on several critical and restrictive assumptions that may not be satisfied or may be satisfied only in the long run. One such assumption is that of constant returns to scale in production. Increasing returns, for instance, might result in the high-wage region attracting both labor and capital, thus leading to divergence. In the extreme, all mobile resources – labor – from the low-wage region are attracted to the high-wage region. Absolute cost differences are another reason for one region to attract most resources from another region. These cost differences could be resource-based – think of the sparse economic activity in northern Sweden – or they could exist because one region is unable to access the same production function as another region – think of the productivity differences between the German Democratic Republic and the Federal Republic of Germany. Consequently, German reunification without changing the economic structure could have resulted in a massive movement of mobile resources to the Federal Republic. As Krugman has pointed out, absolute disadvantages in activities need not cause a country to lose its population because of factor mobility; it is saved by comparative advantage. A region with absolute disadvantages, however, can lose its mobile resources; it is condemned by factor mobility.

Suppose increasing returns are exhausted in the high-wage region but are important in the low-wage region. A situation can arise where the high-wage region attracts labor, but the low-wage region doesn't attract capital incrementally. If a large enough investment were made, increasing returns would make the investment profitable in the low-wage region, but because the required investment is large, atomistic market forces may result in the investment not being made. In this situation, entrepreneurial activity or governmental activity may overcome the atomistic features of the situation through creative risk-taking, finance, or team formation. For instance, suppose the reason for the large required investment is the linkage between introducing a vehicle and introducing the necessary associated fueling system. Coordinated investments may be necessary for both projects to be viable, but there are various methods of achieving that coordination. An entrepreneur with sufficient foresight and financing may start producing the vehicles with the expectation that other entrepreneurs will recognize the potential of the fueling system. At the same time, another entrepreneur could recognize the potential of the vehicle and start developing the fuel system. Both entrepreneurs might act because both projects have great potential. Such joint action is more likely if the entrepreneurs can agree to undertake the projects. The agreement may be informal, but regardless of whether it is formal or informal, it will be easier to reach if the entrepreneurs know each other and have cooperated before. The knowledge and trust necessary for agreements to be effective are more easily developed, if the entrepreneurs are from the same geographical region. Alternatively, one of the entrepreneurs could form a corporation with deep enough pockets to finance the full set of necessary investments.

An important role for entrepreneurs in the discovery process is to determine whether economic growth or economic stagnation is the correct prognosis for a region. They do so by evaluating investment opportunities in a region. That is, the entrepreneur recognizes and acts on profitable opportunities, leading to economic growth in some areas and economic stagnation in others.

The neoclassical model also assumes that information about profitable investments is widely available and the entrepreneurs are quick to take advantage of profitable opportunities. The assumptions regarding information about and response to profitable opportunities may be questioned in the context of peripheral regions, particularly in the enlarged union. One of the functions of entrepreneurs is in fact to generate opportunities and knowledge about these opportunities, but the observed variation in entrepreneurship across countries and regions may result in some regions being more successful than others.

A study of enterprise learning by new private firms in six transition countries – Estonia, former Yugoslav Republic of Macedonia, Hungary, Poland, Romania, and Slovenia – discusses spatial differences in enterprise learning (Petrakos and Tsiapa, 2001). The study identified internal learning (learning-by-doing), learning from the environment and learning from networked firms as three relevant types of enterprise learning. In the authors' view, learning is an interactive process that occurs within the firm as the firm operates, or in interactions between the firm and its external environment, or through interactions with suppliers and customers. To gain an understanding of enterprise learning in transition countries, surveys were distributed to a selection of private firms. Although the sample was not appropriate for drawing statistical inferences regarding spatial differences in enterprise learning, an analysis of the 399 returned surveys leads to some interesting conjectures. One objective of the study was to determine if enterprise learning were more important for firms in the capital regions. If so, we might conclude that entrepreneurial activity will be more effective in these regions. In terms of self-evaluation of their level of knowledge, a higher percentage of entrepreneurs in the capital regions than in the remainder of the country answered that their knowledge of managerial processes was good, very good, or excellent. Similarly, entrepreneurs in the capital regions were somewhat more likely to have introduced different product types, expanded their product line and to have introduced advanced equipment, suggesting a somewhat more entrepreneurial spirit.

The responses in the above-mentioned survey also suggested that firms in the capital region were better situated to take advantage of learning-by-doing. Capital-region entrepreneurs tended to be younger, they and their employees tended to better educated, and their firms were more likely to have formal research and development activities and staff engaged in product design. Not surprisingly, the firms in the capital regions were located in larger cities and thus more likely to have learned from their environment. Indeed, a greater percentage of firms in the capital regions reported learning interactions with universities, research centers, banks, and so on. than did firms in other regions. Being in capital regions and larger cities, these firms are in a diverse environment that provides urbanization economies or what might be termed Jacobs externalities. Firms outside the capital regions, particularly those in regions bordering the EU-15, on the other hand, appear to gain more from interactions with other local firms. A higher percentage of firms outside the capital regions reported potential or actual cooperation with other local firms with regard to production, marketing, or supplies, in contrast to firms in the capital regions, which were more likely to report such activity with firms located elsewhere. In other words, firms outside the capital regions appeared to rely more on local networks or clustering with other local firms, which provides an example of localization economies or what might be termed Marshall–Arrow–Romer (MAR) externalities. These networks of firms generating localization economies are sometimes called regional clusters.

The importance of regional clusters is stressed in a report to the European Commission entitled *Regional Clusters in Europe* (Observatory, 2002b). This report proposes the following definitions for clustering concepts (Observatory, 2002b, p. 14):

1. Regional cluster – 'A concentration of "interdependent" firms within the same or adjacent industrial sectors in a small geographical area.'
2. Regional innovation network – 'More organised co-operation (agreement) between firms, stimulated by trust, norms and conventions, which encourages firms' innovation activity.'
3. Regional innovation system – 'Co-operation also between firms and different organisations for knowledge development and diffusion.'

These concepts have been developed to help understand how a network of smaller firms might yield greater profits and better economic performance than would a similar collection of firms bound together by common ownership. The ideal types might be a Japanese keiretsu, an Italian manufacturing district, or the Silicon Valley. In these networks, firms coordinate through markets and through explicit and implicit long-term contracts. The relevance of regional clusters for entrepreneurship, information and investment follows from the fact that many of them develop spontaneously, as entrepreneurs, inspired by their knowledge of markets and their unique knowledge of opportunities in their local area, establish new small firms (Hayek, 1945). The entrepreneurs recognize that they interact with their fellows in mutually beneficial ways. In particular, they may share information about the market and production processes, and they may rely on each other as customers and suppliers. The initial investment generates a virtuous cycle of increasing information, profitability and investment.

The report (Observatory, 2002b, p. 15) describes the development of a cluster in the following stylized steps:

1. Formation of pioneer firms often based on specific local knowledge, followed by new firm spin-offs.
2. Creation of a set of specialised suppliers and service firms, and a specialised labour market.
3. Formation of new organisations that serve cluster firms.
4. Attraction of outside firms, skilled workers, and fertile grounds for new local companies.
5. Creation of non-market relational assets that foster local circulation of information and knowledge.

The key is the initial establishment of a profitable firm based on the knowledge that entrepreneurs have of their local environment. It may be that someone recognizes that the local labor force has particular skills with machine tools that would be easily transferable to the production of, say, a new-style robot. Or it might be that, by happenstance, a new product is developed in a university laboratory. The entrepreneur may recognize that it is important to keep close ties with the university community and that it would be easy to attract highly skilled workers to the area. From this start, an employee may recognize that she could provide an essential part to the process more cheaply as an independent entrepreneur. She might then establish a new supplier firm that sells parts to the original firm. And so it goes. The regional cluster is established with individual firms in the cluster taking advantage of localization economies. As the cluster grows, the firms may reach more sophisticated agreements that could involve setting up joint ventures to engage in research. Thus, the regional cluster evolves into a regional innovation network. At some point nongovernmental organizations or governments may collaborate with the private firms to promote research and innovation – the establishment of a regional innovation system.

1.3 FIRM BIRTH RATES, REGIONAL CLUSTERS, AND EMPLOYMENT GROWTH

Regional economic structures are always in flux, and usually exhibit a high degree of dynamics in terms of firms or workers. This section summarizes some of what we know about the establishment or birth of new firms. We relate information about new firms to our discussion of regional clusters. Birth rates of new firms for most of the EU and accession countries are presented and discussed in the Observatory of European SMEs report on Business Demography in Europe (Observatory, 2002a). Although these birth rates must be viewed with caution because the data are not harmonized across countries, the huge variability noted in the birth rates is probably accurate. Firm birth rates can be expected to differ across countries and regions because of different economic structures, different aggregate economic performance – income, population, and employment growth – and different attitudes and culture. Differences in entrepreneurship provide another source of varability.

In a multipart study of firm birth rates across labor market regions[1] in the United States, Acs and Armington (for representative examples see Acs and Armington, 2003a, 2003b; Armington and Acs, 2000) are providing important new information about entrepreneurship. In their study of the creation of new firms, they test for both the causes and consequences of differences in birth rates and by implication differences in entrepreneurship. They define the firm birth rate as the number of new firms per 1000 people in the labor force. Their study is based on longitudinal data on an annual basis from the U.S. Bureau of Census for the universe of US private business establishments with employees. By tracking the firms over time, the database allows researchers to observe births and deaths of enterprises. In their study of the birth rates of service firms, they first note the large regional variability in the United States (Acs and Armington, 2003b). The 20 labor market areas with the highest birth rates had an average birth rate three times that of the 20 areas with the lowest rates. These differences in the United States and the apparent previously noted differences in the European Union call for some explanation. Their working hypothesis is that variations across labor market regions of the United States in human capital and in new knowledge generated from existing enterprises are important determinants of the variations in the firm birth rates. They test this hypothesis econometrically with multiple regression analysis that permits them to hold constant other variables, while trying to isolate the effect of human capital and knowledge spillovers.

Clearly, the overall regional economy influences the birth rate of new firms, and the authors introduce variables to control that influence.

Population growth and income growth are included in the econometric model and are found to have the expected positive effect on birth rates. The unemployment rate is included in the model on the grounds that labor-market conditions will influence the choice between working for oneself (creating a new firm) and working for others. The results for this variable are mixed, as it has a positive coefficient in some time periods and a negative coefficient in others. Two variables that have a negative effect on firm formation are the average size of all establishments (employment) and the number of private business establishments per capita. The former suggests small establishments are more likely to be joined by and have local interactions with new small establishments, whereas large establishments will be more vertically integrated – fewer interactions with neighborhood firms. Furthermore, an increase in the number of all-industry establishments per capita dampens new firm formation, perhaps because it implies that a larger percentage of likely entrepreneurs have already established their own businesses.

Acs and Armington's hypotheses that human capital endowments and local spillovers of knowledge are positively associated with entrepreneurship are supported. Startups are positively associated with the proportion of adults that have a university degree and surprisingly with the proportion of adults that have not finished high school. The authors suggest the latter result may reflect the demands for unskilled labor that are generated by new firms.

For our purposes, the results with regard to the number of service establishments and overall population are the most relevant. The number of service establishments per 1000 members of the labor force, an indicator of knowledge spillovers or, more generally, of localization externalities is positively associated with the firm birth rate. Furthermore, the population of the labor market area, an indicator of urbanization economies, is also associated positively with it. In short, this extensive study of the formation of new firms in the United States strongly supports the hypothesis that knowledge spillovers or, more generally, localization and urbanization economies stimulate entrepreneurship and the birth of new firms.

In a related study, Acs and Armington (2003a) find that entrepreneurial activity as measured by the establishment birth rate is positively associated with employment growth in the labor market area. Not only do birth rates differ across regions, they also make a difference. Their approach is to regress annual employment growth rates on entrepreneurial activity (the firm growth rate), industry specialization (establishments per 1000 people in the labor force) and industry density (establishments per square mile) and other control variables. The most striking result is that entrepreneurial activity is positively associated with economic growth, while industry specialization and industry density have negative associations. Putting the two studies together, we find that localization and urbanization economies affect local employment growth, but that the effect is through their impact on firm births rather than some other channel.

1.4   KNOWLEDGE SPILLOVERS, REGIONAL CLUSTERS AND REGIONAL GROWTH

If regional development is the result of a complex multi-hit force field, under which conditions may convergence emerge? Regional clusters of production and innovation with associated knowledge spillovers may be behind some of the regional convergence patterns reported in recent studies of the European Union (Bottazzi and Peri, 2003; Giannetti, 2002 and Carrington, 2003). Giannetti attempts to explain the observed pattern of reduced disparity among EU countries accompanied by increased regional disparities. Carrington takes a different approach to regions. Like Giannetti, she uses NUTS 2 regional data, but in addition to defining regions, she also defines small neighborhoods, which consist of a NUTS region and all contiguous NUTS regions. (She also uses NUTS 3 regional data depending upon availability.) She finds reduced disparities within regional neighborhoods, but increased disparities among neighborhoods. Both studies rely on knowledge spillovers to explain the increasing disparities.

Giannetti (2002) develops a model where each country is composed of two regions, a high-tech region and a traditional region. One country, say A, has a more productive high-tech region and consequently has a higher income per capita than country B. Giannetti's model assumes that the integration of two such countries will result in knowledge spillovers between the two high-tech regions, but the integration does not result in knowledge spillovers to the traditional regions. In particular, the spillover will flow from the high-tech region in country A to the high-tech region in country B. As a result, productivity will grow faster in the high-tech and thus high-wage region of country B. Although her model generates more than one possible equilibrium, the one Ginanetti emphasizes is one where both countries continue to have both a high-tech and a traditional sector. The knowledge spillovers lead to a convergence between the high-tech sectors. The high-tech sector of country B becomes a larger share of its economy. The effect is to narrow the differences between country A and B, while at the same time increasing the differences between the two regions in country B. Giannetti develops and performs econometric tests of these predictions and reports that the results of the tests are consistent with this model.

Carrington (2003) takes a different approach. She assumes that a region receives spillovers from contiguous regions so that income growth in a region is a function of the initial per capita income level in the region and an average of initial per capita incomes in contiguous regions. The effect of income in contiguous regions on the region in question arises from spillovers of physical and human capital. These spillovers are assumed to be greater the greater the research and development (R&D) spending per capita in a contiguous region, other things equal. To introduce this assumption into her empirical analysis, Carrington takes a weighted average of per capita income in the contiguous regions with the weights given by the relative size of R&D spending per capita in the contiguous regions. Upon estimating the convergence model she finds that convergence is occurring within neighborhoods, but that neighborhoods are diverging. The similarity between her results and Ginanetti's results is based on the assumed spillover channels. Carrington assumes that contiguous regions form a neighborhood within which regions converge. Ginanetti's 'neighborhoods' in contrast are formed by regions within the EU with similar levels of technology; her 'neighborhoods' do not necessarily have a geographic component. Like Carrington, she implies that knowledge spillovers are an important part of the regional development process.

1.5 INVESTMENT

Nijkamp (2003) discusses the evolution of regional policies in the context of the increasing integration and enlargement of the European Union. He sees regional policy as moving from the more direct market interventions of the 1960s and 1970s to minimalist regional policies; then, the completion of the single market and the prospective enlargement of the EU heightened interest in a renewal of regional policy. The prospect that either increasing regional disparities or increasing fiscal transfers to relieve regional disparities might hinder the continuing evolution of the EU contributed to this increased interest. The new focus, however, is to reduce the disparities by increasing the competitiveness of lagging regions and countries. This emphasis on improved competitiveness is necessary because the achievement of the single market leaves little room for uncompetitive regions.

Nijkamp emphasizes that the European Union is a network of spatial economies with nodes of innovation and growth. Regional policy, as he sees it, must focus on strengthening the competitiveness of lagging regions by incorporating them more fully into the network. Infrastructure (including education) and innovation policies are key in this effort. Government action to create an appropriate set of infrastructure and innovation policies is not, by itself, sufficient to generate economic growth. The policies, however, may have increased the profit potential for investing in the region. Private investment is necessary to realize that potential.

Nijkamp then discusses two avenues of investment – indigenous industrial development and foreign direct investments. Both avenues presuppose that indigenous industrial development can occur in response to the initial investments. The idea is that under appropriate conditions, the introduction of new business firms into a region can result in a network of new firms based on new linkages.

When local entrepreneurs start new businesses that develop into a network of small and medium-sized enterprises (SMEs), such entrepreneurial activity can generate significant regional growth. It is a particularly strong source of growth if it generates a virtuous cycle of innovation, new establishments, network linkages, and so on. 'Thus, the nurturing of existing (incumbent) business life and the creation of favourable incubation conditions for new business initiations is an important regional development task' (Nijkamp, 2003).

Foreign direct investments can be another important source of regional development. New or existing firms with foreign ownership may be important sources of technology transfer and input–output linkages. A question arises regarding the location of FDI, particularly in the EU accession countries. The latest evidence suggests that the concern that FDI would be concentrated in capital regions and in regions bordering the EU-15 may be unwarranted. Although Dohrn (2001) finds evidence of this concentration, Altomone and Resmini (2001) find a somewhat different pattern. They find that initial investments tended to be located in the central and EU-border regions, but that over time the investments disperse throughout the expansion countries.

Another concern with regard to FDI in Europe has been that the accession countries may not be attracting an appropriate share of inward FDI to Europe. Much FDI in the accession countries, of course, originates in the EU. One reason for the concern about these countries not receiving an appropriate share may be because EU outward FDI to other countries was increasing faster than it was to the accession countries (Resmini and Traistaru, 2003).

1.6 INVESTMENT, ENTREPRENEURSHIP AND REGIONAL SPILLOVERS

This collection of chapters provides new evidence regarding the spatial dimensions of entrepreneurship, information and investment. The first set of chapters deals with FDI in accession countries followed by a study of the effect of EU integration on own-country investment. The second set of chapters treats different dimensions of entrepreneurship, and the final set examines information spillovers, regions and regional clusters.

1.6.1 Investment

Nijkamp and Toth in Chapter 2 provide an analysis of the role of FDI in the accession countries' transition process to a market economy. They apply these general principles to a case study of Hungary. FDI in transition countries provides a catalyst for privatization and employment, while it enhances 'the introduction of innovative production and new production processes'. The two main reasons for the Hungarian initial acceptance of FDI were restructuring and the importance of new capital. Foreign investors created channels that carried a market business and management approach to Hungarian managers, inculcating profit-oriented decision-making. Foreign investors are attracted to investment in these countries by the same forces that attract them to FDI in other countries, forces that would generate increased profitability. Hungary attracted foreign investors early on because of its favourable location, large market potential, its close historical ties to Western Europe, and most particularly its relative success in quickly transitioning to a market economy. As Nijkamp and Toth put it, 'The perception of business risks ... also plays an important role. This risk is, amongst others, dependent on the legal framework and the institutions. In Hungary, the perception of business risk is relatively low'. After discussing the evolution of FDI in Hungary, Nijkamp and Toth discuss the possible effects of increased competition for FDI from other accession countries and the effects of enhanced integration on FDI in Eastern Europe.

In Chapter 3, Cieślik and Ryan analyse Japanese FDI in Europe to examine the proposition that the accession countries are underrepresented in inward FDI from non-EU countries. They argue that Japanese investment in Europe is likely to be attracted to a particular country by its location relative to the overall European market. They measure this location with economic potential, which is simply a distance-weighted sum of each country's GDP. They first regress FDI on economic potential and a dummy variable for accession status. Economic potential has its predicted positive effect on Japanese FDI and accession countries have less FDI than would be predicted on the basis of their economic potential. This would suggest that the accession countries are getting less than their 'share' of Japanese FDI. Adding a variable for past Japanese investment in the country, however, eliminates the negative effect of accession country classification. Indeed, in one regression the accession country effect is positive. Then Cieślik and Ryan estimate their equation with a dummy variable for each country. The results for economic potential and past Japanese investment are qualitatively the same, but this approach reveals substantial heterogeneity among countries in attracting Japanese FDI. Poland, Hungary and the Czech Republic are well above the EU average in attractiveness, whereas most other accession countries are less effective in attracting Japanese investment than warranted by their economic potential.

Pusterla, in Chapter 4, discusses the flows and stock of FDI in Romania in the context of FDI in Bulgaria, Czech Republic, Hungary and Poland. While Romania and Bulgaria have small absolute levels of FDI and stocks of FDI, their value relative to the size of their economy is not very different from the relative values for the other three countries. Her chapter focuses on the profitability of EU firms in Romania with the intent of understanding the evolution of FDI there and of gaining insights about profitability that may be useful in designing policy. The firms are classified into several categories of manufacturing industry, agriculture, construction, services and transport. Pusterla's three most striking results with regard to profitability are: (1) the positive effect of the number of foreign-owned firms in the industry category, (2) the positive effect of exports, and (3) the irrelevance of home country.

The first result is another indication of the importance of agglomeration economies particularly for the smaller firms. These results are similar to those of Cieślik and Ryan regarding the importance of previous FDI for future FDI and presumably profitability. Similarly, the finding that exporting firms are more profitable coincides with the Cieślik and Ryan result that economic potential or location *vis à vis* EU markets is extremely important for the location of FDI. Finally, the result that the location of the home country relative to Romania does not affect profitability shows that the export market and internal conditions in Romania are the chief determinants of profitability.

The focus changes in Chapter 5 from FDI to own-country investment. The issue considered by Hasan is the effect of financial integration on such investment. In his literature review, he demonstrates that in some countries a reason for imposing capital controls, which financial integration effectively eliminates, has been to keep capital in the country and hence increase domestic investment. Thus, their elimination would be expected to reduce domestic investment. Others, as Hasan shows, have argued, however, that the greater economic efficiency that results from financial integration can be expected to lead to increased investment. The empirical evidence is mixed. To provide additional empirical information, Hasan estimates investment function for six Western European countries over the period 1985–2001. He includes in the function deviations from covered interest rate parity as a measure of the intensity of capital controls. For individual countries, he finds that capital controls are associated statistically with increased investment in France and reduced investment in Norway and the United Kingdom, other things equal. Treating the data as a panel and estimating with country dummy variables, he finds that reduced intensity of capital controls – increased financial integration – is associated with increased investment.

1.6.2 Entrepreneurship

The role of entrepreneurship is crucial in considering the effects of EU enlargement on disparities among countries and among regions within countries. One, do the external determinants of successful entrepreneurship exist, in general, in the accession countries? Two, do individuals in the accession countries respond to the external determinants in the same way in the accession countries as in the original countries? And, three, is there a rural disadvantage in entrepreneurship?

Although none of the chapters in this section directly answers these questions, they do provide relevant information. Numerous scholars have examined the external determinants of entrepreneurship. Above we discussed evidence that human capital and development of new knowledge, perhaps from knowledge spillovers, promote the birth of new firms and thus can be considered important for entrepreneurship. As Acs and Armington (2003b) report, holding constant various regional economic performance indicators such as income growth, population growth and unemployment, human capital, localization and urbanization economies are positively associated with the birth rate of new firms. Brixby and Niese examine the external determinants of entrepreneurship with a different methodology. First, they present a shift–share analysis of new firm formation for the 74 planning regions in western Germany. This analysis allows standardization for the number of new firms in a region based on national effects and industry mix. The remaining effect, the regional share of new firm formation, is their measure of the region's entrepreneurial activity.

Their measure of entrepreneurial activity is positively correlated with the birth rates of new firms in surrounding regions (a spillover effect), with the level of human capital in the region, with the proportion of employees in research and development, and with population density. The proportion of employees in small businesses is negatively correlated with the regional share. In a series of multiple regressions that include several control variables, they find that the same factors – knowledge spillovers, population density, human capital and R&D – have positive effects on entrepreneurial activity. To the extent that accession countries and peripheral regions have less favorable levels of these external determinants, they will have a relative disadvantage.

Lescevica's examination of rural entrepreneurship in Latvia takes a micro approach. Her sample of rural entrepreneurs consists of individuals who have consulted with the Latvian Agricultural Consultancy and Training Centre. First her study asks the respondents to identify external and internal success determinants. These rural entrepreneurs indicated that government policies did not seem supportive of their activities, but they also recognized that markets and market institutions were not well developed. A related concern was the difficulty that rural entrepreneurs have in using land as collateral in getting financial capital from the banks. This situation is reminiscent of Hernando de Soto's concept of dead capital in countries where property rights are not well established (De Soto and Litan, 2001). De Soto argues that small entrepreneurs rely heavily on their real estate to finance new activities. As the accession countries continue to develop their financial and legal systems in line with EU requirements, this problem should diminish. Other concerns are with business and transportation infrastructure and availability of raw materials. In terms of internal success determinants, the respondents identify various aspects of management – finance, personnel, marketing and sales – and outdated technology as problems that they must overcome. In short, they recognize that business infrastructure and supply and marketing networks along with some way of accessing improved managerial skills and technology are the elements that could improve their success.

To determine which of these elements are most associated with success, the respondents were asked whether they in fact believed that they were successful. Perhaps not surprisingly, those whose enterprises had larger turnover were more apt to consider themselves successful. Interestingly, those with large land holdings were also more likely to consider themselves successful, although number of employees was not significant. Finally, rural entrepreneurs who considered themselves successful were more likely to be willing to join cooperative societies. It is intriguing that the successful entrepreneurs were the ones that recognized the importance of developing cooperatives, perhaps because they would provide some of the seemingly missing business infrastructure and regional networking.

In the final chapter of this section, Scorsone et al. consider the role of socioeconomic variables in variations in county-level entrepreneurship in Kentucky in the United States. Because it has a large number (119) of diverse counties, the state of Kentucky makes a good laboratory in which to study regional variations in entrepreneurship. The state naturally divides into three regions. The eastern part is rural and mountainous; it is considered part of the Appalachian region. Its poverty rate is almost twice that of the central urban region and of the western rural region and educational levels in the east are substantially below those of the urban region and the other rural region. It has fewer large manufacturing firms per employee, and a higher percentage of its employment in retail, services and the government. In most measures of economic performance the central region ranks as more developed followed by the western region and the eastern one. The east and the west have similar population densities, with the central urbanized region of course having greater densities.

Because of multicollinearity among the independent variables, the authors perform a factor analysis to reduce the number of variables in their primary equations. The variables that combine into a loading called income are essentially socioeconomic variables reflecting education, age, home ownership and poverty. Those that combine into a loading called urban are variables that reflect economic structure and urbanization. They include population density, firm size, percent employed in manufacturing and farm industry, and the county unemployment rate.

The income variable is a significant determinant of the firm birth rate for the east and central regions, but not for the west. This implies that variations in poverty, education, age and home ownership do not affect the birth rate in the west. In the east, on the other hand, the poverty rate and the degree of ruralness inhibit entrepreneurship. Unlike in the central region, counties with a higher percentage of managerial employees have a higher birth rate. The poverty rate inhibits entrepreneurship in both the east and the central regions, and home value and home ownership increase it. The results suggest that in the less-developed region the most rural and the poorest counties have less entrepreneurship, but that this is not true in the west.

The urban variable is significant and of similar value in the three primary equations. Going behind the primary equation the most striking result is that population density is associated with greater entrepreneurship in the west and central regions, but not in the east. In addition, workplace density and the weight of manufacturing in the economy are associated with greater entrepreneurship in all regions. These results confirm the notion that workplace density, perhaps a measure of localization economies or knowledge spillover, and population density, a measure of urbanization economies, promote entrepreneurship. In the less-developed region, human capital – as measured by the proportion of managers in the economy – promotes entrepreneurship. These results are consistent with results discussed above, but more importantly they suggest structural differences between the less-developed rural region and the other rural region. Furthermore the structural differences between the less-developed rural region and the central region are greater than between the other rural region and the central region.

1.6.3 Regional Spillovers

The chapters in this section relate to information and entrepreneurship in the context of spillovers among regions, and more generally in regional clusters or networks. The section starts with Chapter 9, Constantin's analysis of small and medium-size enterprises (SMEs) as they are developing in Romania. Drawing on Armstrong and Taylor (1993), she notes the importance of SMEs in the advanced economies, recognizing their abilities 'to create a diversified and flexible industrial base by creating a pool of entrepreneurs willing and able to take risks, to stimulate competition for small and large firms alike, leading to an enterprise culture, to stimulate innovation'. She describes the emerging network of SMEs in different regions, noting that Bucharest has the most advanced and largest network. Her survey reveals that networking or regional clustering is expanding to interregional and international networking. Survey information reveals that a large percentage of these SMEs have introduced innovations and they interact with other local firms as well as with non-local ones. Interestingly, the firms with some foreign ownership are more likely to have innovated, and the firms that engage in substantive exporting are more likely to network with non-local firms in Romania and with firms in Western Europe.

Kose and Moomaw in Chapter 10 estimate the effect of research and development (R&D) spillovers on regional growth. Kose and Moomaw adapt one of Romer's endogenous growth models to a regional context. They first demonstrate that their estimated output elasticities of labor, physical capital and human capital are reasonable. Another factor that can affect regional growth in their model is R&D activity. They find that private sector R&D within a region promotes growth of the region. Replacing private sector R&D with public sector R&D, they also find that public sector R&D promotes growth.

Their model allows for spillovers from one region to another in two ways. One, it allows economic growth to spill over from one region to another. Two, it allows R&D spending to have spillover effects in other regions. They find that economic growth in one region has a positive effect on growth in surrounding regions. The mechanism of this effect is not established, but it can be expected to consist of input–output linkages and some types of knowledge transfers. They also find that private sector R&D activity has a positive effect on growth in surrounding regions and that public in place of private sector R&D also has a positive effect in surrounding regions. Moreover, even with both spillover effects in the model, the positive effects of both types of spillovers remain statistically significant.

In the last chapter of this section, Chapter 11, van Geenhuizen and Nijkamp examine FDI stocks in the Central and East European transition economies, paying particular attention to institution, cultural, and geographical distance. They use a quasi-experimental approach that classifies the countries as the most advanced in transition as closest to the EU. Close countries include 'Czech Republic, Hungary, Poland, Slovakia, Slovenia, the three Baltic states, and Croatia as a border case'. The countries at 'a large institutional distance are Bulgaria, Belarus, Romania, Ukraine, Moldova, and Albania'.

They note that the countries that are most distant institutionally are also more distant from the EU in both cultural and geographic dimensions. Pairwise comparisons of otherwise similar countries that are classified as close and distant (the quasi-experimental approach) show that distance reduces FDI with the reductions for Bulgaria and Belarus being the largest. Over time Bulgaria, Belarus and Romania improve their FDI standing; in contrast, Albania and Moldova deteriorate.

The chapter proceeds to evaluate the impact that FDI has had in promoting regional innovation systems in the transition economies. A regional innovation system consists of interactions between firms and between firms and other institutions in the development and diffusions of new knowledge and technology. Interactions between firms and other institutions, such as research institutes and the Academy system, were virtually nonexistent under the communist system. With little interaction between the market and the research system, innovation lagged. In addition, firms did not interact in ways that promoted technology development and transfer. In this environment foreign investors and foreign investment have had 'a modest effect on the rise of such spillovers and connected processes of learning and innovation. Most investments to date seem to be in offshore factories, sourcing factories and trading companies, all facing low levels of independent technology development and weak linkages in the regional economy.' They conclude that FDI does not provide an automatic stimulus to the development of regional innovation networks and systems. The chapter closes by discussing policies that could enhance the role of FDI in promoting innovation.

1.7 CONCLUDING REMARKS

Economic integration enhances economic opportunities and generates forces that affect the economic geography of the European Union and its member countries. The accession countries will have opportunities to attract additional direct foreign investments. These investments have the potential to promote technology transfer, including the transfer of management practices. By creating hospitable environments for these investments and perhaps promoting transportation and market infrastructure outside the capital regions, the accession countries may promote economic growth and perhaps reduce geographical disparities within the countries.

An important element in realizing these opportunities is recognizing the importance of entrepreneurship in creating the market infrastructure. Although foreign investments may create opportunities for local suppliers, entrepreneurs must discover and capitalize on the opportunities. By promoting local entrepreneurship and investment, regional supply networks may emerge, and in turn enhance the profitability of the FDIs. This entrepreneurial activity can then stimulate a virtuous cycle, with the initial investment and accompanying local investments serving as a catalyst for the development of a regional innovation system.

NOTE

1. Labor market regions are effectively commuting areas around cities.

REFERENCES

Acs, Z. and C. Armington (2003a), 'Endogenous growth and entrepreneurial activity in cities', Washington DC: Center for Economic Studies, US Bureau of the Census, US Bureau of the Census CES Working Papers No. 2.

Acs, Z. and C. Armington (2003b), 'The geographic concentration of new firm formation and human capital: evidence from the cities', Washington DC: Center for Economic Studies, US Bureau of the Census, US Bureau of the Census CES Working Papers No. 5.

Altomonte, C. and L. Resmini (2001), 'The geography of foreign direct investment in transition countries: A survey of evidence', in A. Tavidze (ed.), *Progress in International Economics Research*, New York: Nova Science Publishers, Inc., pp. 1–36.

Armington, C and Z. Acs (2000), 'Differences in job growth and persistence in services and manufacturing', Washington DC: Center for Economic Studies, US Bureau of the Census, US Bureau of the Census CES Working Papers No. 4.

Armstrong, H. and J. Taylor (1993), *Regional Economics and Policy*, second edition, New York, London: Harvester Wheatsheaf.

Bottazzi, L. and G. Peri (2003), 'Innovation and spillovers in regions: evidence from European patent data', *European Economic Review*, **47** (4), pp. 687–711.

Carrington, A. (2003), 'A divided Europe? Regional convergence and neighborhood spillover effects', *Kyklos*, **56** (3), pp. 381–94.

De Soto, H. and R.E. Litan (2001), 'Effective property rights and economic development: next steps', Brookings-Wharton Papers on Financial Services, pp. 251–71.

Dohrn, R. (2001), 'The impact of trade and FDI on cohesion', background paper for the Second Report on Cohesion, Essen: RWI, April.

Giannetti, M. (2002), 'The effects of integration on regional disparities: convergence, divergence or both?', *European Economic Review*, **46** (3), pp. 539–68.

Hayek, F. (1945), 'The use of knowledge in society', *The American Economic Review*, **35** (4), pp. 519–30.

Nijkamp, P. (2003), 'European regional development policies and foreign direct investments', in R. Domanski (ed.), *Recent Advances in Urban and Regional Studies*, Warszaw: Polish Academy of Sciences, pp. 39–60.

Observatory of European SMEs (2002a), *Business Demography in Europe*, No. 2, Brussels: Enterprise Directorate-General of the European Commission.

Observatory of European SMEs (2002b), *Regional Clusters in Europe*, No. 3, Brussels: Enterprise Directorate-General of the European Commission.

Petrakos, G. and M. Tsiapa (2001), 'The spatial aspects of enterprise learning in transition countries', *Regional Studies*, **35** (6), pp. 549–63.

Resmini, L. and I. Traistaru (2003), 'Spatial implications of economic integration in EU accession countries', in I. Traistaru, P. Nijkamp and L. Resmini (eds), *The Emerging Economic Geography in EU Accession Countries*, Aldershot: Ashgate Publishing Ltd, pp. 3–27.

PART II

INVESTMENT

2. Foreign Direct Investments in EU Accession Countries: A Case Study on Hungary

Peter Nijkamp and Balint Toth

2.1 THE CONTEMPORANEOUS SCENE OF EUROPE

The political history of Europe has been one of wars and conflicts. The idea of a united Europe has almost needed half a century to fully materialize. Tolerance, openness and free market views have at the end been accepted as pivotal instruments to reach freedom and prosperity for all nations in Europe. The geo-political scene in Europe is no longer dominated by military force, but by cooperation and harmonization. Clearly, in an open economy private business is driven by competition, but trust and stability are seen as important factors facilitating a sustainable economic development. In this way, an efficient allocation of resources may be guaranteed without running into the danger of devastating self-centred national policies.

The European integration process is essentially governed by two forces, namely a widening through the enlargement of the EU (horizontal integration) and a deepening through strengthening of mutual interactions (vertical integration). Examples of horizontal integration are: the transition of the European Coal and Steel Community to the European Economic Community (EEC), the extension of the EEC with Great Britain, Denmark, Ireland and Greece, and later on with Spain and Portugal, followed by Austria, Sweden and Finland, and finally complemented with the accession countries. Examples of vertical integration are: development of common foreign trade policies, creation of the Framework Programmes for research cooperation, building of a free market for goods, services, capital and people, or the foundation of a monetary union with a single currency.

Both the horizontal and vertical integration will increase the benefits of cooperation among European countries and regions, by reducing political and institutional uncertainty, monetary and legal risks, or barriers in labour markets or infrastructure, and by offering new economic opportunities through a larger single market, new challenges for innovations and open access to peripheral regions. Clearly, Europe is also facing severe socio-economic challenges, such as cross-border security (see the Schengen agreement), lagging productivity in combination with high wages, or a protected agricultural sector (see also van Geenhuizen and Nijkamp, 1998).

The above-mentioned two types of integration make Europe a unique experiment in the geo-political and socio-economic history of our world. This process has prompted the development of new theories and models on the economics benefits of integration, the socio-political robustness of such major transitions, and the necessary governance structures for such complex democratic entities. The integration of former communist states will contribute to a long-lasting peace process, where security, economic efficiency, technological innovation, stable financial and capital markets, and environmentally sustainable development can flourish.

The recent extension of the EU towards the world's biggest single market (with more than 450 million people) has also induced a debate on the optimal size of a single market (see Kaltenthaler and Anderson, 2001). From an economic perspective, a fully integrated open market will increase the gains of trade and hence the welfare of people. But the real question is one of governance in a multi-country system governed by autonomous states and best restricted by the subsidiarity principle. Consequently, in such a complex constellation the democracy in the EU will become a major issue (for example the position of the European Parliament, the composition of the European Commission, or the issue of majority voting in the Council). The European Commission's White Paper (2001) on this issue offers five principles that should be envisaged in a good governance policy: openness, participation, accountability, effectiveness and coherence. These issues would have to be addressed properly in order to ensure future stability, peace and economic prosperity to all EU countries and regions.

Europe has a great variety of regions with enormous differences in welfare, culture, history, political systems and geo-physical conditions. The regions in the EU have received increasing attention in the past decade and will continue to call for policy interest in the future, mainly because a significant part of the Structural Funds is spent in the regions. Regions have become a focal point of socio-cultural identity, innovative activity and political power. It is therefore no surprise that regions tend to claim increasingly an important role in the complicated European governance structure; witness the well-known statement on the 'Europe of the Regions'. Regions are becoming more and more the spearheads of new economic growth initiatives, for example by mobilizing indigenous forces to attract foreign direct investment (FDI). Such investments are the vehicles through which international access and market orientation leading to regional innovation and development will come about. This chapter will address the issue of FDI in the new acceding countries of the EU, with particular attention for Hungary as an illustrative case. The chapter is organized as follows. We start with a concise description of FDI in general and its relevance for Hungary in particular. The motives of foreign investments – and in particular Dutch investors – will be traced, while an interpretation of the developments of FDI in Hungary will be given in terms of the growth potential of this county as one of the acceding countries for the EU.

2.2 FOREIGN DIRECT INVESTMENT AS A STRATEGIC DEVELOPMENT VEHICLE

FDI is part of international financial transactions. Capital flows can essentially be subdivided into two types of transactions, namely credit type of capital flows in the form of borrowed money and non-credit type of transactions, like investments and grants. Furthermore one may make a distinction between short-term investments and long-term investments comprising portfolio investments and direct investments. Portfolio investments are normally only made for the sake of financial gains – the only aim is to maximize profits on invested money without any regard of or authority in the invested company. In contrast, direct investments grant the investor a more structural involvement and strategic authority in the invested company. Clearly, in the latter case the investor also wants to make money, but the way to achieve this is different because of this involvement in the decision-making process, control and management of the company concerned. As a rule of thumb, it is usually taken for granted that the demarcation line between portfolio investments and direct investment lies in the order of magnitude of 10 percent ownership level. Among the many definitions of FDI we have chosen here the one given by Csösz (2001): 'FDI is a long-term investment in a foreign country through which the investor exercises lasting and direct control in the given economic entity and which usually induces further financial and real investments to sustain the successful development of the business.'

FDI is essentially based on investment in majority- or partially-owned subsidiaries. This may be achieved in two ways, namely acquisition and 'greenfield' investment. In the latter, production facilities are established from the very beginning. Clearly, risks in 'greenfield' investment are different from the ones in acquisition of existing firms. FDI is generally a far-reaching (and less flexible) type of involvement in foreign business, for example, compared with strategic alliances.

The attraction of FDI is considered essential in Eastern Europe in order to pursue improvement of socio-economic conditions. Foreign capital acts as a catalyst for various new developments. It is barely needed in the process of privatization and it helps the creation of new employment (although the initial effect is often the contrary). In addition, FDI enhances the introduction of innovative productions and new production processes. For example, experiences in Hungary indicate that foreign-owned companies spend much more on R&D than domestic ones (see Inzelt, 1994).

FDI plays a critical role in the development of any nation when there is lack of financial capital inside the country. Under such circumstances recruiting foreign investors is a sine qua non for an accelerated growth. This strategy has become a common strategy worldwide, especially among countries in economic transition. One of the countries that has extensively based its new economic and industrial base on foreign capital is Hungary. Since the drastic changes in its economic and political systems, Hungary has attracted relatively the most FDI among all nations in central and eastern Europe. Over the past ten years, more than 25 bn Euros have entered the country in the forms of FDI. This amount makes up almost one third of all FDI in central and eastern Europe during this period. Surprisingly, one of the main investors in Hungary is the Netherlands. Therefore, it is interesting to analyse not only the growth of and motivations for FDI in Hungary, but also the reason for this strong Dutch involvement in the Hungarian economy. We will first offer a concise overview of recent developments in the Hungarian economic policy and the structural reform measures since the major transition in 1989. Next, we will outline the importance of FDI for Hungary and the reason for Dutch financial institutions to invest in this country. Then we will offer a brief statistical account of the forms and the composition of FDI in Hungary, while we will conclude with an exploration of the future development of FDI in Hungary after its accession to the European Union.

2.3 THE ECONOMIC REFORM IN HUNGARY

FDI has been an important source for reducing deficits on the balance of payments of accession countries. Their relatively low cost structure (in particular, low wages and low real estate costs) favoured an enormous influx of FDI. And this, in turn, stimulated their growth potential and competitive advantage. In recent years, however, we have witnessed a decline in FDI in accession countries, sometimes up to a level of more than 35 percent. It is, for instance, illustrative that in 2003 Hungary had an outflow of FDI, to a large extent as a consequence of the rather rapid rise in wages in preceding years. It is thus clear that FDI is only a source of stable growth, if it is supported by low factor (input) costs and an overall favourable investment climate.

From 1956 Hungary was under the strict influence of the Soviet Union. The country had hardly any opportunity to exploit its growth potential and to be at a competitive edge with its neighbouring countries such as Austria. This lasted until 1989 when rigorous economic and political change took place, in parallel with other countries in central Europe. In that year, the economic system started to change from a planned economy to a market-oriented economy. This transition process is of course long-lasting and painful; the transformation process is not yet completed by far, but the country has nowadays a sufficient development potential to become a full member of the EU. The policy of economic reform designed in Hungary after the fall of the iron certain set the tone for a liberal and market-driven economic system which would open up the Hungarian economy to western Europe and which would allow Hungary to remain a gateway to eastern Europe. The new plan was named after the great Hungarian statesman, economist and scientist István Sczéchenyì (1792–1860), and provided a new roadmap for Hungary.

The major economic–political changes in Hungary were facilitated by the significant rise in FDI, which accelerated the structural transformation process. Since 1990, the Hungarian government has pursued building up an open and liberalized market economy and a political system based on western democracy.

During the transformation process, the economic system had to change from a planned command economy to a market economy. One of the main developments in the transition mode was the recognition that an efficient economy could only operate under the conditions of a full restoration of the market. Secondly, the role of economic competition was recognized. To break up the prevailing monopolistic market structure, import liberalization was implemented. In addition, there was a need for deregulation, since the state had to have a less influential role in the market economy. The institutional and legal framework and financial structure of the countries had to be adjusted. And at last, it was recognized that marketization should be combined with privatization in order to be successful (Inzelt, 1994; Lavigne, 1999)..

In the former socialist economy, almost all enterprises were state-owned: a really private sector did not exist. To operate as a market economy, a private sector is necessary. Therefore, privatization was one of the main objectives from 1989 onwards. Privatization may be defined as a legal transfer of property rights from the state to private agents. In a transformation economy, privatization can serve several aims (Antaloczy and Sass, 2001). First of all, privatization forms a new class of entrepreneurs and capitalists. Secondly, privatization returns property to former owners, who often had to give away their property right during the nationalization process. Furthermore, privatization is often combined with more efficiency, which is the result of a better allocation of scarce resources through the vehicle of more competition. Finally privatization generates revenue for the government, which can be used to reduce deficits and debt. By privatization, the welfare and the competitiveness of a country improve, which gives the country a better image and makes it more attractive for FDI. In 2000, the turnover of the private sector as a percentage of GDP in Hungary was about 80 percent (EBRD, 2001b).

The large privatization process was combined with large FDIs in Hungary from 1991 onwards. Many transnational corporations participated financially in Hungarian economic entities, mainly in the form of acquisitions. Hungary has made a rather successful attempt to transform itself into a reasonable modern market-oriented economy (Mihalyi, 2000; 2001). Its entry into the EU will most likely give a new boost to this transformation process.

Case study research indicates that the major motivations to invest in Eastern Europe are cost-related. The most important component in this respect seems to be the low wage level. 'As long as wages are one tenth or less of Western wages, a cost-related investment is always worth' (see Dalmeijer, 1994). Relatively low production costs may also be based on cheap land and cheap equipment. When cost motives dominate, products are usually exported from Eastern Europe. A second group of major motives is market-related. Accordingly, the investing company aims at a location close to (potential) consumer markets. The products are often to satisfy the primary needs of the population, such as from the food industry.

It should be emphasized that the starting position from which companies develop investment plans may be crucial in their search behaviour, negotiation and decision-making on investment. Sensitivity for risk is different between companies performing well in the home market and companies in bad shape (with a downburn in profits) wanting to achieve better results through investment in Eastern Europe. It is also important to note the difference between multinationals, and small and medium-sized enterprises. The latter category is particularly vulnerable, because the firms operate in a small segment (niche) of the market, and have usually little experience in operating abroad.

2.4 REASONS FOR FDI IN HUNGARY

In this section we will first offer a description of the different motivations of the Hungarian state to opt for an accelerated economic growth policy based on FDI. Next, we will highlight concisely the motives of foreign companies to invest in Hungary. And finally, some problems inherent in the use of FDIs will be dealt with.

2.4.1 Main Reasons of Hungary to Accept FDI

After the main economic and political reform, countries in transition were reluctant to accept FDI. They saw the investments as signs or threats of a too large capitalistic influence. But after a while all transition countries turned out to be competing for FDI. The two main motivations for the acceptance of the large foreign investment sums were the need for economic restructuring and the need for capital.

Restructuring needs are generally considered as the main reason to accept FDI. Foreign investors bring in a different kind of management culture and business approach. The formerly state-owned companies were not used to competition, and therefore they did not operate in an efficient and competitive way. Neither innovation nor new technologies were of critical importance in the former period. The foreign investors taught the Hungarian managers to operate in a more profit-driven way and the formerly state-owned enterprise could, by accepting FDI, adjust their management modes to a more market-based approach.

The whole transition process asked for large structure investments. Many investments have to be executed in the development of institutions, infrastructure, the social health system, and so on. By the acceptance of FDI the government was able to obtain a part of the needed capital. The government, receiving cash for shares of the state-owned companies, could invest in the country and decrease the trade deficit. In conclusion, the FDI system was a necessity to make the economy viable and vital.

2.4.2 Motives of Foreign Investors for FDI in Hungary

Many theories have been developed about the motivations of a company to commit FDI. Dunning and Nachum (2000) summarize the reasons for FDI as follows: the sum of the acquired advantages (for example, low cost) and the usefulness of certain advantages (like market potential) have to outweigh the disadvantages (like transportation costs). Besides, the following factors ought to be present in the foreign country to attract FDI: a stable political environment, existence of an operational legal, regulatory and institutional system of a market economy, availability of a proper real and financial infrastructure and presence of an economic policy and structure.

Dunning made a classification of the financial motivators supplying FDI in a given country. These motivators will be described shortly below.

Resource seeking
The potential investor is searching for cheap resources. These resources can be labour, natural resources, knowledge, technology or financial resources.

Market seeking
The foreign investor wants to conquer a new market or wants to increase its market share in a country where he is already present.

Efficiency seeking
The motivation here is to make optimal use of the assets, know-how and technology of the company.

Strategic asset and capability seeking
In this case the investment can contribute to the international corporate advantage or to its national market position.

Escape investment
In this case, FDI is undertaken to overcome regulations of the governments in the home market.

Especially regarding environmental regulations, escape investments are common.

It is clear that these general motives had a particular validity for the former socialist economies. As soon as the reforms in the socialist countries were announced, the big transnational corporations lined up to expand their working field to those countries. Hungary in particular was one of the most favoured nations to invest in. There are several motives for foreign companies to invest their capital in Hungary. The speed and successfulness of the reforms played an important role. The creation of legal frameworks, financial markets and institutions were essential parts of these reforms. Hungary was therefore one of the first transition countries with rising economic and political stability. So Hungary's critical success factors for FDI were already present at an early stage.

Hungary's primary strength for investors is its policy toward foreign investors. In 1988, an act was accepted concerning investments of foreigners in Hungary. The act governs the establishment and operation of companies with foreign participation, and grants special rights and benefits to foreign investors. Besides, for a transnational corporation it is very cost-efficient to operate in Hungary. The highly skilled labour force is on average cheap and also the tax policy is very attractive (with a corporate tax of 18 percent). Secondly, the large market potential in Hungary formed an important attractor; during the socialistic period only uncompetitive state-owned businesses supplied the country. There was no incentive for these firms to focus on quality instead of quantity; there was always sufficient demand. Now for the transnational corporations a whole new market opened up, with willing consumers to spend on 'new' sorts of products. Also the strategic asset and capability-seeking motivation plays an important role. Through the privatization process, it was relatively easy for investors to acquire a strategic position in a given market. During the communist period of the state-owned company, the investor usually got a sort of a monopoly. Besides, there are some geographical motivations; its central location in Europe gives Hungary a gateway function. It is close to Austria and Italy and is easy to access by road and air or via the Danube. The perception of business risks in the country also plays an important role. This risk is, amongst others, dependent on the legal framework and the institutions. In Hungary, the perception of business risk is relatively low. And finally, one can expect a large acceleration of FDI, once a critical mass of FDI is realized; FDIs attract each other. So it seems that FDI has found a favourable seedbed in Hungary.

2.4.3 Problems with FDI

It is clear that the decision of whether to pursue or accept FDI also has a dark side. First of all, for the receiving country, it can be a little bit scary to see large transnational corporations take over its national companies. A part of the economic culture will be lost in this way, especially the stronger parts. A second problem is the difference in goals of a state-owned company and a transnational corporation. The latter operates in a different way, more efficiently, which can result in a large cut in workforce. Furthermore, the Hungarian government was afraid that all profits would flow away to foreign countries. Besides, FDI creates companies that import most of their parts and thus do not help the balance of trade. And finally, well-organized transnational corporations have an enormous lobbying power in Hungary, which could result in inequitable decision-making.

Some problems regarding FDI also showed up for the investor. The investors faced the problem of a totally different culture on the work floor. The working class was not used to a profit-oriented approach. Even the managers of these companies were not motivated, because it really did not matter whether the company was profitable or not. Furthermore, the state-owned companies were not familiar with accounting principles and with using resources in an economical way. The different departments of such a company were in former times not obliged or used to give justification for their expenses, resulting in large spillover and consumption-on-the-job effects. Moreover, the former state companies did not pay any attention to customer satisfaction. During the communist period, all state-owned companies had their own monopoly. The state-owned companies were certain of a given demand and the customers did not have any choice. Under the new market regime, for the foreign investors it was a hard road to change the organizational culture and structure in order to become a successful company. At the beginning, also the language was a problem. That is why the foreign companies often started operating in Hungary in the form of joint ventures. In this way the language and necessary formalities were less problematic. The struggle against corruption, which led to a large waste of money, was however a very hard problem to tackle in the first years after the economic reforms. Gradually, the system of FDI has now stabilized.

2.5 A TYPOLOGY OF FDI IN HUNGARY

FDI is one of the driving forces of the transformation process in Hungary. and can be subdivided into three kinds of investments: a foreign company can decide to operate in another country as a joint venture with a foreign company; they can acquire a foreign company, or can make a greenfield investment (Wright, 2003). In this sector an analysis is given of these different forms of FDI.

2.5.1 Joint Venture

One strategy of combining local and foreign capital is to create a joint venture between a foreign company and a part of a former state-owned company. In this structure the manager of the former state-owned company privatizes a part of the state-owned company. Together with the foreign investor the manager negotiates the business arrangement and the ownership structure. In Hungary many successful firms have been created in this way.

The advantage of this kind of FDI is that it provides the former state company with capital for the daily expenses and investments. In addition, the firm gains easy access to foreign products and foreign markets. These firms have the additional advantage of creating structure of ownership and control, whereby the Hungarian partners effectively control the firms. This structure increases the likelihood of the reinvestment of profits in the local economy and trade with Hungarian suppliers and buyers.

For the foreign investors this structure is a relatively easy way of doing business in Hungary. The Hungarian partner already has the knowledge of doing business in Hungary and is familiar with all the formalities in regard to the state. Besides, one of main problems, the language, is solved. Furthermore, it is less complicated and less laborious than an acquisition or a greenfield investment. One major problem, however, of a joint venture is the non-transparency of the operations in Hungary. Especially in the beginning of the 1990s, there were many cases of fraud and corruption scandals around foreign investment projects by the Hungarian mafia.

2.5.2 Foreign Privatization of Large State-owned Companies

Another form of foreign investment is the mass privatization of Hungarian state-owned companies. This is a more rigorous manner in which to enter the Hungarian market. By the acquisition the foreign company gets full ownership of the former state-owned company. FDI brings new technology, new management techniques, new accounting standards and a new organizational culture into the company. One of the main reasons to acquire a Hungarian company is to utilize the market opportunities. Especially at the beginning of the transformation process, competition was low because all state companies had monopolies. The premium for the acquisition of the state-owned company was favourable most of the time, as the state was not in a position to ask for high premiums.

Furthermore, the foreign company is able to exploit the knowledge of the newly acquired entity. The advantage of an acquisition compared to a join venture is the preservation of the knowledge inside the company. Another advantage of an acquisition is the speed of the potential market gain and ease of the ability to use knowledge of the local formalities and market.

An acquisition has also got some disadvantages. Through the acquisition, the foreign company has to deal with another organizational culture and structure, especially if it has to deal with a former communist state-owned company. This internal transformation process is a long-lasting one and this is one of the main issues which has to be adjusted to the foreign investors' approach. The advantage of the acquisition for the state is the acquisition premium. The state can use this money to invest in the transformation process.

2.5.3 Greenfield Investment

Greenfield investments are investments in new subsidiaries or entities by a foreign investor (Antaloczy and Sass, 2001; Szanyi, 2001). These investments are independent of Hungarian partners. Most of the time, a greenfield investment represents an addition to already existing local facilities in the host economy. It is very profitable for Western European countries to build up manufacturing departments in Hungary. The workforce is still relatively cheap and well trained for the Hungarian economy; greenfield investments are also rather beneficial. New business results in more employment and a higher attractiveness and prestige for other Western countries.

The Hungarian economy has rather successfully tried to attract a portfolio of different FDI schemes towards the country, so that after more than a decade it has a reasonably stable economic structure.

2.6 DEVELOPMENT OF FDI IN HUNGARY

In this section the developments of FDI in Hungary will be described. Special attention is paid to the Dutch FDIs, which became increasingly important for Hungary.

2.6.1 Growth of FDI in Hungary

In 1989 a large privatization project, led by the state Privatization and Holding agency, started in Hungary. In the initial phase of the transformation, all FDIs took the form of foreign privatization, because Hungary started its transformation with a very small private sector. The significant FDI inflows started in 1991, mostly in the form of acquisitions or ventures within the Hungarian privatization programme. In 1995, there was a jump in the amount of FDI, because in this year large strategic companies (banks, energy corporations) were sold to private strategic investors. Most of those strategic investors were large transnational corporations. After 1996 almost all the crown jewels of Hungary were sold and the flow of FDI slowed down.

But Hungary still attracted new foreign investors in the form of the so-called greenfield investments. Many investors did not want to risk the large-scale investments in pioneer projects in an economy in transition and therefore waited for the economy to become more stable. Besides the new foreign investors, there were also follow-up investments of foreign privatized companies. In the year 2000, only a few relatively small-scale privatization projects were completed.

Nowadays about 80 percent of the companies are in private hands. In 2000, FDI amounted to 1.96 billion dollars (EBRD, 2001a). The total amount of all FDI in the last decade is about 23 billion euros. At present, more than 18 000 joint ventures are registered and about 35 of the 50 largest multinationals have subsidiaries in Hungary. In the year 2000, foreign-owned companies generated 33 percent of the Hungarian GDP. The main sectors in Hungary for FDI at this moment are electronics and car manufacturing. The planned liberalization of service sectors, such as telecommunications and energy, will create big opportunities for the investments in the near future.

2.6.2 Development of Dutch FDI

The Netherlands has become one of the biggest investors in Hungary. In 2000, the total FDI made by Dutch companies was about 15 percent of the total investments. Germany (28 percent), the USA (12.2 percent) and Austria (11.7 percent) are the other big investors. From 1998 onwards, the share of Dutch FDI is still growing relatively. Both FDIs by acquisition, joint venture and greenfield investments and buying stocks on the Hungarian stock market have increased. The Netherlands had only a small position in the Hungarian economy before 1998, now several Dutch transnational corporations have large Hungarian branches. Hereafter some of the Dutch investors are described.

Manufacturing sector
With the local subsidiary, Philips Hungary, the Dutch company Philips is one of the leading investors in the Hungarian electronics sector. Philips Hungary consists of 18 entities and is nowadays the fifth largest company and the third largest exporter in Hungary. Philips has already invested a total of 140 million euro, and it continues its expansion with the opening of a new plant in Gyor. The Dutch chemicals and materials group DSM also has several branches in Hungary; Hungary functions as its main port to other Central Eastern Europe countries.

Financial sector
Foreign investments in the Hungarian financial sector are very high. Three Dutch financial companies are strongly present in this sector. In 1996 ABN-AMRO bought the Magyar Hitel Bank. Due to increasing competition the banks were forced to merge to maintain efficiency. That is why the Magyar Hitel Bank and K&H Bank (owned by Belgium's KBC) merged in 2000. Due to this merger, the second largest banking group was created. In the non-banking financial sector, the Dutch companies Aegon and Nationale Nederlanden are active. In December 2000, those companies together had a market share of 16.3 percent and 14.4 percent, respectively, in the insurance sector, and also they belong to the five leading companies in the pension sector.

Telecom sector
In the telecom sector, KPN, the Dutch Royal Telecom Company, is active. With a 62 percent ownership in Pantel, KPN has a very strong position in the Hungarian fixed-line telecom market. KPN also had a 45 percent share in Pannon GSM, the second largest provider in the mobile phone industry. But KPN sold its shares in May 2002.

Food sector

Dutch companies are also active in the Hungarian food sector. First there is Heineken with its popular brand Amstel which is one of the premium beers in Hungary. Heineken is also a popular brand, but is consumed less than Amstel. Heineken operates a brewery in Hungary. Aviko, a Dutch potato company, started a joint venture in 2000, which resulted in Aviko Rt., Vác. Nowadays, this is one of the main companies of the potato industry. Sara Lee/DE has a strong position on the Hungarian coffee market, with its brand Douwe Egberts. A coffee factory of Sara Lee/DE is situated near Budapest. Royal Dutch Numico NV, a company producing healthy food and drinks, also has several entities in Hungary. Unilever has a strong position with several of its brands in Hungary. Knorr, for instance, is one of the popular brands.

Dutch firms have apparently easily found their way to Budapest. Apart from historical links, the geographical accessibility and connectivity of Hungary is very favourable. The country has a good image and a stable political climate, which helps to shape attractive investment conditions.

2.7 PROSPECTS OF FDI IN HUNGARY

In this final section the prospects of FDI in Hungary will be outlined. Two strong forces, that have a decisive influence on the growth of FDI are: the increasing competition in terms of FDIs with other countries, and the new membership of Hungary in the EU.

2.7.1 Competition

It is recognized that the large amount of FDI is a result of the successful reforms, privatization and cheap and good working labour force of Hungary. Nowadays many economists argue that the competitive advantage of Hungary is declining. According to a recent ECOSTAT analysis, which investigated the position of the Hungarian FDI, Hungary can expect more competition from other central and eastern EU countries. If Hungary will not compete for FDI in the near future, the competitive advantage of Hungary will probably be lost. Various other countries in transition offer a more favourable preferential treatment than Hungary to foreign investors.

A main reason is the fact that privatization has just begun to gain importance in the other countries of the region. In the Czech republic and Poland – the countries that are seen as the main rivals of Hungary – large privatization projects have recently started. In addition, another positive point from the viewpoint of the investor can be the market potential of those countries. In Hungary the market consist of 10 million people, while in Poland 40 million consumers are waiting. At this moment Poland already has a higher foreign capital inflow than Hungary.

Another important potential disadvantage of Hungary in the near future could be the shortage of a skilled labour force. In other accession countries, with less FDI, there is still enough labour potential. One of the focal points of public policy must therefore be more investments in the higher education system in order to reduce the potential gap. Furthermore, the wages of the Hungarian labour force rose in the first half year of 2002 by 11 percent, so the advantage of a cheap workforce will be lower in the future.

2.7.2 Membership of the EU

From May 2004, Hungary has been a member of the EU. Membership will favour the free mobility of labour, capital and products across borders, and Hungary will probably get more aid from the EU for the restructuring of the country. As a member of the EU, Hungary will become part of a single market with hundreds of millions of consumers, one of the most influential power centres of international trade. A new market will open up for Hungarian goods and services as well as new opportunities for the inflow of foreign capital from other member states. EU membership will result in direct access to the various development funds of the Union. This will provide vital financial resources for the social transformation, and will probably contribute to further progress in economic performance, growth and competitiveness and also to successful transformation and modernization. And this may exert a positive influence on FDI inflows.

Nowadays investors often seem to prefer the neighbouring Slovakia, where labour is cheaper and unemployment higher, or the Czech Republic, which now attracts far more investments annually than Hungary. Much FDI presently entering Hungary is from existing investors, either reinvesting or meeting new legal requirements for companies to be better capitalized. Yet some existing investors have appeared to be surprisingly resilient, reacting to rising wages by improving productivity and efficiency. Some have even moved manufacturing of higher-value products to Hungary from western Europe (for example, Nokia), while often simultaneously moving the production of lower value products to cheaper locations such as China.

Eastern Europe needs the benefits of FDI, not only to reduce its unemployment but also to help to innovate the production system. Similar to experiences in medium-developed countries in Latin America and the Mediterranean, small companies may play a crucial role in the process of innovation (see Dyker, 1994; Jurickova, 1993). This means taking active steps in order to develop an attractive small business infrastructure, for both domestic and foreign small firms. One major component in such a strategy may be to establish links between strong knowledge sources at universities and foreign small firms. In this setting, Eastern Europe may draw on interesting experiences in Western Europe and elsewhere.

In summary, it is hard to say how the development of FDI in Hungary in the near future will evolve. Much of the development is dependent on the policy of the Hungarian government. The EU membership has both advantages and disadvantages concerning FDI inflows. According to the EU regulations, Hungary is not allowed to give special rights and benefits to foreign investors anymore, but on the other hand a more integrated market and easier trade connections can help Hungary to attract more investments and become a major economic trade centre of Eastern Europe.

REFERENCES

Antaloczy, K. and M. Sass (2001), 'Greenfield investments in Hungary: are they different from privatization FDI?', *Transnational Corporations*, **10**, pp. 39–59.

Csösz, A. (2001), 'Hungary and FDI: an analysis with special reference to Hungary's accession to the EU', www.extra.hu/csanders.

Dalmeijer, M.C.M. (1994), *Samenwerken in Oost-Europa (Cooperation in Eastern Europe)*, The Hague: Sociaal- Economische Raad (Socio-Economic Council).

Dunning, J.H. and L. Nachum (2000), 'UK FDI and the comparative advantage of the UK', *The World Economy*, **23** (5), pp. 701–20.

Dyker, D.A. (1994), 'Technology policy and the productivity crisis in Eastern Europe and the former Soviet Union', *Economic Systems*, **8** (2), pp. 71–85.

EBRD (2001a), *Investments Profile Hungary 2001*, London.

EBRD (2001b), *Transition Report 2001*, London.

European Commission (2001), *European Governance: A White Paper*, Brussels, July 27, 2001.

Geenhuizen, M. van and P. Nijkamp (1998), 'Potential for East–West integration', *Environment & Planning C*, **16**, pp. 105–20.

Inzelt, A. (1994), 'Privatization and innovation in Hungary', *Economic Systems*, **18** (2), pp. 141–58.

Jurickova, V. (1993), 'The role of small and medium-sized enterprises in the economic development of the Slovak Republic', *Local Economy Quarterly*, **2** (3/4), pp. 154–64.

Kaltenthaler, K.C. and C.J. Anderson (2001), 'Europeans and their money', *European Journal of Political Research*, **40**, pp. 139–70.

Lavigne, M. (1999), *The Economics of Transition*, London: Palgrave.

Mihalyi, P. (2000), 'Foreign direct investment in Hungary – the post-communistic privatization story re-considered', *Acta Oeconomica*, **51**, pp. 107–29.

Mihalyi, P. (2001), 'The evolution of Hungary's approach to FDI in post-communistic privatisation', *Transnational Corporations*, pp. 61–72.

Szanyi, M. (2001), 'Privatization and greenfield FDI in the economic restructuring of Hungary', *Transnational Corporations*, **10**, pp. 25–37.

Wright, R. (2003), 'Fresh investors sought', *Financial Times*, 27 May 2003.

Internet sources:
http://www.worldbank.org.hu
http://www.ebrd.com
http://globalf.vwh.net
http://www.mfa.gov.hu
http://www.export.nl

3. European Integration and Japanese Direct Investment in the Central and East European Countries

Andrzej Cieślik and Michael Ryan

3.1 INTRODUCTION

Our study investigates the attractiveness of Central and East European countries (CEEs) to foreign investors. With many CEEs already in the European Union, understanding FDI flows from non-EU countries is important to CEE policymakers wishing to attract such investment. Of particular interest is to determine how these countries compare to their current and future competitors in terms of serving as potential FDI hosts.

With most of the previous research on CEE inward FDI focusing on flows from Western European countries, very little is known about FDI flows from non-European sources. Current and future EU members must begin to determine how EU membership will affect FDI flows both within the CEEs as well as Europe as a whole. Over recent years one candidate country, Poland, has been one of the most attractive investment locations in Europe. It ranks 11th in European OECD FDI inflows, and is well ahead of many of the preenlargement EU members, referred to here as the EU-15. However, Japan, the 6th largest OECD nation in terms of FDI outflows, invests very little, ranking as the 12th largest foreign investor in Poland (CSO, 2000). Similar scenarios describe Japanese FDI to many other CEEs as well.

Studies suggest that FDI into the CEE region is becoming increasingly dependent upon Western European demand, and the EU-15 is Eastern Europe's largest foreign market. Specifically, FDI in Hungary has shifted away from 'local-market activity to export-oriented ventures', while many new foreign investments in Poland are designed not to service the growing domestic market but rather the EU market (World Bank, 1999). In addition, the motivation for Japanese MNEs to invest in the CEEs is different than that of Southeast Asia, another prime location for Japanese FDI. 'Southeast Asia is not a serious competitor of Eastern Europe in attracting FDI. While the main foreign market for Eastern Europe is Western Europe, multinationals settled in Southeast Asia concentrate their export activities on the U.S. and Japanese markets' (World Bank, 1999). From these we can infer that Japanese firms are investing in Europe in order to serve mainly the European markets.

This study examines the puzzle as to what draws FDI from non-EU countries to the CEEs, especially in regard to servicing the EU market. In our study we concentrate on foreign direct investment from Japan. We characterize Japanese firm-level FDI into the CEEs for the period 1990–2000 through the use of an economic potential model. This model recognizes that a host country's FDI attractiveness is based not only on its own domestic market but also its ability (through its geographic location) to serve its 'potential market'. Our study distinguishes itself from previous studies on FDI in the CEEs that were based on a gravity model framework in three ways: (1) we are concerned with FDI originating from a single source (Japan) rather than from multiple sources (Western Europe); (2) we are not concerned with the location of the host country relative to the FDI source, as host-Japan distances vary negligibly across hosts, but are instead concerned with the location of the host country relative to the European market; and (3) we focus on the host country's ability to serve the entire European market rather than simply concentrating only on the local market.

Contrary to previous studies, we find that there exists significant heterogeneity among CEE nations in attracting inward FDI, as several CEE countries are not significantly different in their ability to attract Japanese FDI as compared to EU-15 countries. We also find that in addition to individual country characteristics, the economic potential of the CEE nations plays a significant role in determining inward FDI (with the largest amounts of FDI concentrated in the core EU countries that enjoy the highest economic potential). This suggests that they are receiving the 'correct' amount of inward FDI, having controlled for their economic potential, and that, *ceteris paribus*, their entry into the EU is not likely to significantly increase inward FDI flows. Finally, the presence of previously established Japanese affiliates in the host country seems to affect the present investment decisions of Japanese firms. The lack of previous Japanese investment in the CEEs appears to explain the low levels of Japanese FDI in the region.

The chapter proceeds as follows. Section 3.2 provides a review of previous literature on FDI into the CEEs, with special focus on Japanese FDI in the region. Section 3.3 describes the firm-level data used in this study, while section 3.4 outlines the economic potential index that serves as the basis for our analytical framework. Section 3.5 details the empirical results. Finally, section 3.6 concludes.

3.2 LITERATURE REVIEW: EMPIRICAL STUDIES OF FDI IN CENTRAL AND EASTERN EUROPE

As a result of the transition from central planning to a market economy, inflows of FDI to CEE countries increased significantly throughout the 1990s. This phenomenon raised a great deal of discussion concerning causes and consequences of FDI inflows into the CEEs and stimulated many empirical studies. Broadly, two strands of literature emerged. The first one concentrates on the role of FDI in the context of privatization and the process of industrial restructuring and considers the impact on the host economy. The second focuses on FDI determinants and predicting the volume of investment flows. However, the existing literature in these areas consists mainly of surveys and case studies. Formal quantitative work remains relatively scarce.

Examples of econometric studies that belong to the first genre include Barrell and Holland (2000), Bedi and Cieślik (2002) and Żukowska-Gagelmann (2000). They concentrate on various types of spillovers stemming from the activity of multinational enterprises that may raise the productivity of domestic firms. The second genre, represented by Brenton and Di Mauro (1999), Brenton et al. (1999) and Resmini (2000), to mention just a few, investigates the role of host country characteristics in attracting FDI to Central and Eastern Europe. Our present chapter is related to the second genre.

The general picture that emerges from the latter group reveals a considerable diversification in the destination of investments within the region. The bulk of foreign capital still remains concentrated in three Central European countries: Poland, Hungary and the Czech Republic. Widespread consensus exists as to why these three countries attract most of the region's inward FDI.[1] The primary reason for investing in Central and Eastern Europe has been to secure market access. Poland, Hungary and the Czech Republic are the region's largest markets and were the first to resume economic growth after their periods of transitional recession. Finally, these countries were also the first to launch comprehensive reforms and achieve political and economic stability.

Most previous studies were primarily focused on West European investors and various groups of recipient countries were considered rather than individual locations. Most existing research on Japanese FDI into Europe focuses on EU-15 nations. Formal quantitative studies on Japanese direct investment in particular Central and East European locations have been virtually non-existent. The notable exception constitutes Morita (1998) who adapts Smoker's directional trade ratio macro-level FDI flows to find that Japanese direct investment into Poland is not relatively weaker than its trade position with Japan. Therefore, we hope that our study will complement previous work and contribute to better understanding of how and why Japanese investors are attracted to the CEEs.

3.3 JAPANESE FDI IN EUROPE: THE DATA

The data set on Japanese firm-level foreign direct investment was compiled from three separate volumes (1993, 1995, 2001) of Toyo Keizai Inc.'s *Japanese Overseas Investment: A complete listing by firms and countries* (JOI). For our purposes, we are concerned with the date and location of initial investment into a particular affiliate as well as the verbal description of each affiliate's main business line at the time of investment. During the period 1990–2000, Japanese MNEs made 2072 investments into the 31 countries considered in this study (Table 3.1) of which 523 are in manufacturing with the remaining 1549 affiliates operating in service industries. For purposes of this study, service affiliates operate in the wholesale/retail, financial, real estate, business services, transportation, and engineering/construction industries.

Table 3.1   Countries in survey

European Union (EU-15)		
Austria	Germany	Netherlands
Belgium	Greece	Portugal
Denmark	Ireland	Spain
Finland	Italy	Sweden
France	Luxembourg	United Kingdom
European Free Trade Association (EFTA)		
Iceland	Norway	Switzerland
Central and East European Nations (CEE)		
Bulgaria	Czech Republic	Estonia
Hungary	Latvia	Lithuania
Poland	Romania	Slovakia
Slovenia		
Other countries		
Cyprus	Malta	Turkey

3.3.1 Europe-wide investment

Tables 3.2 and 3.3 detail the complete investment data. Investment into the EU comprised 89 percent of all Japanese investment into the region from

1990 to 2000 (Table 3.2), with the UK, Germany, the Netherlands, and France hosting most of this investment. The CEEs received over 9 percent of total investment, with 77 percent of this investment located in the EU first wave entrants. During the 1990s, the 'Big 3' recipients of Japanese FDI (JFDI) in the region (Czech Republic, Hungary, Poland) received more new investments from Japan (32, 56 and 46, respectively) than 8 EU-15 countries (Austria, Denmark, Finland, Greece, Ireland, Luxembourg, Portugal and Sweden) and three European Free Trade Association (EFTA) countries (Iceland, Norway, Switzerland). With respect to investment timing, total investment into the region declined sharply between 1992 and 1993, and remained relatively constant throughout the remainder of the period. Inward CEE investments followed a similar path, although a peak in first wave entrants is noted in 1997.

Table 3.3 reveals that 96 percent of investment value is located in current EU members, with the CEE nations hosting the remaining 4 percent. The physical location of investment appears far more geographically diverse than investment values suggesting that, on average, CEE affiliates are much smaller in size.[2] Poland and Hungary receive most of the inward CEE investment value, with Poland itself receiving roughly four times the dollar value of investment received by second wave CEE nations. Finally, four countries included in the study, including Latvia and Lithuania, received no Japanese investment during the period.

3.3.2 Focus on the CEEs: Industry, location, and timing

Of the Japanese affiliates in the CEEs since 1979, all but six of these investments were established since 1989 (see Figure 3.1).[3] From 1989 to 1992, a surge of JFDI into the region is noted. This corresponds with the transition of economies in this region as well as increased investment into the EU. Annual investment totals into the region fell between 1993 and 1996, most likely the result of the bursting of the Japanese bubble economy rather than anything that occurred in the region. While a spike of annual investment is noted in 1997, the region has yet to regain the 1991–1992 inward JFDI investment totals. Also note from Table 3.3 that while the number of new investments has fallen in the region, the capital involvement in the region increased. This implies that the average value of a Japanese investment project in the region is growing.

Table 3.2 Total number of investments

	1990	1991	1992	1993	1994	1995	1996	1997	1998	1999	2000	Total
Austria	7	8	3	1	3	2	4	0	1	0	0	29
Belgium	20	17	7	7	6	5	2	6	1	5	2	78
Bulgaria	0	0	1	1	0	0	0	0	0	0	0	2
Cyprus	0	0	0	0	0	0	0	0	0	0	0	0
Czech Rep..	1	6	5	4	4	5	1	4	1	0	1	32
Denmark	5	1	2	1	0	0	0	0	2	1	0	12
Estonia	0	0	1	0	0	0	0	0	0	0	0	1
Finland	1	1	1	1	1	2	2	3	0	1	0	13
France	55	43	28	14	12	8	21	14	11	10	12	228
Germany	88	83	38	27	17	19	15	15	12	16	10	340
Greece	1	0	1	0	0	0	0	0	0	1	0	3
Hungary	6	7	6	6	6	2	3	5	5	4	6	56
Iceland	0	0	0	0	0	0	0	0	0	0	0	0
Ireland	10	2	3	2	2	6	2	3	3	3	1	37
Italy	45	20	11	7	11	5	10	8	7	5	1	130
Latvia	0	0	0	0	0	0	0	0	0	0	0	0
Lithuania	0	0	0	0	0	0	0	0	0	0	0	0
Luxembourg	6	3	4	0	0	0	0	0	0	0	1	14
Malta	0	0	1	0	0	0	0	0	0	0	0	1
Netherlands	69	49	26	19	13	17	16	13	18	12	3	255
Norway	3	1	0	1	0	0	2	1	0	0	0	8
Poland	0	4	6	2	3	4	5	9	6	3	4	46
Portugal	7	4	2	0	1	1	1	1	3	1	0	21
Romania	0	2	4	1	0	1	2	0	1	0	1	12
Slovakia	0	0	0	0	0	0	0	1	1	1	0	3
Slovenia	0	0	0	0	1	0	1	3	1	0	0	6
Spain	18	22	8	6	8	12	8	4	3	2	3	94
Sweden	4	3	4	3	4	3	5	1	2	1	1	31
Switzerland	6	6	3	1	1	0	1	2	4	2	0	26
Turkey	4	4	3	2	3	2	0	1	1	0	0	20
UK	144	97	72	37	37	25	37	28	48	24	25	574
EU-15	480	353	210	125	115	105	123	96	111	82	59	1859
EFTA	9	7	3	2	1	0	3	3	4	2	0	34
CEECs	7	19	23	14	14	12	12	22	15	8	12	158
Total	500	383	240	143	133	119	138	122	131	92	71	2072

Table 3.3 Total value of all investments *

	1990	1991	1992	1993	1994	1995	1996	1997	1998	1999	2000	Total
Austria	6.2	70.6	12.9	5.4	85.8	2.6	1.7	0.0	0.0	0.0	0.0	185.2
Belgium	169.2	82.1	32.1	47.1	5.9	7.0	9.9	1 930.9	0.2	77.6	0.6	2 362.5
Bulgaria	0.0	0.0	23.3	1.8	0.0	0.0	0.0	0.0	0.0	0.0	0.0	25.1
Cyprus	0.0	0.0	0.0	0.0	0.0	0.0	0.0	0.0	0.0	0.0	0.0	0.0
Czech Rep.	346.7	28.4	0.0	5.3	1.6	0.8	99.5	13.6	0.0	0.0	12.1	508.0
Denmark	15.9	0.2	4.9	0.0	0.0	0.0	0.0	0.0	1.1	3.4	0.0	25.4
Estonia	0.0	0.0	0.1	0.0	0.0	0.0	0.0	0.0	0.0	0.0	0.0	0.1
Finland	0.2	0.2	27.2	0.0	3.8	84.0	0.0	530.6	0.0	0.4	0.0	646.5
France	359.2	380.2	169.8	23 922.6	53.3	34.9	121.5	110.9	298.9	79.2	148.3	25 678.8
Germany	8 891.9	3 917.2	309.8	52.2	15.5	205.2	14.0	8.2	19.8	19.6	253.0	13 706.3
Greece	0.1	0.0	0.1	0.0	0.0	0.0	0.0	0.0	0.0	0.1	0.0	0.2
Hungary	5.7	6.7	84.6	8.1	0.9	20.1	14.7	76.5	26.9	3.5	0.2	247.8
Iceland	0.0	0.0	0.0	0.0	0.0	0.0	0.0	0.0	0.0	0.0	0.0	0.0
Ireland	106.0	0.7	9.7	0.9	0.3	27.8	1.4	78.5	88.4	4.7	0.3	318.7
Italy	111.8	63.1	16.2	9.6	9.9	35.6	13.9	7.8	1.2	33.3	0.1	302.7
Latvia	0.0	0.0	0.0	0.0	0.0	0.0	0.0	0.0	0.0	0.0	0.0	0.0
Lithuania	0.0	0.0	0.0	0.0	0.0	0.0	0.0	0.0	0.0	0.0	0.0	0.0

Luxembourg	143.2	63.0	1.2	0.0	0.0	0.0	0.0	0.0	0.0	0.0	0.1	207.5
Netherlands	17 478.9	1 551.9	462.8	318.7	1 347.8	197.0	142.3	194.6	36 057.2	5 003.8	60.0	62 815.1
Norway	11.0	4.5	0.0	0.0	0.0	0.0	15.9	0.1	0.0	0.0	0.0	31.6
Poland	0.0	11.1	1.8	0.2	0.3	23.3	1.0	4 504.0	11.7	1 256.1	12.4	5 821.9
Portugal	11.1	19.1	2.6	0.0	4.4	2.7	6.5	0.0	3.8	26.4	0.0	76.6
Romania	0.0	0.0	0.7	0.1	0.0	0.3	2.8	0.0	16.8	0.0	0.1	20.8
Slovakia	0.0	0.0	0.0	0.0	0.0	0.0	0.0	3.2	0.2	1.3	0.0	4.7
Slovenia	0.0	0.0	0.0	0.0	0.0	0.0	0.1	0.2	0.0	0.0	0.0	0.2
Spain	89.8	85.9	37.9	44.6	40.2	32.7	10.9	2.8	0.4	0.6	0.3	346.2
Sweden	4.6	0.3	0.3	3.6	24.1	9.8	3.8	0.1	0.9	0.2	0.1	47.8
Switzerland	4.3	18.6	15.9	0.4	0.1	0.0	0.2	0.4	7.1	94.8	0.0	141.8
Turkey	30.9	9.5	56.8	2.6	979.6	24.4	0.0	14.5	2.3	0.0	0.0	1 120.6
UK	46 526.4	2 146.2	12 677.7	216.4	443.2	989.9	493.2	29 673.7	1 806.8	2 689.3	2 351.4	100 014.2
EU-15	73 914.6	8 380.7	13 763.9	24 621.1	2 034.1	1 629.3	819.1	32 538.1	38 278.7	7 938.6	2 814.2	206 732.4
EFTA	15.4	23.1	15.9	0.4	0.1	0.0	16.1	0.5	7.1	94.8	0.0	173.4
CEECs	352.4	46.2	110.5	15.5	2.8	44.5	118.1	4 597.5	55.6	1 260.9	24.8	6 628.6
Total	74 313.2	8 459.5	13 948.3	24 639.5	3 016.6	1 698.3	953.2	37 150.6	38 343.7	9 294.3	2 839.0	214 656.3

Note: * In millions of 1996 US$. The value of the 1992 investment into Malta is unknown.

At the individual host-country level, Figure 3.1 reveals that Poland, after a period of transition recession in the early 1990s, started to receive substantial FDI inflows. Hungary, in part because of its relative economic stability, received a relatively stable amount of JFDI inflows throughout the period covered by our data. Surprisingly, Japanese investors were not very active in the Czech Republic, although with the Czech authorities introducing special investment packages for foreign investors in the late 1990s, annual investment totals should begin to rise over the next few years.

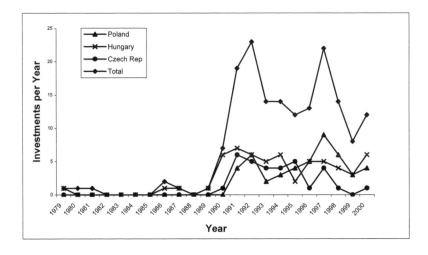

Figure 3.1 Time series of Japanese FDI into the CEEs

Having discussed the distribution of JFDI across the region, we now move to investigating country specialization patterns. Our focus lies in country–industry breakdown to verify whether investment patterns across CEEs are similar or different. Table 3.4 highlights the industry affiliation and location choice of JFDI into the CEEs at the 2-digit NACE level. Fifty-four percent of JFDI into the region is into wholesale and retail distribution affiliates, with a majority of these investments located in wholesale trade excluding automobiles (NACE 51) and automobile wholesale (NACE 50). Only three other industries received more than ten investments, including NACE 29 (Machinery and Equipment, n.e.c.), NACE 32 (Radio, TV, and Communications Equipment) and NACE 74 (Other Business Activities).[4] In fact, of the 33 industries receiving investment, 16 received two or fewer investments.

Table 3.4   Location of JFDI in the CEECs by affiliate industry membership[*]

	NACE	BUL	CZE	EST	HUN	POL	ROM	SLO	SVK	Total
Agriculture	01	0	1	0	0	0	0	0	0	1
Manufacturing	17	0	1	0	0	0	0	0	0	1
	19	0	0	0	1	0	0	0	0	1
	20	0	0	0	0	0	0	0	0	0
	23	0	0	0	0	0	0	0	0	0
	24	0	0	0	2	0	0	0	0	2
	25	0	0	0	1	0	0	0	0	1
	26	0	2	0	2	0	0	0	0	4
	27	0	0	0	1	0	0	0	0	1
	28	0	1	0	1	1	0	0	0	3
	29	0	2	0	6	3	1	1	1	14
	31	0	2	0	2	3	0	0	1	8
	32	0	4	0	5	2	0	0	2	13
	33	0	0	0	2	0	0	0	0	2
	34	0	0	0	2	0	0	0	0	2
	35	0	0	0	1	0	0	0	0	1
	36	0	0	0	0	0	2	0	0	2
Electricity &	40	0	0	0	1	0	0	0	0	1
Construction	45	0	0	0	2	3	0	0	0	5
Wholesale,	50	1	9	1	5	10	4	0	1	31
Retail &	51	1	13	0	17	21	5	1	2	60
Hotels	52	0	0	0	0	2	0	0	0	2
	55	0	0	0	1	0	0	0	0	1
Transport &	63	1	0	0	0	0	0	0	0	1
Commun.	64	0	0	0	0	0	0	0	0	0
Financial	65	0	0	0	1	1	0	0	0	2
Services	67	0	0	0	2	0	0	0	0	2
Real Estate,	70	0	0	0	0	0	0	0	0	0
Renting, &	71	0	0	0	0	0	0	0	0	0
Bus.	72	0	0	0	0	0	0	0	0	0
Services	73	2	0	0	3	2	0	0	0	7
	74	0	1	0	3	2	1	0	0	7
Social Work	85	0	0	0	0	0	0	0	0	0
Total Manufacturing		0	12	0	26	9	3	1	4	55
Total Services		5	23	1	35	41	10	1	3	119
Total		5	36	1	61	50	13	2	7	175

Note: [*] *Excludes four investments for which the affiliate's main business line is unknown*

Manufacturing investment appears more concentrated than the overall investment and primarily located in the Czech Republic, Hungary and Poland, which combined receive 85 percent of manufacturing investment in the region. While some manufacturing industries have chosen to locate throughout the region, several industries have agglomerated in a particular country that maintains a comparative advantage in those industries. Hungary (26 investments), which receives over one-third of the region's manufacturing investment, hosts one-half of JFDI into automobile manufacturing (NACE 34) and is also the largest recipient of investment into radio and TV manufacturing (NACE 32). Poland, recognized for its exports of electrical machinery and highly abundant specialized workforce, is the largest recipient of investment into electrical machinery manufacturing (NACE 31). With investment in miscellaneous manufacturing (NACE 29) diversified among the Czech Republic and Hungary, a closer examination reveals that each country has appeared to specialize within this broad industry classification. Hungary received all manufacturing investment into cooling and ventilation equipment (NACE 2923) and weapons and ammunition (NACE 2960). Manufacturing of pumps and compressors (NACE 2912) split its location choice evenly across the Czech Republic, Hungary and Poland.

While manufacturing JFDI to CEE countries appears highly concentrated in the three main host nations, JFDI into services appears less concentrated. However, a closer inspection of this service trade is warranted. We split services into two categories: wholesale and retail affiliates ('consumer services') and financial and business services ('producer services'). We make this division, as the motivation for these investments is somewhat different. Consumer service investments are often associated with facilitating Japanese export trade into the region, while producer services are often used as inputs by future JFDI into the region, and are not necessarily related to exports. In addition, goods markets are viewed to be far less segmented than those for producer services, which may in turn have implications on location choice for investments in each industry.

The Czech Republic (24%), Hungary (24%), and Poland (33%) host the majority of wholesale and retail trade investments. Not surprisingly, general wholesale trade (NACE 51) affiliates are located throughout the region, although they are primarily located in the 'Big 3' nations. Automobile wholesale affiliates are primarily located in Poland and the Czech Republic, suggesting that Japanese automobile MNEs have fragmented the automobile production-distribution process. Although Hungary serves as the largest host for vehicle manufacturing it does not appear (from the number of affiliates) to serve also as the distribution center for the region. Also, unlike other wholesale/retail investments, such as those in Poland that might be more focused on the CEE nations, FDI into the Czech Republic may be designed to serve both EU and CEE markets. This may be the result of the Czech Republic's centralized geographic location and its proximity to Western markets. Finally, service affiliates comprise 19 of the 175 (11%) investments into the region, with nearly half of this investment into Hungary and Poland.

The timing of investment into each industry also reveals important information on JFDI into the region. Figure 3.2 reveals that annual investment into wholesale/retail distribution affiliates is somewhat more volatile than investment into either services or manufacturing. Investment into manufacturing appears to be a more recent phenomenon, while investment into services has somewhat waned since the early 1990s. Much of this service investment was into market research and financial services affiliates, and given the nature of this service investment, it does appear that manufacturing searches for locations with previously established service investments. In fact, while the average date of investment into manufacturing is 1995, the average date of investment into service affiliates was 1992, suggesting that these investments were intended to gain market information for use in subsequent manufacturing FDI.[5]

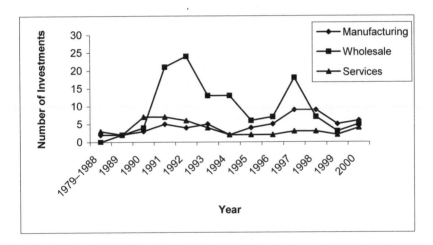

Figure 3.2 Japanese FDI into CEEs by affiliate industry affiliation

3.3.3 Characteristics of Japanese investing firms

While the previous section details general investment characteristics, this section focuses on the Japanese MNEs that undertake these investments. As suggested by the aforementioned World Bank (1999) article, EU–CEE integration is an important factor in JFDI into the CEEs. We choose to investigate parent characteristics, as we are interested in examining the type of firm that invests in the CEEs in addition to understanding how previous investment into the EU may affect JFDI into the CEECs. From the Toyo Keizai data, 127 Japanese MNEs invested in the CEEs up through 2000 (Table 3.5). Investing firms average close to two investments, although this number may be inflated by the multiple investments made by the *soga shosa*, the large Japanese trading companies that appear to have blanketed the region with wholesale affiliates. In fact, some 80 percent of investing firms have two or fewer investments in the region, with most of these firms manufacturing MNEs.

Table 3.5 details the industry affiliation of the investing Japanese MNEs.[6] A majority of the investing firms are in the machinery and equipment (NACE 29) industry, specifically, in pumps and compressors (NACE 2912), machine tools (NACE 2940) and electric domestic appliances (NACE 2971). Other major manufacturing investing industries are photographic chemicals (NACE 2464), measuring devices (NACE 3320), automobiles (NACE 3411) and automobile parts (NACE 3430). A majority of the 15 investing firms in wholesale trade (NACE 51) are *soga shosha*. In total, of the 35 industries with investing firms, 23 of these industries have two or fewer investing firms, indicating that a majority of Japanese FDI into the CEEs originates from firms in a limited number of industries. From this list, it appears from that the focus of JFDI into the region is from firms interested in establishing a location to produce parts and components that may serve as intermediate inputs for other Japanese firms operating in Europe.

Table 3.5   Stylized facts about Japanese multinational enterprises with CEEC investments

Total number of investing firms:	127
Average number of investments	1.93
Median number of investments	1
Maximum number of investments	11
Number of firms with:	
1 investment	83
2 investments	19
3 investments	6
4 investments	10
5+ investments	9

A closer examination of the investing firms finds that 38 percent of investments into the region have their capital originate from the EU-based affiliates of the Japanese parent company.[7] Thus, while sales data on the final customers do not exist, it does appear that Japanese parents are often using investments into the CEEs as overseas production sites to provide intermediate goods for their other EU-based affiliates. In fact, '[Japanese] companies with manufacturing facilities [in Europe] are looking for lower cost areas [to produce]...Central Europe is of particular interest'.[8]

The average date of a firm's first investment into the region was 1994, and firms that chose to invest again did so with an average duration to second investment of 21 months. In fact, over one-half of the multiple investors establish a second affiliate within one year of the first. In 29 of the 43 'multiple investor' cases, the second investment was into a different host country. The quick duration and diverse location choices may be in part attributable to these firms' investment experience, or the delay in making these investments in relationship to the opening of these economies. For many of the Japanese MNEs, the CEE investments may play a significant role in their entire European market servicing plans, as 71 percent of these firms had previous investment experience in Europe (EU). There appears no one significant characteristic of non-experienced firms, as they are evenly split between manufacturing and non-manufacturing firms.

For firms with single investments into the region, most MNEs have chosen to locate in Hungary and Poland. 'Single-investor' firms with investments in wholesale distribution and financial services are primarily located in Hungary, while manufacturing is primarily located in Hungary and Poland. Of the 69 single-investor Japanese MNEs for which their industry affiliation is known, 58 percent of the firms chose to establish affiliates of similar main business lines.[9] A majority of the firms that did choose to 'diversify' were manufacturing firms establishing wholesale/retail distribution affiliates, suggesting that firms investing in the CEECs follow a similar investment pattern as those investing in other regions: diversification in affiliate main business lines occurs at later stages of the investment process. This is true even for those firms with previous investment experience in Europe, suggesting a limited spillover of market information occurred, and firms chose to gain CEE investment experience in the same way they did earlier for the EU-15: early investments were into wholesale & retail affiliates, followed then by manufacturing, and lastly by producer service investments. This is the view of Belderbos (1997), among others, who suggests that firms use wholesale and retail investment as a stepping-stone for future manufacturing investment. For JFDI into the CEEs, it appears that we can also add service investment to that primary step.

For firms with multiple investments, a majority of initial investments are into the Czech Republic. Of the 43 multiple investors in the sample, only 5 do not diversify their holdings away from their (broadly defined) main business line. Closer investigation of these multiple investors finds that 10 manufacturing firms have only non-manufacturing investments, while 11 of these firms have both manufacturing and non-manufacturing investments. Finally, all 12 of the wholesale/retail multiple investors have non-wholesale/retail investments.

Table 3.6 JFDI investment into CEECs by parent's industry affiliation

NACE Codes	Description	No. of Investors[*]
01–05	Agriculture, Hunting, Fishing	2
15–39	Manufacturing	77
45	Construction	3
50–51	Wholesale & Retail Trade	17
55	Hotels & Restaurants	1
61–63	Transport, Storage & Communications	3
65–67	Financial Intermediation	5
70–74	Real Estate, Renting & Business Service	8
Total		116

Note: [*] Excluding 11 Japanese firms for which industry affiliation is unknown.

3.4 ECONOMIC POTENTIAL FRAMEWORK

Developed by economic geographers, the index of economic potential first appeared in the work of Stewart (1947). At that time, however, the concept lacked formal microfoundations and instead was based on solid intuition developed by the physics literature on electrical potential. Subsequent use of the index (e.g. Harris, 1954; Clark, 1966; Rich, 1978) centered on population distribution and industrial location analysis. Clark et al. (1969) first introduced the economic potential index in a European context. Their study raised two important issues. First, the attractiveness of various Western European regions to foreign manufacturers was determined. Second, it attempted to measure the likely effect of the EC enlargement. Keeble et al. (1982) eventually revised and updated the study.

In its simplest form a typical index of economic potential for location i can be calculated as a weighted sum of a measure of economic activity of all other locations j with the weights declining with distance:

$$P_i = \sum_{j=1}^{n} \frac{M_j}{D_{ij}} \qquad (3.1)$$

where P_i = the economic potential of location i, M_j = a measure of the volume of economic activity in location j, D_{ij} = a measure of the distance between locations i and j.

The summation over all n locations yields an economic potential value for each location expressed in terms of economic activity per unit of distance. Therefore, economic potential values represent a given location's access to economic activity after the cost of covering the distance to that activity has been accounted for (Keeble et al., 1982).[10]

Despite its early use among geographers, economists viewed the index of economic potential as lacking clear theoretical underpinnings. It is only recently, through tools developed from the 'new trade theory' literature, that economic potential has been incorporated into mainstream economic analysis. Krugman (1992) refers to Harris (1954) and argues that the index of economic potential can be derived from a model of the interaction of economies of scale at the plant level with transportation costs. More specifically, Krugman (1992) renames economic potential as 'market potential' and concentrates entirely on the role of a forward linkage – the proximity of firms supplying final goods to consumers. Krugman's (1992) framework serves in turn to underpin empirical work by Hansen (1998) and Head and Mayer (2000).

Unfortunately, empirical work that uses only one-way linkages to generate the index of economic potential is seriously incomplete and it is always subject to identification problem. Previous economic geography studies (such as Keeble et al., 1982) argued that locations with higher economic potential have a comparative advantage over locations with lower potential, as they have greater access to economic activity. The advantage of higher accessibility due to shorter distance can be related to demand- and supply-side factors. Shorter distances reduce costs of supplying final goods to consumers (forward linkage), while also lowering the costs of intermediate input acquisition (backward linkage). Concentration of economic activity may also give rise to external effects in the form of technological or information spillovers that decrease the costs of conducting business activity (Fujita and Thisse, 1996).

At present, there is no easy way to link geographers' concept of economic potential to highly simplified models developed by economists. Concentrating on only one aspect of economic activity in a simple empirical framework, such as Krugman (1992) and Head and Mayer (2000), cannot fully explain a location's economic potential. Furthermore, identification problems exist since several forces may work simultaneously to drive the empirical results. For example, economic potential may be related to backward and forward linkages as well as spillovers. A convincing test to disentangle these effects has yet to be devised, although Midelfart-Knarvik et al. (2000) have taken the first steps in this direction.

Instead of trying to distinguish directly between various factors that affect location of firms, this chapter takes the indirect approach by using an economic potential index. By assuming that all factors that influence firm investment decisions are reflected in the computed value of economic potential,[11] identification problems are avoided. Our estimating equation expressed in logs becomes then:

$$\ln X_{it} = \alpha \ln P_{it} + \mu_i + \lambda_t + \varepsilon \tag{3.2}$$

where X_{it} = a measure of foreign involvement in location i at time t, P_{it} = the economic potential of location I at time t, μ_i = a location-specific individual effect, λ_t = a time specific effect, and ε_{it} = a white noise disturbance term.

In addition, while this chapter chooses not to focus on agglomeration economies per se, we wish to net out the Japanese generated externalities from all other agglomeration effects that are reflected in the computed values of the economic potential index. Empirical evidence suggests that firms in the same industry tend to cluster in the same geographical area. The 'just-in-time' delivery system common to Japanese supplier relationships and the prevalence of local manufacturing content requirements in many countries provide incentive for upstream firms to follow their downstream final goods suppliers to new markets. This result can be extended, in the case of Japanese MNEs, to include firms with common keiretsu ties.[12] Keiretsu membership is believed to provide several potential FDI advantages including long-term supply relations with fellow group members, close ties with the group's principle bank, and frequent information exchanges between firms on new markets and products. These relationships potentially provide the firm with easier access to investment capital as well as foreign market information acquired by other group members.[13]For these reasons, the location choice of new investors may in part be determined by the FDI location choices of previous investors. The technological, pecuniary and market-information externalities that arise from such location choices often create an environment of 'circular agglomeration', where increased industrial activity spurs future investment into the area (Baldwin, 1999). These externalities may arise due to local conditions or via the investment choices of foreign (Japanese) firms. In analyzing how 'history matters' to future FDI location choice, we examine the extent to which firm location is determined by a self-reinforcing 'circular' investment process among Japanese investors. For the CEEs, ideological, political and economic factors contributed to the region's poor investment conditions in the 1980s and early 1990s, significantly impacting the number and amount of inward FDI. If an FDI agglomeration effect does exist, such a finding may help explain why current Japanese investment is still relatively low, indicating a persistence to the investment climate that may take the region's economies some time to overcome.

Our *second* general estimating equation expressed in logs becomes:

$$\ln X_{it} = \alpha \ln P_{it} + \beta A_{it} + \mu_i + \lambda_t + \varepsilon \qquad (3.3)$$

where A_{it} = a measure of previous Japanese investment in location i at time t. A description of the data used in this study is provided in the data appendix.

3.5 EMPIRICAL RESULTS

The empirical results section proceeds as follows. First, we use a traditional OLS dummy variable approach on the pooled dataset and investigate the robustness of the OLS estimation using fixed and random effects. Then we proceed with panel data analysis and net out the Japanese generated externalities from all other agglomeration effects that are reflected in the index of the economic potential. Finally, we compare individual effects for particular locations before and after controlling for investment history. Estimates of individual country effects allow us to rank particular countries according to their attractiveness to Japanese investors, having controlled for their economic potential. The OLS economic potential model estimates are reported in columns (1)–(5) of Table 3.7.

3.5.1 OLS Approach

We begin by estimating the simplest possible version of the economic potential model by regressing the logged yearly investment inflow value on the log of the economic potential and the constant. The estimation results for this specification are presented in column (1). We find that economic potential (*Lpotential*) exerts a significant influence on FDI location choice. This suggests the important role that 'export-ability' plays in attracting inward FDI. However, it has been frequently claimed that Central and Eastern European countries are less attractive for the Japanese investors than their Western counterparts and receive 'too little' investment. Usually this claim is verified by adding into the estimating equation a dummy variable for these countries (e.g., Brenton and Di Mauro, 1999). We follow this approach and add into the estimating equation a dummy variable for CEEs. The estimation results are presented in column (2). As expected, the coefficient on the CEE variable is negative and statistically significant. We examine the robustness of our estimates by including into the estimating equation a set of indicator variables for particular years to control for individual time effects (see column (3)). The time dummies allow us to control for potential business cycle effects on FDI into the region. It turns out that our previous conclusion basically remains unchanged, although the coefficients on our explanatory variables are now more accurately estimated.

Table 3.7   Economic potential model estimates: pooled data OLS dummy variable approach (t-statistics in parentheses)

Specification Variable	(1)	(2)	(3)	(4)	(5)
Lpotential	14.138	13.730	14.463	10.457	4.811
	(8.653)	(8.743)	(9.261)	(7.207)	(3.318)
CEE dummy		−8.883	−8.847	1.423	7.860
		(5.461)	(5.517)	(0.798)	(4.329)
LaggTotal				1.221	
				(9.417)	
LaggService					0.709
					(6.257)
LaggManufacturing					0.982
					(8.673)
Constant	−323.103	−310.825	−324.166	−232.603	−101.229
	(8.568)	(8.568)	(8.996)	(6.953)	(3.025)
Time specific effects	No	No	Yes	Yes	Yes
R^2 adjusted	0.179	0.243	0.264	0.419	0.523
N	341	341	341	341	341

Note: CEE (Central or Eastern European Country): Czech Republic, Hungary, Poland, Slovakia, Slovenia, Bulgaria, Estonia, Latvia, Lithuania, Romania.

We also include variables that control for possible agglomeration externalities generated by Japanese firms. In column (4) we present estimates when we control for the total investment history, while in column (5) we split Japanese investment into services and manufacturing. It turns out the when we control for investment history the negative sign associated with the CEE variable simply disappears. Moreover, previous Japanese investment (*LaggTotal, LaggService, LaggManufacturing*) significantly affects future location choices. Including previous investment history in the analysis decreases the magnitude of economic potential's significant influence on inward FDI.

Although the model based on the pooled data OLS dummy variable approach is instructive, panel data and individual effects for particular countries may be the appropriate estimation format. A panel data approach allows for individual heterogeneity while also addressing the omitted variable problem, a distinct advantage over OLS. Thus in the next subsection, we turn to determining the correct panel data approach.

3.5.2 Panel Approach

In this subsection we present empirical results obtained from the implementation of panel data techniques on our estimating equations (3.2) and (3.3). The main proposition of our model is that Japanese investors are attracted to countries with high values of economic potential, and individual differences that exist across European countries in their ability to attract inward investment can be modeled as country-specific effects.

Allowing for individual country and time effects, we estimate equations (3.2) and (3.3) via fixed and random effect models to determine the appropriate estimation framework, allowing for individual country and time effects. Including individual country effects allows us to formally verify whether CEE countries are less or more attractive for Japanese investors compared to well established Western economies.

Base-case fixed and random effects estimates of equation (3.2) are presented in columns (1) and (2) of Table 3.8, respectively. The estimated parameter on economic potential variable has the expected sign under the random effects specification only, however in the case of the fixed effects it is not statistically significant. Although both the F-test for the fixed effects estimator and Breusch-Pagan LM test for the random effects estimator confirm the appropriateness of allowing for individual heterogeneity across countries, the Hausman test suggests the use of a random effects framework.

Table 3.8's columns (3) and (4) present the fixed and random effects estimates of equation (3.3) that controls for investment history effects. Now, the estimated parameter on economic potential variable has the expected sign under both specifications, however it is not statistically significant in the case of the fixed effects model. Investment history is found under both model specifications to significantly affect FDI location choice. Similar to our base case, F and LM tests confirm the importance of individual country effects while the Hausman test again does not allow us to reject random effects in favor of fixed effects.

An important advantage of panel data estimation as compared to the traditional dummy variable approach is that it allows for estimation of individual country-specific effects without the necessity of estimating dummies for often very heterogeneous country 'groups'. A panel approach allows us to compare directly the individual effects estimated for various European countries and verify the common claim that post-communist

Central and Eastern European countries still receive too little Japanese foreign investment compared to other European countries. The individual country random effects estimates for the model specifications presented in columns (2) and (4) of Table 3.9, respectively.

Table 3.8   Economic potential model estimates: panel data fixed and random effects approach (t-statistics**)*

Specification Variable	(1)	(2)	(3)	(4)
Lpotential	−3.464	14.842	53.399	8.489
	(0.036)*	(3.483)	(0.553)	(2.932)
LaggService			0.411	0.506
			(2.386)	(3.419)
LaggManufacturing			0.287	0.545
			(1.457)	(3.799)
Constant	85.322	−335.743	−1220.136	−185.776
	(0.039)	(8.568)	(0.549)	(2.781)
Country specific effects	Fixed	Random	Fixed	Random
Time specific effects	YES	YES	YES	YES
R2 adjusted	0.009	0.224	0.288	0.509
F-test	15.389		6.403	
(p-val)	(0.000)		(0.000)	
LM-test		549.220		164.240
		(0.000)		(0.000)
Hausman test		0.040		7.850
		(1.000)		(0.853)
N	341	341	341	341

Before controlling for investment history effects, individual country effects estimated for EU-15 members are on average higher than those for Central and East European countries. Individual effects are positive for four CEEs: Hungary, Poland, Romania and the Czech Republic, while the other CEEs close the list. Differences between CEE and EU-15 members in regard to individual effects become much less pronounced if one controls for investment history. The estimated values of individual effects for the EU-15 members become smaller while the estimated values for the CEE countries go up.[14]

Table 3.9   Individual country-specific random effect estimates before and after controlling for investment history

'History effect' excluded in analysis			'History effect' included in analysis		
Country	Estimate	Rank	Country	Estimate	Rank
Spain	15.395	1	Poland	11.110	1
Turkey	15.058	2	Spain	7.678	2
Sweden	12.714	3	Hungary	7.406	3
Ireland	11.940	4	Sweden	6.546	4
Hungary	11.738	5	Ireland	6.492	5
Portugal	11.419	6	Turkey	6.222	6
Italy	9.952	7	Czech Rep.	4.892	7
Finland	9.934	8	UK	4.733	8
UK	9.240	9	Italy	4.591	9
Poland	8.836	10	Portugal	4.286	10
France	8.006	11	France	4.074	11
Netherlands	6.080	12	Finland	3.850	12
Germany	5.735	13	Romania	3.732	13
Romania	3.053	14	Netherlands	3.636	14
Belgium	1.587	15	Germany	2.258	15
Czech Rep.	1.585	16	Belgium	0.673	16
Austria	−0.960	17	Lithuania	−1.523	17
Switzerland	−1.222	18	Latvia	−1.603	18
Greece	−3.812	19	Switzerland	−2.796	19
Iceland	−4.918	20	Slovenia	−2.853	20
Cyprus	−5.515	21	Bulgaria	−3.188	21
Norway	−5.730	22	Austria	−3.377	22
Bulgaria	−7.319	23	Cyprus	−3.732	23
Denmark	−10.852	24	Iceland	−3.964	24
Malta	−12.004	25	Estonia	−4.765	25
Estonia	−12.931	26	Malta	−5.210	26
Lithuania	−14.623	27	Slovak Rep.	−5.934	27
Latvia	−14.776	28	Norway	−8.536	28
Slovenia	−15.679	29	Greece	−8.929	29
Slovak Rep.	−15.933	30	Denmark	−10.946	30
Luxembourg	−15.997	31	Luxembourg	−14.825	31

3.6 CONCLUSION

This chapter employs an economic potential framework to investigate how Japanese firm-level investment flows into Central and East European

Countries (CEEs) during the 1990s differ from that of the EU for both manufacturing and service FDI at country and sectoral levels. We focus on the industry, location and timing of affiliate establishment in order to characterize the type of investing parent and investigate the entry-mode choices of investing firms. Empirical estimation is based on a model of economic potential rather than a gravity-type model, as foreign investments into the region are designed not only to service the growing domestic market but also the EU market as well.

From this framework, significant heterogeneity among CEE nations in their ability to attract Japanese FDI is revealed. The 'Big 3' countries (Czech Republic, Hungary, Poland) are not significantly different from many EU-15 nations in their ability to attract inward FDI. In fact, these countries receive more FDI than their EFTA-member counterparts. This suggests that entry into the EU will not have a significant impact on Japanese FDI into these countries However, future membership alone is not enough to generate significant inward FDI, as it appears that economic potential, political and economic stability, and previous investment history play an important role in attracting Japanese FDI to the region. These results fail to support the assertion by Sinn and Weichenrieder (1997) that FDI into the CEEs is 'too small', at least for investors from Japan. In fact, we find that the amount of FDI into the region appears 'correct' in relation to nations' economic potential.

NOTES

1. See *International Financial Statistics*, IMF, 2001.
2. From the data, median affiliate size in the CEE countries is $537 647, while median affiliate size for affiliates in the EU is $811 659.
3. Of these six 'original' investments, three were located in Hungary and three in Bulgaria. The Bulgarian investments were into market research firms, while the Hungarian investments were into manufacturing and financial services. The presence of manufacturing in Hungary is not surprising given its early opening to foreign investors.
4. This includes market research, advertising, and legal activities, among others.
5. For wholesale and retail affiliates, the average date of investment was 1993.
6. For a more disaggregated examination of industry affiliation for Japanese investing firms, see the appendix.
7. Approximately one-half of investments into the Czech Republic, Hungary and Poland have as their primary investing parent an EU-based affiliate of a Japanese MNE.
8. Interview with Koicho Akatsu, general director of JETRO Warsaw. *Warsaw Voice* (16 December 2001). http://www.warsawvoice.pl/v686/Business06.html
9. Here we measure similar business lines at a broad industry classification (manufacturing, wholesale/retail, business services, financial services, agriculture). There is some degree of diversification across industries at more disaggregated levels.
10. It is easy to notice that there is a straightforward relationship between the index of economic potential and the gravity model used in previous studies of FDI flows. A gravity model measures only local economic activity while an economic potential index also considers

economic activity at other locations. Therefore, the economic potential model seems better suited for investigation of FDI inflows than a simple gravity equation, employed for example by Brenton and Di Mauro (1999).

11. By analogy with macroeconomics, the index of economic potential can be interpreted in the similar way as Tobin's q in Hayashi's Theorem.

12. There exists a well-established literature on how agglomeration economies affect Japanese investment patterns for members of the same industry as well as keiretsu. For inter-industry agglomeration linkages, see Gross et al. (2001).

13. For a more detailed summary on keiretsu structure, see Aoki (1988).

14. Hungary, which began allowing foreign joint ventures (on a limited basis) in 1972, is the only exception to this rule.

REFERENCES

Aoki, M. (1988), *Information, Incentives, and Bargaining in the Japanese Economy*, Cambridge: Cambridge University Press.

Baldwin, R. (1999), 'Agglomeration and endogenous capital', *European Economic Review*, **43**, pp. 253–80.

Barrell, R. and D. Holland (2000), 'Foreign direct investment and enterprise restructuring in Central Europe', *Economics of Transition*, **8**, pp. 477–504.

Bedi, A.S. and A. Cieślik (2002), 'Wages and wage growth in Poland: the role of foreign direct investment', *Economics of Transition*, **10**, pp. 1–27.

Belderbos, R. (1997), 'Antidumping and tariff jumping: Japanese firms' DFI in the European Union and the United States', *Weltwirtschaftliches Archiv*, **133**, pp. 419–57.

Brenton, P. and F. Di Mauro (1999), 'The potential magnitude and mpact of FDI flows to CEECs', *Journal of Economic Integration*, **14**, pp. 59–74.

Brenton, P., F. Di Mauro and M. Lücke (1999), 'Economic integration and FDI: an empirical analysis of foreign investment in the EU and in Central and Eastern Europe', *Empirica*, **26**, pp. 95–121.

Clark, C. (1966), 'Industrial location and economic potential', *Lloyds Bank Review*, **82**, pp. 1–17.

Clark, C., F. Wilson and J. Bradley (1969), 'Industrial location and economic potential in Western Europe', *Regional Studies*, **3**, pp. 197–212.

Central Statistical Office (CSO) (2000), *Activity of Ventures with Foreign Capital Participation in Poland in 1999* (in Polish), Warsaw: Zakład Wydawnictw Statystycznych.

Fujita, M. and J.-F. Thisse (1996), 'Economics of agglomeration', *Journal of the Japanese and International Economies*, **10**, pp. 339–78.

Gross, D., H. Raff and M. Ryan (2002), 'Intra- and inter-industry linkages in foreign direct investment: evidence from Japanese investment in Europe', University of Kiel Working Paper.

Hansen, G. (1998), 'Market potential, increasing returns and geographic concentration', NBER Working Paper No. 6429.

Harris, C. (1954), 'The market as a factor in the localization of industry in the United States', *Annals of the Association of American Geographers*, **44**, pp. 315–48.

Head, K. and T. Mayer (2000), 'Market potential and the location of Japanese Investments in the European Union', mimeo, University of British Columbia.

Keeble, D., P.L. Owens and C. Thompson (1982), 'Regional accessibility and economic potential in the European community', *Regional Studies*, **16**, pp. 419–32.

Krugman, P. (1992), 'A dynamic spatial model', NBER Working Paper No. 4219.

Midelfart-Knarvik, K.H., H.G. Overman and A.J. Venables (2000), 'Comparative advantage and economic geography: estimating the location of production in the EU', Bergen: Norwegian School of Economics and Business Administration Discussion Paper 18.

Morita, K. (1998), 'On determinants of Japan's foreign direct investment in Eastern Europe: the case of Poland', *Journal of East-West Business*, **4**, pp. 141–8.

Resmini, L. (2000), 'The determinants of foreign direct investment in the CEECs: new evidence from sectoral patterns', *Economics of Transition*, **8**, pp. 665–89.

Rich, D.C (1978), 'Population potential, potential transportation cost and industrial location', *Area*, **10**, pp. 222–6.

Sinn, H.W. and A.J. Weichenrieder (1997), 'Foreign direct investment, political resentment and the privatization process in Eastern Europe', *Economic Policy*, **24**, pp. 179–210.

Stewart, J.Q. (1947), 'Empirical mathematical rules concerning the distribution and equilibrium of population', *Geographical Review*, **37**, pp. 461–85.

World Bank, Development Economics Research Group (1999), 'Transition Newsletter: The Newsletter About Reforming Economies' (http: www.worldbank.org/html/prddr/trans/so99/pgs7–8.htm).

Żukowska-Gagelmann, K. (2000), 'Productivity spillovers from foreign direct investment in Poland', *Economic Systems*, **24**, pp. 223–56.

DATA APPENDIX. ECONOMIC POTENTIAL DATA

Economic activity – We use national GDP expressed at market prices and measured in constant 1995 US$. This data comes from the *World Development Indicators 2002* annual database complied by the World Bank available on a CD-Rom.

Distance – We measure distance by calculating an 'as the crow flies' distance between European capitals (expressed in kilometers). This data is provided on-line by http://www.indo.com/distance.

Self-potential – This is the contribution to the economic potential of region *i* of its own economic mass value. For this we need to find a measure of internal distance for region *i*, D_{ii}. We follow a simple theoretical method proposed by Head and Mayer (2000). They assume that each region can be approximated as a disk in which all production concentrates in the center and consumers are uniformly distributed throughout the rest of the area. Following their calculations, $D_{ii} \approx 0.376\sqrt{A}$.

Previous Japanese Investment effects: or 'History matters' effect – 'Previous Japanese investment' is measured as the cumulative number of previous investments in that host country prior to the year in question. Each year, three such variables are created for every host country: (1) the cumulative amount of previous Japanese FDI, regardless of industry; (2) the cumulative amount of previous Japanese manufacturing FDI; and (3) the cumulative amount of previous Japanese service FDI. We chose to take the log of these totals as there exists a diminishing marginal return to such economies as more firms choose to invest.

4. Foreign Direct Investment Profitability: EU Firms in Romania

Fazia Pusterla

4.1 INTRODUCTION

Foreign capital flows towards Central and Eastern European countries (CEECs) have an important role in enhancing economic transition and development. The literature concerning foreign investment is very rich and provides a complete analysis of the role and the effects, both direct and indirect, of foreign direct investment (FDI) on host economies (Blomstrom and Kokko, 1996 and 1999). Moreover, many empirical studies have lately concentrated specifically and extensively on these countries, thus underlining the great interest they raise.[1]

In the last decade investment flows towards CEECs have increased constantly, but they are far from being distributed homogeneously: almost 60 percent of flows are directed to Central Europe and the Baltic States, among which the main recipients are Hungary, Poland and the Czech Republic, the former 'Visegrad' countries.[2]

During the 1990s, investment flows grew from 479 million USD in 1990 to 25.4 billion in 2000, reflecting, on the one hand, the host countries' creation of a safe and appealing investment environment and, on the other hand, origin countries' interest in such emerging economies. However, when it comes to the relative importance of FDI in CEECs and in developing countries as a group, discrepancies can be noticed: with regard to FDI as a percentage of GDP in 2000, developing countries minus China accounted on average for 30.9 percent while CEECs for 19.9 percent (UNCTAD, 2002) only. This should not be surprising considering that Central and Eastern Europe (CEE) was a latecomer in attracting FDI compared to other countries. Even though CEEC were late in the FDI competition, expectations of their ability to attract further foreign investments were exuberant.

In fact, it now seems to be the accepted position that the volume of FDI into CEECs has not been as great as these countries could have expected. The reason might be that severe constraints upon FDI inflows are present in these countries and that their removal will lead to a surge of FDI. However, this interpretation does not hold for all the CEECs. Indeed, it has been demonstrated (Brenton and Di Mauro, 1999) that once one takes into account the key determinants of FDI flows, then the amounts invested in the more advanced CEECs from individual European countries are not below their potential level. Conversely, FDI flows to Bulgaria and Romania remain substantially below their potential level.[3]

It is important to understand the causes of these differences and particularly how countries lagging behind, like Romania and Bulgaria, can catch up. It is also fundamental to evaluate FDI performance and see what went wrong and what can be improved for the future. To this end, a micro level approach can give more significant results than an aggregate level approach, such as an industry level analysis, because most of the economic effects of foreign investment take place at the firm level (King, 1999).

Given the recognized importance of the role of FDI, less-attractive host countries have to deal with two problems: i) how to attract more foreign investment and ii) how to select ex ante investment that best fits the country's potentialities and expectations of development.

Besides incentives and special laws, foreign investors are attracted by a safe, stable and competitive economic environment, which can guarantee positive and increasing profits. Thus, the presence of groups of highly profitable foreign enterprises, regardless of their size, can be a signal of such an environment and contribute to further increase in foreign investments. So it could be said that once the second problem is solved, the solution to the first one could be found more easily. That is, agglomeration effects should be desirable.

The objective of this chapter is to focus on FDI performance in Romania. In particular the analysis aims at studying the determinants of the profitability of European Union (EU) direct investments, using such variables as export intensity, firm size, activity and home country. This analysis should lead to the identification of best performing foreign enterprise typologies active in the country that could be useful in giving an answer to the two problems mentioned above.

The decision to focus only on EU FDI derives from two facts: on the one hand, in Romania EU investments cover 60 percent of total FDI in terms of capital invested, and, on the other hand, the geographic proximity and the future accession[4] of the country into the EU should make Romania an attractive recipient for EU investments.

The rest of the chapter is organized as follows. Section 4.2 contains an overview of FDI in Romania from the beginning of the 1990s. A concise theoretical and empirical framework on profitability is presented in section

4.3. Data are described in section 4.4, while sections 4.5 and 4.6 concern the econometric analysis. Some brief remarks conclude the chapter.

4.2 OVERVIEW OF FDI IN ROMANIA

Several characteristics make Romania an attractive destination for foreign enterprises willing to invest abroad. Among these, the most important ones are geographical location, the candidature as member of the EU by 2007, and the size of the internal market (over 23 million inhabitants, second only to Poland among the CEECs). These characteristics, together with the presence of a well-skilled and low-cost labour force, could have attracted important investments if they had been accompanied by clear and stable laws and by a solid economy, especially during the first years of the transition process.

When comparing FDI flows (Figure 4.1) for the period 1993–2001 in the Czech Republic, Hungary, Poland, Bulgaria and Romania, we see the lack of enthusiasm shown by investors towards the last two countries. Between 1996 and 1998 Romanian FDI inflows increased, pulling ahead of Bulgaria. However, they fell again in 1999. Poland's inflows have kept growing since 1996 and the country attracts more FDI than any other CEE country.

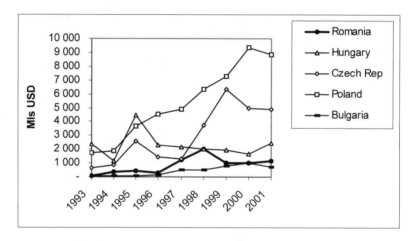

Source: Author's elaboration from UNCTAD, 2002.

Figure 4.1 FDI inflows 1993–2001

FDI stocks (Figure 4.2) confirm the trend seen for FDI flows in Romania and Bulgaria. From 1995 onwards the strength of the former 'Visegrad' countries is clear and continues up to now, even though in 2001 there is a hint of a saturation effect (decreasing FDI inflows).

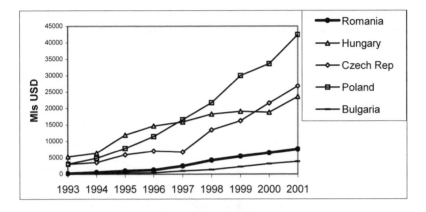

Source: Author's elaboration from UNCTAD, 2002.

Figure 4.2 FDI stocks 1993–2001

The weight of FDI stocks as a percentage of gross fixed capital formation (Figure 4.3) is more balanced since 1998 with Bulgaria and Romania performing more like the other CEECs and Hungary, Poland and Czech Republic, in turn, showing a more typical balance between domestic and foreign investments.

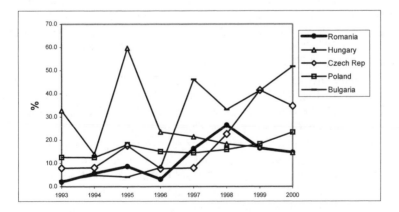

Source: Author's elaboration from UNCTAD, 2002.

Figure 4.3 FDI stocks as a percentage of gross fixed capital formation

Figure 4.4 shows the trend of FDI inflows as a percentage of gross domestic product. When comparing Figures 4.3 and 4.4, 1998 seems to be a year of considerable convergence for both inflows in percentage of GDP and gross investment. However, from the subsequent year each country follows its own trend, which seems independent of the others, giving no more signs of convergence.

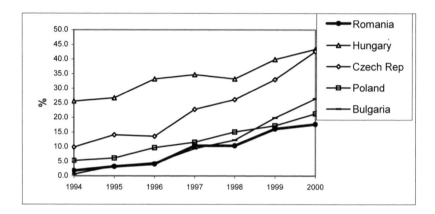

Source: Author's elaboration from UNCTAD, 2002.

Figure 4.4 FDI inflows as a percentage of gross domestic product

Most Romanian economists believe that without a critical mass of FDI, Romania cannot overcome the present state of economic decay (Serbanescu, 2000). The critical mass should reach 9–10 billion USD; in other words the present stock of 6.7 billion should increase by 50 percent. In 2001, the FDI stock was 7 636 million USD, 4.7 percent of total FDI stock in CEE, whereas in 1995 it represented only 2.9 percent.

The main investors in Romania are the Netherlands, Germany, USA, France and Austria, which altogether account for 53 percent of total flows in the country. As far as the number of foreign firms is concerned, the first five countries are Italy, Germany, Turkey, China and Iraq.

The European Union is the major foreign investor, representing more than 45 percent of total capital flows and about 37 percent of foreign firms localized in Romania. We can see (Table 4.1) that Italy and Germany are the first two investors for number of firms and among the first five for invested capital, while the Netherlands and France are the first two in terms of financial capital, with 26.7 percent and 24 percent of total invested capital respectively. Their contribution, however, is very small when considering the number of firms, which represent respectively 4.2 percent and 7.6 percent of the total number of EU firms presently operating in Romania.

This distribution shows that Dutch and French foreign investments have been undertaken by large firms, whereas Italian and German firms are mostly small and medium-size.

Table 4.1 Invested capital and number of firms in the period 1990–2001 in Romania

Invested Capital	EU (%)	Number of firms	EU (%)
EU	100.0	EU	100.0
1 Netherlands	26.7	1 Italy	34.3
2 France	24.0	2 Germany	27.6
3 Germany	19.3	3 France	7.6
4 Austria	10.1	4 Austria	6.8
5 Italy	8.4	5 Greece	6.6
6 UK	5.3	6 Netherlands	4.4
7 Luxemburg	1.9	7 UK	4.2
8 Sweden	1.4	8 Belgium	2.8
9 Belgium	1.1	9 Sweden	2.2
10 Spain	0.6	10 Spain	1.3
11 Ireland	0.5	11 Denmark	0.6
12 Greece	0.4	12 Luxemburg	0.5
13 Portugal	0.2	13 Ireland	0.4
14 Denmark	0.1	14 Portugal	0.2
15 Finland	0.0	15 Finland	0.2

Source: National Trade Register Office of Bucharest.

Examining the FDI distribution by sector (Table 4.2), shows that the majority of firms, mainly micro and small size, are active in the trade sector (both wholesale and retail) accounting for 62 percent of the total number of investments, whereas only 20 percent of the total number foreign firms belongs to the industrial sector. When looking at the value of the invested capital, these figures are reversed: 47 percent of foreign capital goes to industry, while only 22 percent is directed to the trade sector.

Table 4.3 examines the regional distribution of FDI within Romania comparing that from the EU with the total from the world. The agglomerating role played by the capital region, Bucharest-Ilfov, is evident when considering both invested capital and number of firms. EU FDI seems to be slightly less concentrated in this region than investments from the rest of the world, whose percentage is above 50 percent of total non-EU FDI.

Table 4.2   Distribution of EU FDI in Romania by sector

Type of activity	Invested capital (%)	No. of firms (%)
Industry	47.1	19.8
Trade (wholesale)	15.3	41.9
Services	14.9	7.9
Transports	9.1	3
Trade (retail)	7	20.9
Tourism	4	3.6
Construction	2.5	2.4
Agriculture	0.1	0.5
Total	100	100

Source: National Trade Register Office of Bucharest.

Table 4.3   Regional distribution of FDI: invested capital and number of firms

	Invested capital (%)		No. of firms (%)	
	EU	World	EU	World
North-East	2.8	5.1	4.6	3.8
South-East	4	3.7	5.1	5.8
South	18	8.9	4.8	3.5
South-West	2.2	4.2	3.2	2.2
West	9.7	9.4	18	9.8
North-West	7.9	5	14	6
Centre	13.2	6.2	12.8	8
Bucharest-Ilfov	42.2	57	37.5	60
Total	100	100	100	100

Source: National Trade Register Office of Bucharest.

As far as the other regions are concerned, the South, West and Centre are significant FDI recipients. The South seems to be particularly attractive for EU firms, especially in terms of capital invested (18 percent, only second after Bucharest–Ilfov) with respect to 8.9 percent of total non-EU FDI.

4.3 A FRAMEWORK ON PROFITABILITY

The traditional literature on FDI was established on the solid theory that foreign firms decide to invest abroad and perform better than domestic firms because they hold capabilities, which their local counterparts do not have (Hymer, 1967; Dunning, 1993; Porter, 1992). Conversely, recent studies find opposite results (King, 1999; Chhibber and Majumdar, 1999) that suggest that domestic firms' performance is better than foreign firms' performance for reasons such as the ability to exploit already established network ties and the superior knowledge of the local economic environment.

Some mixed evidence on the relation between performance and ownership was also found in the case of Romania. According to Konings (2000), in Romania there is no sign of a positive foreign ownership effect, but Boscaiu et al. (2000) finds that foreign firms perform better than domestic ones, especially if they are export oriented.

Since the dataset used in this analysis only covers foreign enterprises that invested in Romania, it is impossible to compare foreign and domestic firm performance. However, the analysis of foreign firms' performance should lead to interesting results concerning the determinants of their profitability, which, through further research, could be compared with that of domestic firms.

Hence, the analysis is carried out following Chhibber and Majumdar (1997), who adopt a very interesting framework to explain the impact of foreign ownership (measured as percentage of capital assets), on Indian firm profitability. As a measure of performance the authors use two different variables: return on sales (ROS) and return on assets (ROA).[5]

The variables they use to explain firm-level performance are of particular interest. Firstly, in order to pick up competitive conditions, export intensity[6] is introduced as a regressor. Secondly, firm size, classified according to sales level, is used to measure how organizational factors can influence performance. Thirdly, a variable representing capital intensity[7] is used to account for variations in firms' input structures. Finally, industry-specific controls are introduced for five sectors (chemicals, engineering, finance, foods, mining, textile, agriculture and others). The results of their study show a positive relation between export intensity and performance, as well as between size and performance. An increasing and positive relationship between ownership and profitability is found to be significant, that is, the higher the percentage of capital assets belonging to the foreign investors, the higher is the firm's profitability.

Mutinelli and Piscitello (1997) have similar findings in their study on Italian FDI in CEE, finding that export intensity and profitability of Italian firms investing abroad depend positively on firm size.

The relationship between size, export intensity and performance has also been explored in some other studies with mixed results. No direct link between firm size and export performance was found by Moen (1998), even if small highly specialized and competitive firms seem to be as successful in international markets as larger exporting firms. Lu and Beamish (2001) measure the performance of Japanese firms using ROA and ROS as dependent variables and several other measures, such as export intensity, size, FDI activities and joint ventures, as independent variables. They find that firm size is negatively related to performance, while exporting and FDI activity have a positive and increasing effect on profitability.

4.4 DATA DESCRIPTION

Recall that the analysis aims at highlighting differences in profitability related to home country, firm size and economic activity, in order to identify best performing enterprise typologies among EU firms active in Romania in the second part of the 1990s. The FDI database created by the Chamber of Commerce and Industry of Bucharest, which contains all balance sheet information concerning foreign enterprises in Romania since 1990. is ideal for this purpose. The database records FDI of each size i (micro, small, medium and large) in each sector j over home country n at time t. Size is measured according to the number of employees and corresponds to the EU classification. Micro, small, medium and large firms are defined as firms with 1–9, 10–49, 50–249 and over 250 employees.[8]

Firms are sorted into specific sectors using NACE rev.1 classification of economic activities. I have ten sectors, namely agriculture, construction, mining and quarrying, food beverage and tobacco, basic metals, pulp paper and products, textile leather and footwear, other manufacturing products, services, transport. In spite of its importance in terms of number of investments, the trade sector was excluded from the analysis, because of data unreliability.

In addition, four countries (Ireland, Finland, Portugal and Spain) had to be excluded from the analysis because of the small number of foreign firms recorded in the database.

As can be noted in Table 4.4, the distribution of foreign firms by size is dominated by micro firms, decreasing constantly, but in 2000 still representing 82 percent of total number of firms and 77.2 percent of total number of EU firms. The presence of large firms has been constant through the years, increasing only slightly and reaching 2.8 percent of the total number of firms in both groups of countries.

Table 4.4   Foreign firms by size (percentage distribution)

	1994		1997		2000	
Size	World	EU	World	EU	World	EU
Micro	88.9	86.0	85.3	80.3	82.0	77.2
Small	6.7	8.3	10.2	13.6	11.0	14.4
Medium	1.9	2.3	2.6	3.8	3.8	5.5
Large	2.2	2.5	1.7	2.2	2.8	2.8
Total	100	100	100	100	100	100

Source: Author's calculation from Chamber of Commerce database.

Figure 4.5 shows the trend of performance by firm size, measured by return on investments (ROA), following Chhibber and Majumdar. ROA is decreasing in time for all firms sizes, with the exception of large firms, whose ROA has remained more or less constant over time. It is interesting to notice that, though at the beginning of the transition process the level of profitability was quite heterogeneous among firms of different size, and very high, especially for small and medium enterprises, in 2000 it has become much more homogeneous and convergent to lower levels (around 8 percent).

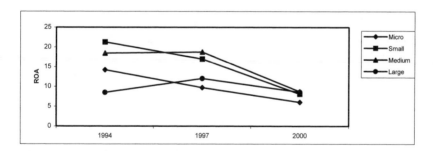

Source: Author's calculation from Chamber of Commerce database.

Figure 4.5 EU FDI return on assets (ROA) by size

Figure 4.6 describes the trend of export intensity according again to firm size. Export intensity, calculated as the ratio of exports and turnover, is constantly increasing among all groups of firms: in 2000 all EU firms in Romania exported on average more than 25 percent of their total sales, while in 1994 less than 15 percent. Large firms are more export oriented in comparison to the others, which reached in 2000 approximately the same export intensity (approximately 28 percent).

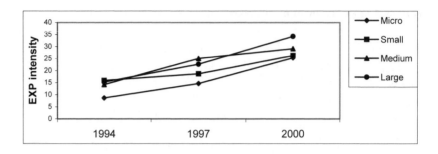

Source: Author's calculation from Chamber of Commerce database.

Figure 4.6 EU FDI export intensity by size

The distribution of EU FDI by sector is represented in Table 4.5. It is worth underlying the trend of the food sector, where a remarkable increase has occurred in the year 2000. At the same time the decrease in the service sector is quite significant. The remaining sectors keep growing.

Table 4.5   EU FDI distribution, ROA and export intensity by sector

Sector	Distribution			ROA (%)			Export intensity (%)		
	1994	1997	2000	1994	1997	2000	1994	1997	2000
Agriculture	143	196	398	6.7	5.7	2.3	12	11	17
Construction	199	310	118	22.8	14.4	6.9	2	2	3
Mining	19	14	404	14.1	8.1	3.8	4	11	2
Food	285	517	2961	13.4	11.7	5.4	3	6	9
Basic									
metals	92	183	618	11.9	15.3	9.1	13	18	33
Pulp, paper	120	171	598	18.4	22.7	9.3	4	2	6
Textiles	340	528	876	17.4	17.5	9.9	30	54	75
Other	596	969	948	13.0	11.2	6.9	22	28	33
Services	1297	2029	1566	20.9	13.1	9.1	7	18	22
Transport	350	609	641	17.0	17.4	10.7	27	36	52

Source: Author's calculation from Chamber of Commerce database

The same table shows the trends for ROA and export intensity. In all sectors a strong decrease of ROA is registered in 2000. The strongest declines of ROA were registered in the textile, pulp and paper, and construction sectors. As far as export intensity is concerned, it grew in all sectors, except for mining. The textile, leather and footwear industry export on sales ratio reached 75 percent.

The distribution of EU FDI by country (Table 4.6) shows clearly that in 2000 German and Italian enterprises, whose presence in the country dominates that of all other countries, are the least profitable and the most export oriented, together with the Belgian ones.

Table 4.6   EU FDI distribution, ROA and export intensity by country

Countries	Distribution			ROA (%)			Export intensity (%)		
	1994	1997	2000	1994	1997	2000	1994	1997	2000
Austria	277	408	488	18.9	6.4	16.6	12	34	23
Belgium	92	167	197	19.2	19.9	7.3	25	15	33
Denmark	19	35	97	6.0	8.9	19.9	23	18	4
France	311	446	849	14.9	5.9	12.9	11	24	15
Germany	1397	2077	3601	14.5	15.3	6.9	20	17	25
UK	107	208	256	7.9	17.7	21.0	29	19	12
Greece	111	224	526	16.7	9.0	12.9	7	23	13
Italy	828	1499	2540	10.7	9.1	8.5	24	16	31
Luxemburg	39	67	122	7.7	9.4	10.5	40	18	17
Netherlands	201	296	319	12.2	5.3	13.4	17	23	22
Sweden	59	99	133	17.1	19.5	16.0	14	7	21

Source: Author's calculation from Chamber of Commerce database.

4.5 ECONOMETRIC MODEL

In order to obtain a homogeneous database and be able to compare data, I grouped foreign firms in four categories, according to their size (micro, small, medium and large) and used average values by each group of firms. The total number of observations is 595 covering 10 industries,[9] in 11 EU home countries,[10] over three years (1994, 1997, 2000).

The dependent variable is ROA, as suggested by similar works on firms' performance (Chhibber and Majumdar, 1999; Lu and Beamish, 2001). ROA measures the average net profit as a percentage of net worth in each industry and country, so it shows the ability of firms (or of group of firms, as in this case) to create returns on the investment base of their business.

The independent variables are:

- NUMFIRMS = number of foreign firms in each industry, size, and year.

- EXP[11]   = exports/sales ratio measured by total exports on turnover
- KL[12]   = capital/labour ratio measured by the assets per employee
- LC   = labour costs measured by the average monthly wage per employee in each industry and year

NUMFIRMS by industry and size may measure competition effects or agglomeration (concentration) effects: if total number of foreign firms increases, profitability should decrease in the first case and increase in the second. This variable has been lagged one period in order to avoid introducing simultaneity into the regressions.

Export-oriented enterprises are more profitable than market-oriented enterprises and small- and medium-size firms tend to be labour seeking, while market-seeking enterprises are generally large (Mutinelli and Piscitello, 1998). I expect that these relations should be confirmed by the econometric analysis, i.e. the coefficient of EXP should be positive and decreasing when firm size increases.

Including the firm's capital intensity (KL) in the regression is particularly significant in a country such as Romania, where the debate on the determinants of FDI is still wide open. In other words, this variable should help to shed light on the question whether profitability is more affected by capital intensity or labour intensity.

Finally, labour costs (LC) are usually considered as a determinant for the decision to invest abroad, but here LC represents one of the determinants of the firm's performance: one can expect that the relation between LC and profitability is significant and negative, because availability of cheap labour should have a positive effect on profits.

Two dummy variables were also included in order to control for sector and country fixed effects.

4.6 ECONOMETRIC RESULTS

First, I run a general regression on the pooled sample. Then a fixed effect regression is estimated in order to control for size effects. And finally I run a variable slope coefficient model in order to analyse and compare the explanatory power of the exogenous variables in relation to firm size.

The regression results are presented in Table 4.7. Column I contains the results for the base regression, while column II shows the fixed effect regression results. All but the labour cost variable are significant. In columns III, IV and V the sector and the country dummy variables are included.

A positive relation between NUMFIRMS and profitability is displayed, indicating that foreign firms take advantage of the presence of other already established foreign firms in the same sectors and with the same size.

The export on sales ratio has a positive sign and, in column II, weak statistical significance (10 percent). This might indicate that foreign firms' profitability does not completely depend on exports, but is likely to rely also on the domestic market conditions. Nevertheless it would be too strong to generalise such a result for all the sectors of the economy and for all firms, regardless of their sizes.

The findings on capital intensity are quite interesting: the coefficient of KL variable is negative and statistically significant at the 1 percent level. Such a result confirms the evidence found by Boscaiu (2000) concerning the high performance of low capital-intensive foreign firms in Romania for the year 1998. The explanation that could be put forward for this result is threefold. First, capital-intensive firms need a longer period of time to assess their activity and become profitable. Second, capital-intensive FDI could be the result of some privatization operations that imply considerable restructuring activities, both from a financial and time perspective. Third, it could be that the characteristics of the domestic environment better fit the needs of labour-intensive firms, which take advantage of it in terms of profitability.

Although the labour cost coefficient is not always statistically significant, its negative sign is consistent with expectations. Labour costs have an inverse relation with profitability.[13]

After including home country and sector dummies (columns III, IV and V) all coefficients maintain the same result. Apparently, profitability is not affected by the country of origin of the firms (country dummies are never significant), while sector dummy variables (which are always significant) play an important role in determining profitability along with the other determinants.

Model IV is my preferred model because it has the significant sector dummies and because it, like all of the models except the first one, has firm fixed effects. Although firm size is not controlled in Model IV, the fixed effects reduce the effect of size on heterogeneity. Notice that coefficients generally are estimated more precisely in the presence of sector dummy variables and firm fixed effects. In this estimate the coefficients on export intensity and labour costs have the expected signs and are significant at the 0.05 level. The coefficients of the number of firms and capital intensity are estimated even more precisely and have signs indicating the importance of localization economies and the importance of adopting labour-intensive methods of production to take advantage of labour abundance.

Finally, as we will see in the variable slope coefficient model (Table 4.7), size-specific effects may exist, suggesting data heterogeneity.

Table 4.7 Pooled and fixed-effects estimates

Variable	I	II	III	IV	V
Numfirms	0.084**	0.111***	0.110**	0.103***	0.087*
	(0.034)	(0.038)	(0.45)	(0.038)	(0.051)
Exp	0.459**	0.396*	0.408*	0.637**	0.620**
	(0.230)	(0.244)	(0.225)	(0.301)	(0.304)
KL	–0.314***	–0.288***	–0.295***	–0.265***	–0.270***
	(0.042)	(0.042)	(0.042)	(0.041)	(0.042)
LC	–0.071	–.100*	–0.099	–0.178**	–0.173**
	(0.066)	(0.073)	(0.071)	(0.076)	(0.077)
const	6.02***	5.87***	6.12***	5.28***	5.51***
	(0.532)	(0.521)	(0.523)	(0.533)	(0.548)
Country dummies	no	no	yes	no	yes
Sector dummies	no	no	no	yes***	yes***
n. obs.	595	595	595	595	595
R–sq	0.15	0.14	0.17	0.20	0.22
F-test		2.81**	1.67*	4.83***	2.19*

Notes:
*** indicates statistical significance at 0.01 level.
** indicates statistical significance at 0.05 level.
* indicates statistical significance at 0.1 level
Robust standard errors in parentheses

In order to better understand the role of the effects of size, I apply the variable-slope regression model. In this estimate the coefficient for NUMFIRMS is positive for micro, small and large firms, while it is negative, though insignificant, for medium-size ones. Therefore, it can be said that the micro and small firms enjoy localization externalities, while medium firms seem to suffer from competition effects. Although the coefficient is positive for large firms, it is very small and insignificant. As expected, the export on sales ratio's coefficient is positive and significant, confirming the importance of exports for profitability of foreign firms. This result does not hold for small and medium firms, as suggested by the negative sign of the estimated coefficients.

As far as capital intensity is concerned, the results are in line with those shown in Table 4.8: the estimated coefficients are negative and significant in all groups of firms.

Finally, results for labour costs are consistent with the regression results; in the absence of sector controls, they are not significant but have a negative sign.

Table 4.8   Variable slope coefficient model

Variable		Micro	Small	Medium	Large
Numfirms		0.128**	0.218**	–0.103	0.008**
		(–0.056)	(0.070)	(0.091)	(0.135)
Exp		–0.866**	–0.248	–0.248**	0.083**
		(–0.43)	(0.422)	(0.613)	(0.691)
KL		–0.304***	–0.436***	–0.040***	–0.182***
		(0.062)	(0.102)	(0.134)	(0.109)
LC		–0.153	–0.023	–0.088	–0.049
		(0.112)	(0.152)	(0.235)	(0.212)
R-sq	0.20				
F-test	1.64**				
n.obs	595	178	174	134	109

Notes:
Constant omitted.
*** indicates statistical significance at 0.01 level.
** indicates statistical significance at 0.05 level.
Robust standard errors in parentheses.

4.7   CONCLUSIONS

The goal of identifying best performing enterprise typologies is very ambitious and such an analysis cannot lead to an unequivocal result. In this chapter I find that profitability of EU FDI in Romania depends positively on agglomeration effects, generated by the presence of other foreign firms of the same size, and exports and negatively on capital intensity. The failure to find home-country effects on profitability is in contrast to the descriptive findings that German-, Italian- and Belgian-owned firms are the least profitable, a negative finding of some consequence.

These results are suggestive in terms of the roles of clustering, learning networks, and entrepreneurship in the Romanian economy. Foreign-owned firms of different size survive and they benefit by the existence of other such firms in their sector. This indication of localization economies suggests that clustering of foreign-owned firms and by extension domestic firms in a sector benefits from surrounding industry infrastructure and from the interaction of similar activities. The fact that these firms are attracted to the capital region supports this extension and may be indicative of a learning network.

The importance of entrepreneurship is also by implication. First, the country of origin does not seem to affect profitability. Thus, differences in profitability are more likely to be due to differences in conditions, such as market infrastructure and entrepreneurship, within Romania. If foreign-owned firms are to have a domestic market infrastructure to rely on, this infrastructure must be provided by both government and the private sector. This infrastructure consists both of public-utility services and the provision by the private domestic sector of business services and on-the-job training to develop a pool of effective labour. The latter clearly requires domestic entrepreneurship and the positive effect of labour intensity on profitability suggest that these entrepreneurs will be most successful with small, labour-intensive firms.

The preliminary look at firm size effects is also suggestive. The profitability of micro, small and large firms seems to be positively affected by localisation economies (with firms of the same size and sector) and by export intensity, while medium-size firms do not seem to take advantage of these two variables.

In spite of the expectation that larger firms' performance would depend positively on capital intensity, no firms gain positive effects on profitability from capital intensity. Moreover, they all seem to be much better off when their activity is rather labour-intensive.

These results could be a signal of the need to keep attracting firms (micro, small and large) that are efficiency seeking and export oriented, rather than focusing on the creation of attractive policies for FDI in high value added sectors or that are market oriented, which do not seem to be able to get any profit advantages from producing in Romania.

Needless to say, further analysis might help in strengthening these conclusions. In particular, it seems necessary to explore more in depth the performance of firms over a longer period of time and across different manufacturing sectors. The further analysis of the service sector, given its increasing importance in the Romanian economy, and the comparison of firms' performance in the two main branches of the economic activity should lead to more detailed results.

NOTES

1. See Konings (2001), Szanyi (1997), Alessandrini (2000), Resmini (1999), Altomonte and Resmini (2002), Bevan and Estrin (2000) among many other interesting empirical studies.
2. According to the European Bank for Reconstruction and Development, CEECs are divided into Central Eastern Europe and Baltic States (CEB), including the Czech Republic, Estonia,

Hungary, Latvia, Lithuania, Poland, Slovakia and Slovenia; South-Eastern Europe (SEE), including Albania, Bulgaria, Bosnia Herzegovina, Croatia, Yugoslavia, Macedonia and Romania; and the Commonwealth of Independent States (CIS) including Armenia Azerbaijan, Belarus, Georgia, Kazakhstan, Kyrgystan, Moldavia, Russia, Tajikistan, Ukraine and Uzbekistan.

3. The decreasing FDI inflows registered in Czech Republic, Hungary and Poland from 2000 (UNCTAD, 2003) can be interpreted as supporting the finding of Brenton and Di Mauro.
4. Romania should become a member of the EU in 2007, together with Bulgaria.
5. ROS is calculated as profit after depreciation, interest and taxes as a ratio of net sales. ROA is calculated as profit after depreciation, interest and taxes as a ratio of total assets
6. Export intensity is calculated as the ratio of exports to total sales of each company.
7. The authors use NET FIXED assets, calculated as the ratio of net fixed assets to total assets, to control for capital intensity in firms' operations.
8. This classification has been incorporated in the Romanian law. See law 133/1999, regarding the stimulation of the private entrepreneurs to set up and develop small and medium enterprises (SMEs).
9. The sectors correspond to the NACE classification.
10. As said before Ireland, Finland, Portugal and Spain are excluded because of the low level of investment in comparison to the other Member States.
11. Rojec and Stanojevic (2001) use this variable to compare foreign firms and domestic firms in Slovenia.
12. Blomstrom and Lipsey (1986) use the capital labour ratio to study the propensity of firms to produce abroad according to their size.
13. The result concerning labour cost could be affected by the data used, which are national averages derived from the Statistical Year Book edited by the National Office of Statistics.

REFERENCES

Alessandrini, S. (2000), *The EU Foreign Direct Investments in Central and Eastern Europe*, Milan: Giuffrè Editore.

Altomonte C. and L. Resmini (2002), 'Multinational corporations as a catalyst for industrial development: the case of Poland', *Scienze Regionali, The Italian Journal of Regional Science*, no.2, pp 29–58.

Bevan A. and S. Estrin (2000), 'The determinants of foreign direct investment in transition economies', CEPR, DP2638.

Blomstrom, M. and R. Lipsey (1986), 'Firm size and foreign direct investment', NBER Working paper series, WP no. 2092.

Blomstrom, M. and A. Kokko (1996), 'How foreign investment affects host countries', World Bank Policy Research WP no. 1745.

Blomstrom, M. and A. Kokko (1999), 'The determinants of host country spillovers from foreign direct investment: review and synthesis of the literature', SSE/EFI WP no. 239.

Boscaiu V., D. Liusnea, C. Munteanu and L. Puscoi (2000), 'Impact of the FDI productivity in Romanian manufacturing industry', Romanian Center for Economic Policies, WP no. 22

Brenton, P. and F. Di Mauro (1999), 'The potential magnitude and impact of FDI's flows to CEECs', *Journal of Economic Integration,* **14** (1), pp 59–74.

Chhibber, P.K and S.K. Majumdar (1999), 'Foreign ownership and profitability: property rights, strategic control and corporate performance in Indian industry', *Journal of Law and Economics,* **42** (1), pp. 209–39.

Dunning, J. (1993), 'Multinational enterprise and the global economy', Wokingham, England: Edison-Wesley Publishing Company.

Hymer, S. (1976), 'The international operations of national firms: a study of direct foreign investment', Phd. Dissertation M.I.T.

King, L. (1999), 'The developmental consequences of foreign direct investment in the transition from socialism to capitalism: the performance of foreign owned firms in Hungary', The William Davidson Institute, WP no. 277.

Konings, J. (2001), 'The effects of direct foreign investment on domestic firms: evidence from firm level panel data in emerging economies', *Economics of Transition*, **9** (3), pp. 619–34.

Lu, J.W. and P.W. Beamish (2001), 'The internationalization and performance of SMEs', *Strategic Management Journal*, **22**, pp. 565–86.

Moen, O. (1998), 'The relationship between firm size, competitive advantages and export performance revisited', *International Small Business Journal*, **18** (1), pp. 53–71.

Mutinelli, M. and L. Piscitello (1997), 'The influence of firm's size and international experience on the ownership structure of Italian FDI in manufacturing', *Small Business Economics*, **11** (1), pp. 43–56.

Porter, M. (1992), *The Competitive Advantage of Nations*, London: The MacMillan Press Ltd.

Resmini, L. (1999), 'The determinants of foreign direct investment into the CEECs: new evidence from sectoral patterns', LICOS, DP 83/1999.

Rojec, M. and M. Stanojevic (2001), 'Slovenia: factor cost seeking FDI and manufacturing', in G. Gradev (ed.) *CEE Countries in EU Companies: Strategies of Industrial Restructuring and Relocation*, Brussels: European Trade Union Institute, pp. 137–71.

Serbanescu, I. (2000), 'Can the vicious circle be broken?', in C. Ruhl and D. Deianu (eds) *Economic Transaction in Romania, Proceedings of the Conference 'Romania 2000, Ten Years of Transition'*, Bucharest: World Bank and Romanian Center for Economic Policies, pp. 77–94.

Szanyi, M. (1997), 'Experiences with foreign direct investment in Eastern Europe: advantages and disadvantages', Institute for World Economics, Hungarian Academy of Sciences, WP no. 85.

UNCTAD (2002), *World Investment Report 2002, Transnational Corporations and Export Competitiveness*, New York: United Nations.

UNCTAD (2003), *World Investment Report 2002, FDI Policies for Development: National and International Perspectives*, New York: United Nations.

5. Financial Integration and Investment Performance in the European Union

Hasan Vergil

5.1 INTRODUCTION

Integration among European financial markets has increased in recent years. European countries have lowered their capital market barriers as a part of broad liberalization or deregulation of domestic financial markets and adopted a single currency that has increased trade in goods within Europe and has provided easier access to their capital markets. The studies dealing with the real effects of financial integration have yielded mixed results (Blecker, 1999 and Checchi, 1992). On one hand, a number of studies support the view that open capital markets increase a reallocation of productive resources, enhance financial services and impose discipline on policy makers. On the other hand, many economists criticize financial integration using arguments such as the destabilizing effects of capital flows and reduced economic policy autonomy.

Part of this debate concerns the effect of financial integration on domestic investment. Many theoretical and empirical works have analyzed this relationship, but this literature is marked by conflicting results.

Sweeney (1997), Ries (1997), and Bacchetta (1992) link the relationship between financial integration and investment by assessing the information-providing role of the financial system. They argue that when capital markets are open, investors can use the information efficiently in the market to assess risks and improve their evaluations about projects. On the other hand, Tornell (1990) and Razin and Sadka (1991) make a theoretical case for capital controls to increase domestic investment. They analyze capital controls as emergency measures in the presence of distortions. Tornell (1990) presents a model in which Tobin taxes can increase real investment by reducing the variance of domestic interest rates caused by rumors unrelated to economic fundamentals.[1] Razin and Sadka (1991) argue that when it is difficult to tax foreign-source income, it may be optimal to impose restrictions on capital outflows to generate over-investment domestically.

Keynesian theories recognize institutions and structures in economies that make financial markets inefficient. Thus, according to these theories, government should control capital markets to guide the economy successfully. For example, using a Keynesian framework, Epstein and Schor (1992) argue that expansionary monetary and fiscal policies can in the presence of capital controls increase investment and employment.

The results of the theoretical models differ because they assume different channels through which capital controls affect investment. The empirical studies also reach conflicting results. For example, Lemmen and Eijffinger (1996) find that greater financial integration leads to lower investment and Klein and Olivei (1999) find that the effect of financial liberalization on investment is positive for industrialized countries and negative for developing countries. Grilli and Milesi-Ferretti (1995) find that capital controls reduce real interest rates but also raise inflation rates. They do not test for the effects of capital controls on investment, but their results suggest that they could encourage investment through a lower interest rate.

The main purpose of this chapter is to estimate the effects of the degree of financial integration, or more precisely of the intensity of capital controls, on private investment for the six European countries (France, Germany, the Netherlands, Norway, Sweden and the United Kingdom) over the period 1985:1–2001:4. The degree of financial integration is estimated by calculating covered interest rate differentials. Two investment models (the individual time-series version of the model and the panel data fixed-effects model) are built up using empirical investment models based on factors affecting private investment rates.

This chapter improves the previous studies by Lemmen and Eijffinger (1996) and Grilli and Milesi-Ferretti (1995), which investigate the determinants of financial integration and Klein and Olivei (1999), which investigates the effect of capital liberalization on economic growth through its effect on financial depth. One criticism of the empirical studies is that, except for Lemmen and Eijffinger (1996), their cross-country regression analyses proxy for capital controls with dummy variables constructed using the IMF's *Exchange Arrangements and Exchange Restrictions*. In this study, deviations from covered interest rate parity are used as a proxy for financial integration. In addition, this chapter focuses on directly testing the effects of financial integration on investment, which only a few previous studies have done.

The chapter is organized as follows. Section 5.2 provides a discussion of measuring financial integration and the method of estimating covered interest rate differentials. Section 5.3 presents an empirical model along with the theoretical background. In this model, covered interest rate differentials are specified as one of the determinants of private investment. Section 5.4

presents the empirical results. The last section contains a summary and conclusions.

5.2 MEASURING THE INTEGRATION OF CAPITAL MARKETS

Financial integration has been analyzed in the literature in a number of ways. First, in their seminal paper, Feldstein and Horioka (1980) argued that in a world of perfect capital mobility, there should not be any correlation between the rate of saving in one country and the rate of investment in that country. On a sample of 21 OECD countries over the 1960–74 period, they found that investment and national saving rates are closely correlated suggesting an absence of international capital integration. This approach has been by those who are not convinced that saving/investment correlations can adequately reflect the degree of international capital mobility.[2]

A second approach focuses on the idea of 'the law of one price' to test for financial integration of capital markets (for example Frankel and MacArthur, 1988; Lemmen and Eijffinger, 1996). In a perfectly integrated asset market, a single price should prevail over all markets for given assets with the same characteristics. One way of assessing the degree of integration of markets is to look at deviations from covered interest rate parity between any pair of Eurocurrency rates. Covered interest rate parity asserts that if the return on any instrument denominated in different currency is adjusted for the cost of cover in the forward exchange market, then the returns on instruments with the same characteristics should be just equal to each other. That is:

$$COVERED\ INTEREST\ RATE\ PARITY:\quad i_{k,t} = i_{w,t} + f_t \qquad (5.1)$$

where $i_{k,t} = \ln(1+$ nominal interest rate denominated in currency k), $i_{w,t} = \ln(1 +$ nominal interest rate denominated in currency w), and $f_t = \ln(F_t / S_t)$ (where F_t is the forward exchange rate, and S_t is the spot exchange rate, both denominated in currency k/currency w).

If both interest rates are expressed in the same currency, the forward premium is omitted. Since no currency risk is involved, the comparison of offshore and onshore interest rates is sufficient to measure the degree of capital controls. That is:

$$COVERED\ INTEREST\ RATE\ PARITY:\quad i_{k,t} = i_{b,t} \qquad (5.2)$$

where $i_{k,t} = \ln(1+$ Eurocurrency rate denominated in currency k) and $i_{b,t} = \ln(1+$ nominal interest rate denominated in currency k)

A third methodology to test for financial integration is based on deviations from uncovered interest rate parity. Uncovered interest rate parity states that equilibrium in international financial markets occurs whenever domestic and foreign assets have equal expected returns. That is:

$$UNCOVERED\ INTEREST\ RATE\ PARITY: i = i^* + \square s^e \qquad (5.3)$$

where i and i^* are domestic and foreign interest rates on comparable assets and Δs^e is the expected rate of change of the domestic currency. When the parity holds, the anticipated rate of change of the domestic currency, Δs^e, will be equal to the nominal interest rate differentials among similar assets denominated in domestic and foreign currencies. The deviations from parity reflect barriers to investing abroad including capital controls.

Most of the literature follows an indirect approach to measure the degree of intensity of capital controls in that they estimate covered interest rate differentials (for example Ito, 1983; Frankel and MacArthur, 1988; Marston, 1995; Lemmen and Eijffinger, 1996). However, some of the literature constructs dummy variables to measure the degree of financial integration using the International Monetary Fund's *Annual Report on Exchange Arrangements and Exchange Restrictions* (Epstein and Schor, 1992; Grilli and Milesi-Ferretti, 1995; Razin and Rose, 1994). For example, Razin and Rose (1994) use the *Annual Report* of IMF by taking the country-specific annual dummy variables as a proxy for restrictions on capital account. If a country has a restriction on capital account, they assign it a value of 1; otherwise it gets a value of 0.

The problem with the use of dummy variables is that they provide no measure of the intensity of capital controls (Epstein and Schor, 1992, p. 143; Grilli and Milesi-Ferretti, 1995, p. 525; Lemmen and Eijffinger, 1996, p. 434). A related problem with the dummy variable approach is that restrictions are not always effective. The private sector generally finds ways to evade capital controls internationally, such as by using leads and lags for exports and imports. In countries with restrictions on capital mobility, the private sector can prepare 'faked' invoices by under-invoicing of exports and over-invoicing of imports to evade legal controls on capital flows. Therefore, it might be a mistake to conclude that the market is segmented when there are significant differences between the actual and legal intensity of controls.

Covered interest rate differentials can arise for any of four reasons. First, costs in the financial transaction and in the acquisition and sale of foreign currency generate deviations from covered interest rate parity. Second, domestic capital market imperfections, such as regulations of returns on domestic securities, might prevent financial markets from reaching equilibrium. Third, the market may be segmented by the imposition of government intervention and regulation, including controls on international capital flows or foreign exchange transactions. Finally, there is the possibility that political risk associated with investment in a foreign country might generate deviations from parity. Political risk arises because of the concern that a foreign government can intervene in financial markets and freeze foreign investment in their markets. Although covered interest rate differentials can arise for reasons other than capital controls, we argue that covered interest rate differentials can be used as reasonable proxies for capital controls.

Covered interest rate differentials for Norway and Sweden are calculated by comparison of national interest rates in any currency with Eurodollar rates using one of Ito's (1983) arbitrage measures. Marston (1995), Frankel and MacArthur (1988), Lemmen and Eijffinger (1996), and many others employ similar formulations. Formally, the measure is defined as follows:

$$CD = \{\ln(1 + EURO\$ / 400) + \ln(F/S) - \ln(1 + INT / 400)\} * 400 \quad (5.4)$$

where $EURO\$$ is the three-month United States Eurodollar deposit rate, F is the three-month forward exchange rate measured in national currency per dollar, S is the spot exchange rate measured in national currency per dollar, INT is the three-month national interest rates and ln is the natural logarithm. Since the interest rates are for three-month maturities expressed in percent per annum, the interest rates are divided by 400 for comparison with three-month (90 day) forward premia, and then the results are multiplied by 400 to express the per-quarter gain as an annual percentage yield.

The representative three-month Eurocurrency rates are available for the following EU countries: the United Kingdom, the Netherlands, France and Germany and Euro Area from the IMF IFS (quarterly series). The covered interest rate differentials for these countries are estimated by comparison of national interest rates and Eurocurrency rates in the same currency using the formula below:

$$CD = \{\ln(1 + EUROCURRENCY / 400) - \ln(1 + INT / 400)\} * 400 \quad (5.5)$$

where $EUROCURRENCY$ is the three-month Eurocurrency Deposit Rate, INT is the three-month national interest rate and ln is the natural logarithm.

Table 5.1 shows correlations among the deviations from covered interest rate parity. Correlations are calculated from quarterly data over the period 1991:1–1998:4. Except for Germany, deviations from covered interest rate differentials of the United Kingdom are negatively correlated with deviations from covered interest rate differentials of the other countries. Correlations are higher between the deviations of Sweden and Norway and France and the Netherlands compared to the correlations among other countries.

Table 5.1   Correlations of the covered interest rate differentials

	France	Germany	Norway	Netherlands	Sweden	UK
France	1	0.24	0.17	0.64	0.42	–0.49
Germany	0.24	1	–0.13	0.29	0.01	0.25
Norway	0.17	–0.13	1	–0.07	0.54	–0.09
Netherlands	0.64	0.29	–0.07	1	0.12	–0.30
Sweden	0.42	0.01	0.54	0.12	1	–0.17
UK	–0.49	0.25	–0.09	–0.30	–0.17	1

Table 5.2 reports statistics on the covered interest rate differentials for six countries over the period starting from 1985:1. On average, except Norway, the sample countries have positive differentials, which suggest that there could be capital controls or transaction costs currently operating to discourage capital from flowing out of the country. Although it is very small, on average, Norway's interest rate differentials are negative. Of the six countries, France and Sweden have higher covered interest rate differentials. The differentials averaged only 0.05 percent per annum for Germany, 0.03 percent per annum for the Netherlands, and 0.06 percent per annum for the United Kingdom over the sample periods. Although the means of Germany, the Netherlands and the United Kingdom are statistically significant at the 5 percent level, they are not economically significant since the differentials are most likely in the transactions cost band.[3] In other words, the deviations from the covered interest rate parity in these countries are most likely due to transactions costs. Similarly, Norway's differential is effectively zero. Therefore, it can be concluded that while Germany, Norway, the Netherlands and the United Kingdom have financially integrated capital markets, France and Sweden impose some barriers discouraging capital outflow over the sample periods.

5.3   THE EMPIRICAL INVESTMENT MODEL

This section uses an investment model that synthesizes the results of previous empirical estimates of investment functions in cross-country studies. The usual methodology in these studies is to employ combinations of economic, institutional and political variables that are econometrically significant in explaining private investment. The factors included in these models have proven to be successful in explaining private investment. More specifically, the empirical models generally include some kind of proxy for accelerator effects as well as other variables.

Table 5.2   Means and standard deviations of covered interest rate differentials

Country	No. of obs.	Mean[a]	Standard deviation
France[b]	68	0.209	0.654
Germany[b]	44	0.054	0.136
Norway	56	−0.005	0.781
Netherlands[b]	56	0.030	0.069
Sweden	56	0.102	1.023
United Kingdom[b]	68	0.062	0.061

Note: [a]indicates that negative (positive) sign corresponds to controls on capital inflows (outflows) and [b]indicates that sample mean is different from zero with 95 percent confidence.

Most of the cross-country studies that have tested for the determinants of investment have largely focused on developing countries, while the sample of countries in this study consists of industrialized countries. However, many of these factors (such as macroeconomic uncertainty and the trade share of GDP) could also be relevant in industrialized countries. As will be shown below, these variables generally have the expected signs in our results. In any case, the empirical model sufficiently tests the impact of the financial integration on private investment for our sample of countries.

5.3.1 The Specification of the Model

This section discusses the determinants of private investment besides financial integration variable in order to examine the relationship between financial integration and private investment. Based on the previous research surveyed below, the following variables will be employed as determinants of private investment: (1) the lagged percentage change in real GDP (GR), as a proxy for the income accelerator; (2) the ratio of public sector investment to GDP (IG); (3) inflation volatility (INFV), as a proxy for macroeconomic uncertainty; (4) the trade share (OPEN); and (5) the covered interest rate differentials (CD). The theoretical and empirical motivations for using each of these factors are explained in the following subsections.

Income accelerator
There is little doubt that the income accelerator is an important determinant of investment. Almost all investment models include one form of income

accelerator and they all emphasize the importance of the positive relationship between changes in output and the level of investment. As Bosworth (1993, p. 84) asserts, 'at the empirical level most studies have confirmed a part of the model in that they have consistently found a strong correlation between investment and changes in output'.

One commonly used measure of the income accelerator effect is the percentage change in real GDP. A relationship between income growth and investment can be derived from flexible accelerator investment models in which it is assumed that the desired (or optimal) capital stock is a linear function of output. Similarly, many studies use the percentage change in per capita GDP as a proxy for the income accelerator effect. In any case, population growth rates are low and stable in all of the sample countries, and therefore the use of per capita GDP growth rates makes little difference to the results. The investment studies that include the percentage change in GDP and GDP per capita, such as Greene and Villanueva (1991) and Oshikoya (1994), find a positive impact on investment.

The ratio of public sector investment to GDP
Theoretically, the effect of government investment on private investment is ambiguous. The effects of public investment on private investment can go in two different directions. On the one hand, public investment may complement private investment by raising demand for private output and expanding aggregate demand thereby raising the productivity of capital by creating infrastructure and other externalities. On the other hand, public investment may crowd out private investment by producing products that compete with private output, or by competing with private investment for physical or financial resources thereby causing higher interest rates, credit rationing, and a higher tax burden. The net effect of public investment on private investment depends on the relative strength of these various effects.

The empirical studies on this issue reflect this controversy. Aschauer (1989) found that public and private investments are complementary for the United States over the period 1925–1985. Greene and Villanueva (1991), and Oshikoya (1994) found a positive effect of public investment in developing countries. On the other hand, Balassa (1993) found a negative relationship between public and private investment. The relationship between private and public investment is still a debatable issue.[4]

Inflation volatility as a proxy for macroeconomic uncertainty
The irreversible nature of investment suggests that once investment is made, installed capital cannot be used in another economic activity without incurring a substantial cost. Therefore, private investors take into account uncertainty about the economic, social and political environment before

installing capital. A large recent literature shows that the option to wait rather than invest because of irreversibility can significantly affect investment decisions.

In this study, the level of macroeconomic uncertainty is represented by the volatility of the percentage change in the country's consumer price index. Empirical studies such as Serven and Solimano (1993), and Serven (1997) provide evidence that inflation volatility has a negative impact on domestic investment. In this study, following Serven (1997), we calculated inflation volatility as the standard deviation of the percentage change in the country's consumer price index over a four-quarter period (t, $t - 1$, $t - 2$, and $t - 3$). This provides relatively smooth volatility rates since the coefficient of variation would become extremely large at very low or very high inflation rates.

Trade share
The previous literature supports the hypothesis that there is a strong positive relationship between investment and openness. Baldwin and Seghezza (1996a, 1996b) explain the reasons as follows: first, traded goods and services are more capital-intensive relative to non-traded goods and services, hence, trade liberalization stimulates the demand for capital. Second, investment-goods production uses imported intermediates, and therefore an increase in trade lowers the price of capital goods. Third, trade liberalization increases competition in the international market for machinery and equipment and thus lowers the cost of capital. Empirical studies, such as Levine and Renelt (1992) and Vamvakidis (1998), also find a positive link between openness and investment. In most of the studies, openness is measured by the percentage trade share of GDP, which we define as *OPEN* = [(*exports* + *imports*) / *GDP*]*100.

5.4 EMPIRICAL RESULTS

The discussion above suggests the following equation:

$$IP_t = \beta_0 + \beta_1 IG_t + \beta_2 GR_{t-3} + \beta_3 INFV_t + \beta_4 OPEN_t + \beta_5 CD_t + u_t \quad (5.6)$$

where,

IP = the ratio of private investment as a percentage of GDP;
CD = the covered interest rate differential;
IG = the ratio of government investment as a percentage of GDP;
GR = the percentage change in real GDP;

INFV = inflation volatility;
OPEN = trade share as a percentage of GDP;
and *u* = disturbance term.

Based on the discussion in the introduction, the effects of financial integration variable proxied by covered interest rate differentials are ambiguous. The percentage change in real GDP and the trade share, however, should have positive effects on private investment. In contrast, inflation volatility is expected to have negative effects on private investment and the effect of the ratio of government investment to GDP on private investment is ambiguous.

Before proceeding to discuss the results of the time-series estimations, it is necessary to check the possibility of non-stationary data. Table 5.3 reports the unit root test results. According to the ADF test results, most of the variables are stationary at the 1, 5 and 10 percent levels. The results of the ADF test statistics indicate that financial integration variable (CD) is stationary in all countries, private investment is non-stationary in five countries, and the other variables are generally stationary. Econometric theory suggests using non-stationary variables in first differences while using the stationary variables in levels. The model is specified according to the suggestion of the econometric theory.

Table 5.3   ADF unit root test results

Country	France	Germany	Netherlands
CD	-3.93^{*}	-3.16^{**}	-8.52^{*}
INFV	-2.85^{**}	-4.38^{*}	-3.59^{*}
GR	-5.87^{*}	-4.74^{*}	-5.55^{*}
IG	-1.78	-1.49	-3.55^{*}
IP	-1.79	-0.29	-2.25
OPEN	-0.75	-0.22	-3.65^{*}
Country	Norway	Sweden	UK
CD	-4.61^{*}	-3.47^{**}	-4.27^{*}
INFV	-4.18^{*}	-1.71	-3.72^{*}
GR	-3.61^{*}	-2.86^{***}	-2.19
IG	-2.81^{***}	-2.78^{***}	-1.29
IP	-1.53	-2.31	-3.10^{**}
OPEN	-3.15^{**}	-0.41	-2.21

Notes:
The order of lag is determined by the Akaike Information Criterion.

*, ** and *** indicate that the variable is stationary at the 1 percent, 5 percent and 10 percent level, respectively.

The equations are tested using the OLS for France, Germany, the Netherlands, Norway, Sweden and the United Kingdom over the period starting from 1985:1, and then, the relationship is estimated using the fixed-effects panel data model. Quarterly data is employed in all the estimations.

Tables 5.4 and 5.5 show the estimation results of the individual time-series models with the financial integration variable proxied by covered interest rate differentials. Each model fulfills the conditions of serial non-correlation and homoscedasticity, and parameter stability (except Germany for which the instability might be due to the inadequate sub-sample size). The signs of the coefficients for the variables are mostly as theoretically expected. In order to avoid a simultaneity problem, the growth rate of GDP is specified with lags. The lag is two for Sweden and three for the other countries because these lags give the best results.

Growth in GDP has a significantly positive sign for four countries and is insignificant for two. Public investment also enters with a positive sign, significant in two countries and insignificant in four. This finding supports the results of Aschauer (1989) and Greene and Villanueva (1991) suggesting that public sector investment is complementary to private sector investment for the industrialized countries in the sample. As theoretically expected, inflation volatility is negatively signed in four countries, being significant for Norway at the 10 percent level and the United Kingdom at the 5 percent level; it is positive but insignificant in two countries. The estimated coefficient for the openness (OPEN) is positive and significant for three countries and is insignificant for the other three countries with reverse sign for two. These results suggest that for three countries in the sample trade liberalization increases private sector investment.

Finally, the financial integration coefficient (CD) enters with a negative sign, significant for Norway at the 1 percent level and the United Kingdom at the 5 percent level; however, it enters with a positive and significant sign for France at the 1 percent level. The CD coefficients for the other countries are not significant. The coefficients for Norway and the United Kingdom indicate that 1 percentage point rise in capital export restrictions would reduce private investment 0.73 and 2.02 percentage points, respectively. The coefficient for France indicates that 1 percentage point rise in capital export restrictions would increase private investment 0.09 percentage point. In other words, while an increase in financial integration has positive effects on private investment in Norway and the United Kingdom, an increase in financial integration has negative effects on private investment in France for the sample periods. For the rest of the countries, the impact of the covered interest rate differentials on percentage private investment ratio is insignificant. The time-series estimations indicate that financial integration has varying effects in different country regressions. The estimations do not provide uniform strong conclusions about the effect of short-term integration on private investment.

Table 5.4   Regression results for investment models

Dependent variable: private investment as a percentage of GDP			
Country	France	Germany [	Netherlands
Period	(1985:1–2001:4)	(1992:1–2001:4)	(1985:1–1998:4)
# of Observations	68	40	56
Variables			
CD	0.091*	−0.378	0.283
	(2.86)	(−0.72)	(0.28)
INFV	−0.011	0.057	0.176
	(−0.29)	(1.12)	(1.52)
GR($t-3$)	0.004*	−0.0004	0.139***
	(3.17)	(−0.07)	(1.66)
IG	0.851*	0.862	0.384
	(2.80)	(1.27)	(0.74)
OPEN	0.059*	0.117***	0.002
	(3.67)	(1.88)	(0.25)
Summary Statistics			
Adj R^2	0.53	0.18	0.17
DW	2.02	1.92	1.97
Serial Corr	$\chi^2[2] = 4.38$	$\chi^2[2] = 2.04$	$\chi^2[2] = 0.24$
NORM	$\chi^2[2] = 1.21$	$\chi^2[2] = 0.02$	$\chi^2[2] = 2.41$
CHOW	$F[8, 52] = 1.40$	$F[7, 26] = 3.01$	$F[7, 42] = 2.17$

Notes:
Non-stationary variables are in first differences. Figures in parentheses are the t-statistics.
*, ** and *** indicate that the variable is statistically significant at the 1 percent, 5 percent and 10 percent level, respectively. Constants and AR adjustments are not reported. [indicates that the White Procedure was applied for heteroscedasticity. Serial Corr χ^2 [2] is the second order Breusch-Godfrey Serial Correlation LM Test. NORM χ^2 [2] is the Jarqua-Bera normality test of the residuals. CHOW is the Chow parameter instability test using the mid-point of the sample period as the potential breakpoint.

Equation (5.6) is also estimated using the fixed-effects panel data model to test the robustness of the findings in the time-series estimations. Standard panel data models take the intercept of Equation (5.6) to be the same for all countries and, thus, do not take into account unobservable country-specific effects such as culture and institutional factors that might be correlated with the right-hand side variables of the equation. This chapter controls this bias using the fixed-effects panel data model, which allows intercept to be different for each country.

Table 5.5 Regression results for investment models

Dependent variable: private investment as a percentage of GDP			
Country	Norway	Sweden	UK
Period	(1986:1–1998:4)	(1985:3–1998:4)	(1985:1–2001:4)
# of Observations	52	54	68
Variables			
CD	-0.731^{*}	0.005	
	(-2.72)	(0.06)	(-2.35)
INFV	-0.401^{***}	-0.06	-0.160^{**}
	(-1.76)	(-1.04)	(-2.42)
GR(t–3)$^{\square}$	0.171^{*}	0.129^{*}	0.002
	(3.10)	(10.94)	(0.10)
IG	0.227		0.447
	(0.54)	(1.46)	(2.67)
OPEN	-0.068	0.069^{***}	-0.061
	(-1.05)	(1.84)	(-1.42)
Summary Statistics			
Adj R^2	0.43	0.75	0.90
DW	2.03	2.04	1.78
Serial Corr	$\square^2[2] = 1.33$	$\square^2[2] = 0.12$	$\square^2[2] = 5.66$
NORM	$\square^2[2] = 0.95$	$\square^2[2] = 1.16$	$\square^2[2] = 0.94$
CHOW	$F[7,38] = 1.66$	$F[6, 42] = 1.35$	$F[7, 54] = 1.15$

Notes:
Non-stationary variables are in first differences. Figures in parentheses are the t-statistics. γ shows that the lag order of GR is 2 for Sweden. Constants and AR adjustments are not reported. Serial Corr χ2[2] is the second order Breusch-Godfrey Serial Correlation LM Test. NORM χ2[2] is the Jarqua- Bera normality test of the residuals. *, ** and *** indicate that the variable is statistically significant at the 1 percent, 5 percent and 10 percent level, respectively. CHOW is the Chow parameter instability test using the mid-point of the sample period as the potential breakpoint.

Therefore, the specification of Equation (5.6) with the fixed effects is:

$$IP_{it} = \beta_{0it} + \beta_1 IG_{it} + \beta_2 GR_{i\,t-2} + \beta_3 INFV_{it} + \beta_4 OPEN_{it} + \beta_5 CD_{it} + u_{it} \quad (5.7)$$

where β_{0it} is the country-specific intercept. The sample period covers 14 years from 1985 to 1998 for the six countries (France, Germany, the Netherlands, Norway, Sweden and the United Kingdom).

Table 5.6 reports the estimates of Equation (5.7). Sample I is an unbalanced panel because the data for Germany are missing before the 1991 period and the sample II is a balanced panel that excludes Germany. The relevant data is expressed in the percentage GDP ratios for all the countries. Thus, it is appropriate to use them in the panel data fixed-effects model. Samples I and II indicate that the overall fit of the equation is fairly good, and the models fulfill the conditions of serial non-correlation and homoscedasticity.

Chow's stability test for the parameter estimates is conducted for samples I and II. The resulting F-statistic values are 2.60 and 3.33 suggesting the existence of instability (at the 5 percent level) in the parameter estimates. These unstable parameter estimates might be only temporally, only across countries, or both. In order to figure out the source of instability, one way is to check the parameter estimates of the individual time-series regressions. Tables 5.4 and 5.5 indicate the existence of stability for the countries, except Germany. An inadequate sub-sample size might yield unstable parameter estimates for Germany. Thus, the stable individual time-series regressions suggest that the lack of cross-country uniformity possibly accounts for the observed instability in the equation.

As expected theoretically, the GDP growth rate enters with a positive and significant sign. Government investment has a significantly positive effect on private investment suggesting that private sector and government investment are complementary. Inflation volatility and trade share coefficients are insignificant and enter with a negative and positive signs, respectively. These results are in conformance with the theoretical expectations and the results obtained from the time-series estimations.

Interestingly, the financial integration coefficient has a negative sign and is statistically significant at 10 percent level in samples I and II. The coefficients indicate that 1 percentage point rise in the capital export restrictions would reduce private investment 0.18 percentage point for the sample countries. These overall results suggest that greater financial integration leads to higher private investment.

5.5 SUMMARY AND CONCLUSIONS

This chapter tests the relationship between financial integration and private investment, developing empirical time-series and panel data investment models for six European countries over the period 1985:1–2001:4. The deviations from covered interest rate parity are used as a proxy for financial integration. The analyses of the covered interest rate differentials indicate that, on average, the deviations from the covered interest rate parity of Germany, the Netherlands, Norway and the United Kingdom are most likely due to the transactions costs, suggesting that they have financially integrated capital markets over the sample period. In contrast, on average, France and Sweden impose some barriers discouraging capital outflows.

Table 5.6 Fixed-effects panel data results

Period # of Observations	Sample I (1985:3–1998:4) 288	Sample II (1985:3–1998:4) 260
	Variables	
CD	-0.181^{***}	-0.184^{***}
	(−1.76)	(−1.77)
INFV	−0.067	−0.079
	(−0.94)	(1.01)
GR_{t-2}	0.027^{***}	0.027^{***}
	(1.87)	(1.89)
IG	1.323^{*}	1.322^{*}
	(4.50)	(4.39)
OPEN	0.030	0.026
	(0.82)	(0.70)
	Summary Statistics	
Adj R^2	0.88	0.87
DW	2.04	2.03
CHOW	$F[13, 262] = 2.60$	$F[12, 236] = 3.33$

Notes:
Figures in parentheses are the White Heteroscedasticity consistent t-statistics. The fixed-effects constants and AR adjustments are not reported.
*, ** and *** indicate that the variable is statistically significant at the 1 percent, 5 percent and 10 percent level, respectively. CHOW is the Chow parameter instability test using the mid-point of the sample period as the potential breakpoint.

Having taken into account the non-stationary behavior of the variables, the time-series estimations indicate that capital export restrictions have significant negative effects on private investment for Norway and the United Kingdom and significant positive effects on private investment for France. The individual time-series regressions suggest that financial integration can affect private investment in a variety of ways and the effect of financial integration policies may depend on the economic structure of the country and overall economic policy regime in each country.

In the panel data fixed-effects model, the covered interest rate differentials variable has a negative sign and is statistically significant suggesting that greater financial integration leads to higher private investment. The positive relationship between financial integration and private investment can be explained by the fact that liberalized short-term capital might move around the globe and re-enter the original economy with increased returns. Since the sample includes only the industrialized countries, this augmented capital might benefit the home country. This overall conclusion conforms with previous studies that find a positive relationship between financial integration and private investment.

NOTES

1. The Tobin tax is a proposed tax on international currency transactions that aims to discourage short-term flows relative to long term flows.
2. Tsoukis and Alyusha (2001) review the criticisms on this approach.
3. Clinton (1988) calculated transactions cost band associated with covered interest rate transactions using bid-ask spread in the spot market. He estimated that the transactions cost band is ± 0.06 percent per annum from parity between the US dollar and the five Eurocurrencies over the period 1985–1986.
4. Even though there is no a priori reason to believe that they are necessarily substitutes or complements, most of the empirical evidence finds that a positive relationship between public and private investment dominates in developing countries.

REFERENCES

Aschauer, D.A. (1989), 'Does public capital crowd out private capital?', *Journal of Monetary Economics*, **24**, pp. 171–88.
Bacchetta, P. (1992), 'Liberalization of capital movements and of the domestic financial system', *Economica*, **59**, pp. 465–74.
Balassa, B. A. (1993), *Policy Choices for the 1990s*, New York: New York University Press.
Baldwin, R.E. and E. Seghezza (1996a), 'Trade-induced investment-led growth', *National Bureau of Economic Research Working Paper*, No. 5582.
Baldwin, R.E. and E. Seghezza (1996b), 'Testing for trade-induced investment-led growth', *National Bureau of Economic Research Working Paper*, No. 5416.
Blecker, Robert A. (1999), *Taming Global Finance: A Better Architecture For Growth and Equity*, Washington, DC: Economic Policy Institute.
Bosworth, B.P. (1993), *Saving and Investment in a Global Economy*, Washington, DC: Brookings Institution.
Checchi, D. (1992), 'What are the real effects of liberalizing international capital movements?', *Open Economies Review*, **3**, pp. 83–125.
Clinton, K. (1988), 'Transactions cost and covered interest arbitrage: theory and evidence', *Journal of Political Economy*, **96**, pp. 358–70.
Epstein, G.A. and J.B. Schor (1992), 'Structural determinants of economic effects of capital controls in OECD countries', in T. Banuri and J. B. Schor (eds), *Financial*

Openness and National Autonomy, Opportunities and Constraints, Oxford: Clarendon Press, pp. 136–61.

Feldstein, M. and C. Horioka (1980), 'Domestic saving and international capital flows', *The Economic Journal*, **90**, pp. 314–29.

Frankel, J.A. and A.T. MacArthur (1988), 'Political vs. currency premia in international real interest rate differentials: a study of forward rates for 24 countries', *European Economic Review*, **32**, pp. 1083–121.

Greene, J. and D. Villanueva (1991), 'Private investment in developing countries', *IMF Staff Papers*, **38**, pp. 33–58.

Grilli, V. and G.M. Milesi-Ferretti (1995), 'Economic effects and structural determinants of capital controls', *IMF Staff Papers*, **42** (3), pp. 517–51.

Ito, T. (1983), 'Capital controls and interest rate parity', *National Bureau of Economic Research Working Paper*, No. 1187.

Klein, M. and G. Olivei (1999), 'Capital account liberalization, financial depth, and economic growth', *National Bureau of Economic Research Working Paper*, No.7384.

Lemmen, J.J.G. and S.C.W. Eijffinger (1996), 'The fundamental determinants of financial integration in the European Union', *Weltwirtschaftliches Archiv*, **132**, pp. 432–56.

Levine, R. and D. Renelt (1992), 'A sensitivity analysis of cross-country growth regressions', *American Economic Review*, **82**, pp. 942–63.

Marston, Richard C. (1995), *International Financial Integration: A Study of Interest Rate Differentials Between the Major Industrial Countries*, New York: Cambridge University Press.

Oshikoya, T.W. (1994), 'Macroeconomic determinants of domestic private investment in Africa: an empirical analysis', *Economic Development and Cultural Change*, **42**, pp. 573–96.

Razin, A. and A.K. Rose (1994), 'Business cycle volatility and openness: an exploratory sectional analysis', in L. Leiderman and A. Razin (eds), *Capital Mobility: the Impact on Consumption, Investment and Growth*, Cambridge, UK: Cambridge University Press, pp. 48–75.

Razin, A. and E. Sadka (1991), 'Efficient investment incentives in the presence of capital flight', *Journal of International Economics*, 31, pp. 171–81.

Ries, C.P. (1997), 'Capital controls and investment behavior', in C.P. Ries and R.J. Sweeney (eds), *Capital Controls in Emerging Economies*, Boulder, Colorado: Westview Press, pp. 89–110.

Serven, L. (1997), 'Irreversibility, uncertainty and private investment: analytical issues and some lessons for Africa', *Journal of African Economies*, **6**, Supplement, pp. 229–68.

Serven, L. and A. Solimano (1993), 'Economic adjustment and investment performance in developing countries: the experience of the 1980s', in L. Serven and A. Solimano (eds), *Striving for Growth After Adjustment: The Role of Capital Formation*, Washington, DC: World Bank, pp. 147–79.

Sweeney, R.J. (1997), 'The information cost of capital', in C.P. Ries and R.J. Sweeney (eds), *Capital Controls in Emerging Economies*, Boulder, Colorado: Westview Press, pp. 45–61.

Tornell, A. (1990), 'Real vs. financial investment: can Tobin taxes eliminate the irreversibility distortion?', *Journal of Development Economics*, **32**, pp. 419–44.

Tsoukis, C. and A. Alyousha (2001), 'The Feldstein-Horioka puzzle, saving-investment causality and international financial market integration', *Journal of Economic Integration*, **16** (2), pp. 262–77.

Vamvakidis, A. (1998), 'Explaining investment in WAEMU', *IMF Working Paper*, No. 99.

APPENDIX

Variable Sources and Definitions

Data for covered interest rate differentials

Interest rates

Interest rates are selected to match as closely as possible the three-month term of the forward exchange rates and the Eurodollar deposit rate to which they were compared. Also, interest rates are chosen among those that have similar market determined characteristics. Table 5A.1 shows the countries, sources, definitions and periods used for interest rates.

Table 5A.1 Sources and definitions of interest rates

Country	Source	Interest Rate	Period
France	OECD MEI	3-month Pibor	1980:1–1998:4
	IMF IFS	3-month Treasury Bills	1999:1–2001:4
Germany	OECD MEI	3-month Fibor	1991:1–1998:4
	IMF IFS	Call Money Rate	1999:1–2001:4
Netherlands	OECD MEI	Call Money Rate	1980:1–1985:4
	OECD MEI	3-month Aibor	1986:1–1997:4
Norway	OECD MEI	3-month Nibor	1985:1–1998:4
Sweden	OECD MEI	3-month Treasury Discount Notes	1985:1–1998:4
United Kingdom	OECD MEI	3-month Interbank Rate	1980:1–2001:4

Note: OECD MEI = OECD Main Economic Indicators and IMF IFS = IMF International Financial Statistics.

Spot and forward exchange rates

Spot and three-month forward exchange rates were obtained from the Datastream International database at Princeton University, New Jersey, the United States. Those data are collected from other sources such as Barclays Bank International and HSBC Midland. Three-month forward rates and spot exchange rates are collected by Barclays Bank for Norway and Sweden. The United States Eurodollar rates are 3-month US Dollar deposit rates obtained from the Datastream International database.

Eurocurrency rates

The representative three-month Eurocurrency rates are available for the following EU countries: the United Kingdom, the Netherlands, France and Germany and Euro Area from IMF IFS (quarterly series). The three-month Eurocurrency rates for the United Kingdom are Paris interbank offer rates on deposits denominated in pounds sterling and the 3-month Eurocurrency rates for Germany, France and the Netherlands are London interbank offer rates on deposits denominated in French francs, Deutsche mark and the Netherlands Guilders. Starting from 1999:1, the Euro Area three-month Deposits Libor rates are used for France and Germany.

The dependent and other independent variables

IP   the ratio of private investment as a percentage of GDP.
     Sources: Private investment data is non-government gross fixed capital formation from OECD National Accounts. GDP data is from OECD National Accounts.

IG   the ratio of government investment as a percentage of GDP.
     Source: Government investment data is general government gross fixed capital formation from OECD National Accounts.

G   the percentage change in real GDP, $(GDP_t - GDP_{t-1})/GDP_{t-1})*100$.
     Source: GDP and consumer price index are from IMF IFS.

INFV   inflation volatility, defined as $INFV = \sqrt{(CPI_t - CPI_{t-3})^2}$; where CPI is changes in consumer prices from IMF IFS.

OPEN   trade share as a percentage of GDP; whole data is from IMF IFS.
OPEN={(exports of goods and services + imports of goods and services)/GDP}*100.

PART III

ENTREPRENEURSHIP

6. The Determinants of Regional Differences in New Firm Formation in Western Germany

Udo Brixy and Michael Niese

6.1 INTRODUCTION

The variation of the differences in regional new firm formation has attracted the interest of researchers since the 1980s (Armington and Acs, 2002). Usually regressions are calculated to explain the variation of new firm formation rates or sometimes count data models are used. But the influence of the regional industry mix on the amount of newly founded business is well known (Fritsch and Niese, 2002). The standard approach for dealing with the spatial influence of different regional industry structures is the shift–share analysis. Therefore in a first step we calculated a shift–share analysis. This yields three shares: the national or total share, the industry mix share and the regional or local share. The latter describes the extent to which factors unique to the region have caused growth or decline in the regional performance. As a residual the regional share contains the number of newly founded firms in a region, which is not influenced by its size and industry structure.

The outcome of the shift–share analysis, however, is that the influence of the industry structure is not as great as one might have expected. The influence of the industry structure share is just 2.9 percent and that of the regional share is 7.6 percent. So combined they account for only 10.5 percent. This means that nearly 90 percent of all regional differences can be explained by the national standard and just arise from the differences in regional size.

Nevertheless the regional variation is quite considerable. The regional share varies between −20.7 percent and 12.1 percent, the structural share between −9.4 percent and 8.1 percent. To examine the factors that influence the birth of new business apart from industry structure and regional size, we use the regional share as a dependent variable in regression models. Hence it is possible to estimate models with independent variables that should explain differences in regional entry apart from industry structure and size. Its value can be negative or positive. In the first case it means that there are fewer firms founded than expected and vice versa. The analysis is restricted to western Germany during a ten-year period from 1987 until 1997.[1]

6.2   FACTORS THAT MIGHT INFLUENCE THE VALUE OF THE REGIONAL SHARE

Factors with a possible influence on the regional share are manifold. Usually they are categorised into three classes: first, indicators of the level of regional demand; second, indicators of the regional reservoir of entrepreneurs (supply-side); and third, indicators of structural differences between regions other than industry structure and size.

6.2.1 Indicator of Regional Demand

Regional demand is of great importance for young firms. Most of them trade on regional and local markets only. This is especially true of firms in the service sector, to which more than 50 percent of all newly founded firms belong. As an indicator of regional demand during the analysed period at regional level only the development of the number of employees is available. Therefore the development of the number of employees is included in the estimations with a lag of one year.

However, the relationship between the two variables is not straightforward. That is because the change in the level of employment can stimulate or hinder the development of newly founded firms (see for example Keeble and Walker, 1994). A positive trend promotes regional demand and improves the economic prospects of the newly founded firms. This increases the motivation of entrepreneurs to found new firms and raises the survival prospects of the new firms. If the growing number of employees is connected with an increase in population (in-migration), then this indicator has a supply-side influence as well. Young and well-educated people are most likely to migrate and are moreover most likely to establish a firm. Therefore, with a positive migration balance the number of possible entrepreneurs increases disproportionately. But prospering regions offer attractive employment alternatives to potential entrepreneurs. Thus the opportunity costs for setting up a new business rise with the economic success of a region. This could lead to a negative correlation between the development of employment and the regional shares. The bivariate correlation coefficients show no significant effect. This could be because both possible relationships offset a correlation.

6.2.2 Indicators of the Regional Reservoir of Entrepreneurs

The qualification level of the population is of great importance for assessing the size of the pool of likely entrepreneurs. According to a study conducted by Brüderl, Preisendörfer and Ziegler (1996: 85) in the greater Munich region, 23 percent of new entrepreneurs hold a university degree. This is distinctly more than the average of all employees (16 percent). This result is similar to other studies (see Storey, 1994 and literature mentioned there).

Spatial data on the qualification level of the whole labour force is not available for this period. We therefore took the qualifications of employees liable to social insurance and the unemployed together and calculated the share of people with university education overall.

An unfavourable situation on the labour market is associated with low opportunity costs because of a lack of alternatives. This might result in 'entrepreneurs of need' (Bögenhold and Staber, 1990; Gerlach and Wagner, 1994), which means that people set up their own businesses because they see no other way to get work. But empirical studies have not proven this connection; there was no evidence of a larger share of entrepreneurs among the unemployed in several studies (Brüderl, Preisendörfer and Ziegler, 1996; Preisendörfer, 1999: 54; Fritsch and Falck, 2002). But if, in spite of these outcomes, an influence of 'entrepreneurs of need' exists, then such start-ups can be expected to occur more often in times of rising unemployment. For this reason the rate of change in unemployment is also included in the estimations with a lag of one year.

On the other hand the rate of unemployment is widely seen as a sign of quantitative and structural problems on the labour market (Fritsch, 1992; Gerlach and Wagner, 1994; Storey, 1994). Problems of the regional labour markets lead to lower levels of spending power and hence to lower levels of demand. This would result in a negative influence on the value of the regional share.

Besides the number of potential entrepreneurs, there are habitual factors that are much more difficult to measure. In part these are based on regional traditions and attitudes which gave rise to the 'incubator thesis'. This assumption states that people employed in smaller firms are more likely to set up a business of their own. It is thought that smaller firms allow a deeper insight into the running of a firm, whereas work in larger firms is more specialised. To measure this effect, the share of employees working in small firms is integrated in the estimations.

Table 6.1   The dependent and independent variables

Variables	Description and calculation	Expected relationship
	1. Indicators of regional demand	
Change in employment	Change in employment in the previous year of employees liable to social insurance	Positive: increasing demand Negative: alternative employment for potential entrepreneurs in prospering regions
	2. Indicators of the reservoir of entrepreneurs	
Proportion of highly-qualified employees	Proportion of employees liable to social insurance with university degree	Positive
Unemployment rate	Average unemployment rate	Positive
Change in the unemployment rate	Change in the unemployment rate in the previous year	Positive
Proportion of employees in small businesses	Proportion of employees liable to social insurance in firms with fewer than 50 employees	Positive
	3. Structural indicators	
Population density	Average employees liable to social insurance in 1995 per square kilometre (log)	Positive
Employees in R&D	Proportion of engineers, mathematicians and scientists among all employees liable to social insurance	Positive
Technological regime	Proportion of engineers, mathematicians and scientists in firms with fewer than 50 employees divided by the share of employees with these qualifications among all employees	Positive
Survival rate	Proportion of firms that survive at least three years	Negative
	4. Controlling for spatial autocorrelation	
Spill-over effect	Mean of the founding rates (new firms divided by the labour force) of the bordering regions	Positive
Residuals	Mean of the residuals of the bordering regions	Positive, if unobserved relationships exist ?

6.2.3 Indicators of Structural Differences Between Regions

An important structural indicator is the population density. It is used to assess the effect of urbanization. Regions that have a positive regional share presumably also include those that are known as 'innovative regions'. Newly founded firms are widely seen as pioneers with the development and use of innovations. To quantify the regional innovative potential, two indicators are calculated. First the share of scientists and engineers is taken. If this share is above the average, it is assumed that the regional level of innovations is accordingly higher than the average, too. But, according to the 'incubator thesis', it is more important for the regional entrepreneurial potential – if the scientists and engineers are working in smaller firms. Audretsch (1995) introduced the so-called 'technological regime' as an indicator of the innovative potential of the small-firms sector of industries. This approach is used for regions in a similar way (Audretsch and Fritsch, 2002). So the regional share of scientists and engineers working in SMEs is taken into the estimations. The higher its value, the greater the importance of the small-firm sector for innovative activities in the regions and the higher the entrepreneurial character of the regions.

As a fourth indicator of structural differences between regions we included the average three-year survival rate. If survival rates are low, this could have a discouraging effect on potential entrepreneurs. But results from Brixy and Grotz (2006) suggest a negative relationship between entry and survival. The cause is presumably competition, which increases with the number of competitors in the region.

6.2.4 Controlling for Spatial Autocorrelation

Spatial autocorrelation can cause the standard deviation of the estimated coefficients to be calculated too low. With these inefficient estimators it is not possible to calculate the significance of the coefficients (Anselin and Rey, 1991). Two variables are integrated to deal with this problem. First the mean of the regional share in the regions bordering each region. This indicator should have a positive influence with the dependent variable, because closer regions can be expected to have more in common than those further away. This indicator, which also measures the amount of spill-over effects, should therefore estimate the quantity of spatial autocorrelation. The second variable contains the means of the residuals of the neighbouring regions. With the help of this indicator it is to be measured whether there are factors which are not considered but which influence these regions equally.

6.2.5 Bivariate Correlations

The important descriptive statistics of the independent variables are shown in Table 6.2. For most of the independent variables chosen a significant bivariate relationship exists with the dependent variable, which is in line with expectations (see Table 6.3). Exceptions are the development of employment and the development of unemployment, both of which have no significant correlation with the regional share. Furthermore, the indicator of the regional technological regime shows a significant negative relationship with the regional share, which is contrary to expectations. This might be due to correlations between the independent variables.

Table 6.2 Summary statistics for the regional variables

	Mean	Standard deviation	Median
Change in the unemployment rate	−0.95	16.02	−3.18
Unemployment rate	8.02	2.88	7.73
Change in employment	1.63	1.89	1.69
Population density (log)	4.39	0.81	4.24
Technological regime	13.46	9.13	11.49
Proportion of employees in small businesses	40.69	5.90	40.26
Proportion of highly qualified employees	4.88	1.84	4.43
Employees in R&D	0.02	0.01	0.02
Birth rate	6.15	1.00	6.03
Survival rate	57.91	2.57	57.88

6.3 RESULTS OF THE ESTIMATIONS

The structure of the data (one observation per year and region) would suggest to estimate panel models with fixed effects. But it was not possible to estimate reliable models. This was obviously because of a high degree of multicollinearity between the independent variables and the regional error term (fixed effects). We therefore estimated the regional shares with pooled OLS models.[2]

Table 6.3   Correlation coefficients of the variables

	Regional share	Spill-over effect	Change in the unemployment rate	Unemploy- ment rate	Change in employment	Survival rate
Spill-over effect	0.412**	1.000				
Change in the unemployme nt rate	0.002	–0.053	1.000			
Unemployment rate	0.341**	0.442**	0.211**	1.000		
Change in employment	–0.045	–0.035	–0.727**	–0.335**	1.000	
Survival rate	–0.334**	–0.174**	–0.121**	—0.266**	0.102*	1.000
Population density	0.342**	0.305**	0.065	0.062	–0.145**	–0.043
Technological regime	–0.223**	–0.048	–0.070	0.083*	0.075	–0.074
Proportion of employees in small businesses	–0.318**	–0.100*	0.024	0.003	0.012	–0.107*
Proportion of highly qualified employees	0.357**	0.061	0.156**	–0.137**	–0.118**	–0.117*
Employees in R&D	0.250**	–0.035	0.133**	–0.187**	–0.106*	–0.034

	Population density	Technological regime	Proportion of employees in small businesses	Proportion of highly qualified employees	Employees in R&D
Technological regime	–0.606**	1.000			
Proportion of employees in small businesses	–0.767**	0.754**	1.000		
Proportion of highly qualified employees	0.623**	–0.619**	–0.590**	1.000	
Employees in R&D	0.610**	–0.758**	–0.679**	0.879**	1.000

Notes: *significant at 5 percent level   **significant at 1 percent level

The results of the estimations are shown in Table 6.4. It can be observed that there is a stable positive relationship between the population density and the regional share (models I–III). Thus the regional share can be partly explained by positive urbanization effects. The proximity of customers on the one hand and suppliers on the other hand in densely populated areas offer entrepreneurs a favourable environment. Additionally the recruitment especially of highly educated employees is easier, too. This is underpinned by the likewise positive relationship of the share of employees in R&D and, even more significant, the share of highly educated employees. The share of highly qualified employees, as well as a high share of employees in R&D, are a locational advantage for the setting up of new businesses. Both variables are highly correlated with the population density, so they can shed some light on the factors that are behind the urbanization effects. The availability of knowledge in a region is a factor that has a positive influence on the number of newly founded firms. Regions with a large share of highly educated people have an advantage in the use of new technologies and in the adaptation to customers' changing preferences. Often this knowledge is utilized by setting up a new business.

However, this does not hold in regions with above-average survival rates. The negative coefficient of this indicator shows that the survival chances for the new firms decrease as the number of newly founded firms rises. This indicates that factors which increase the number of newly founded firms have the opposite influence on the survival chances of new businesses and vice versa. Evidently a growing regional share is an indicator of increasing competition between the newly founded firms and is hence associated with declining survival rates. But this means that obviously low rates of firm survival do not deter entrepreneurs from starting new businesses.

The level of unemployment shows a positive effect. This points to the existence of 'entrepreneurs of need'. It should be kept in mind that the influence of different regional industry structures is excluded. Therefore differences in the industry structure between regions with a high or low unemployment rate have no influence, which underpins the relevance of these results.

Table 6.4 *OLS estimates of the regional shares with robust standard errors*

	I	II	IIa	III	IV	V	VI	VII
Change in the unemployment rate	-0.90** (2.73)				-0.64 (1.92)	-0.96** (2.91)	-1.43** (3.83)	-1.23** (3.70)
Change in employment		10.43** (4.03)	8.01** (2.74)	2.77 (1.37)				
Survival rate	-16.12** (6.64)	-16.09** (6.71)	-14.59** (5.71)	-19.33** (7.38)	-18.32** (6.60)	-17.79** (5.96)	-13.33** (5.95)	-15.34** (6.27)
Unemployment rate	12.97** (3.43)	14.11** (3.61)	10.16** (2.56)		12.66** (3.53)	14.28** (3.91)	17.61** (5.25)	16.81** (5.07)
Population density	56.67* (2.29)	58.32* (2.38)	51.77* (2.04)	56.26* (2.26)				
Proportion of employees in small businesses					-888.51** (3.64)			
Technological regime						-4.03** (3.19)		
Proportion of highly qualified employees							31.52** (3.37)	
Employees in R&D								5317.80** (2.48)
Residuals	0.40** (3.50)	0.42** (3.70)		0.52** (4.69)	0.50** (4.59)	0.46** (3.83)	0.38** (3.25)	0.46** (4.16)
Spill-over			0.30** (2.26)					
Observations	592	592	592	592	592	592	592	592
R²	0.33	0.33	0.32	0.30	0.37	0.32	0.38	0.35
F-Test	21.00** (5.73)	17.97** (5.73)	18.62** (5.73)	20.58** (4.73)	19.47** (5.73)	16.70** (5.73)	18.49** (5.73)	18.34** (5.73)

Notes: *significant at 5 percent level   **significant at 1 percent level.

The negative influence of the development of unemployment is not in line with our expectations. We expected a rise in entrepreneurial activity due to an influx of people into unemployment who then choose to establish a business of their own ('entrepreneurs of need'). A reason for the absence of this connection could be that shortly after becoming unemployed, most people still hope to find a new job. Only after some time of unsuccessful searching do they try to start a business of their own. The negative influence of the development of unemployment is, however, a sign of a negative influence of the deterioration of the economy. Correspondingly a prospering economy, measured by the development of employment, seems to foster the creation of new firms (model II). But this holds only if the level of unemployment is considered, too (model III). The limited validity of the development of employment is certainly caused by the negative correlation with the unemployment rate (see Table 6.3). One explanation could be that an improving economy raises the number of newly founded firms, especially in those regions with high unemployment.

Contrary to our expectations, the share of employees working in small firms has a declining impact on the regional share (model IV). After the exclusion of industry-specific effects there seems to be no spatial influence left. That means we found no proof of the existence of a 'seed bed effect'. This could be because the share of employees working in SMEs is especially large in rural and peripheral areas. For this reason a large proportion of SMEs is not only an indicator of the entrepreneurial qualification of the employees but much more an indicator of a lack of urbanization advantages. The same applies for the 'regional technological regime', which shows a significant negative coefficient, too (model V). The technological regime, like the share of employees in SMEs, shows a strong negative relationship with the population density (see Table 6.3). The values of this variable increase along with the values of the technological regime. So it can be assumed that, contrary to initial expectations, the share of scientists and engineers in SMEs measures the weight of SMEs in the regional economy and not the innovative capacity of SMEs.

The two variables that control for spatial autocorrelation could not be included in the same estimation, because they are highly correlated. The positive relationship between the spill-over effect and the residual effect causes very similar estimations in both cases (models II and IIa). This leads to two conclusions. On the one hand there are only few differences between neighbouring regions as locations for new businesses. Regions in close proximity have similar economic conditions. The positive influence of the residuals on the regional share shows on the other hand that factors which are not considered in the estimations influence neighbouring regions in an equal way.

Taken together one can state that there are five main results. First, urbanization effects have a strong influence on the regional variation in the number of newly founded firms. Whereas in densely populated regions the environment is especially favourable for entrepreneurs, the regional share in rural and peripheral regions is lower on average. One reason for this is presumably the spatial concentration of knowledge that is relevant for setting up new firms. Moreover, urbanization effects dominate the relationship between the regional share and other regional indicators, such as the share of employees in small firms or the technological regime.

Second, factors that have a positive influence on the number of newly founded firms seem to have a negative influence on the survival of new firms. In regions with a high level of new firm formation, competition between new firms, which typically focus on local demand, is presumably high. This leads to relatively low levels of surviving firms.

Third, only the level of unemployment but not the development of unemployment has a stimulating influence on new firm formation. A lack of opportunities on the labour market encourages unemployed people to set up their own firms. This does not happen immediately after a rise in unemployment, though, but after realizing further prospects.

Fourth, there is no evidence for a 'seed-bed-function' of regions with a high proportion of SME.

Fifth, we found a high degree of spatial autocorrelation. Neighbouring regions can be expected to have similar economic conditions in many aspects. It would be interesting to investigate the background of these factors on the number of newly founded firms.

NOTES

1. Eastern Germany is excluded because of insufficient data for most of the period. More recent data than 1997 could not be used, due to the introduction of the NACE industry classification in 1998, which could not be transformed into the old classification.
2. The temporal autocorrelation was controlled by using grouped observations (= 74 standard statistical areas) and the use of robust standard errors (Software: Stata 7).

REFERENCES

Anselin, L. and S. Rey (1991), 'Properties of tests for spatial dependence in linear regression models', *Geographical Analysis*, **23**, pp. 112–30.

Armington, C. and Z.. J. Acs (2002), 'The determinants of regional variation in new firm formation', *Regional Studies*, **36** (1), pp. 33–45.

Audretsch, D. B. (1995), *Innovation and Industry Evolution*, Cambridge, MA: MIT Press.

Audretsch, D. B. and M. Fritsch (2002), 'Growth regimes over time and space', *Regional Studies*, **36**, pp. 113–24.

Bögenhold, D. and U. Staber (1990), 'Selbständigkeit als ein Reflex auf Arbeitslosigkeit? [Entrepreneurship as a result of unemployment?]', *Kölner Zeitschrift für Soziologie und Sozialpsychologie*, **42**, pp. 265–79.

Brüderl, J., P. Preisendörfer and R. Ziegler (1996), *Der Erfolg neugegründeter Betriebe [The success of newly founded firms]*, Berlin: Duncker and Humblot.

Brixy, U. and R. Grotz (2006), 'Regional patterns and determinants of the survival of new firms in western Germany', IAB Discussion Paper 2006, forthcoming, download at http://www.iab.de/asp/order/vvzdokuOhne.asp?doktyp=dp

Fritsch, M. (1992), 'Regional differences in new firm formation: evidence from West Germany', *Regional Studies*, **25** (3), pp. 233–41.

Fritsch, M. and O. Falck (2002), 'New firm formation by industry over space and time: a multi-level analysis', Working Paper 2002/11, Faculty of Economics and Business Administration, Technical University Bergakademie Freiberg.

Fritsch, M. and M. Niese (2002), 'Vergleich auf gesamtwirtschaftlicher und sektoraler Ebene' [Comparison of founding rates on the overall economy], in M. Fritsch and R. Grotz (eds), *Das Gründungsgeschehen in Deutschland - Darstellung und Vergleich der Datenquellen* [Newly founded firms in Germany - Description and comparability of different databases], Heidelberg; Physica, pp. 141–64.

Gerlach, K. and J. Wagner (1994), 'Regional differences in small firm entry in manufacturing industries: Lower Saxony, 1979–1991', *Entrepreneurship and Regional Development*, **6**, pp. 63–80.

Keeble, D. and S. Walker (1994), 'New firms and dead firms: spatial patterns and determinants in the United Kingdom', *Regional Studies*, **28** (4), pp. 411–27.

Preisendörfer, P. (1999), 'Zugangswege zur Selbständigkeit und die Erfolgschancen neugegründeter Unternehmen. [Ways into self-employment and the chances of new firms]', in L. von Rosenstiel and T. Lang-von Wins (eds), *Existenzgründung und Unternehmertum [New businesses and Entrepreneurship]*, Stuttgart: Schaeffer-Poeschel, pp. 49–71.

Reynolds, P., D. Storey and P. Westhead (1994), 'Cross-national comparisons of the variation in new firm formation rates: an editorial overview', *Regional Studies*, **28** (4), pp. 343–46.

Storey, D. J. (1994), *Understanding the Small Business Sector*, London: Routledge.

7. Rural Entrepreneurship Success Determinants

Maira Lescevica

7.1 INTRODUCTION

Latvia is going through the same rapid development of a market-oriented economy as other East European and CIS countries, making it another of the so-called transition countries. Gradual economic development is observed, but is sadly lacking in rural parts of the country. The main business in the countryside – agriculture – is diminishing. Over recent years, the Ministry of Agriculture and the Ministry of Environmental Protection and Regional Development have emphasized the importance of employment in rural Latvia by setting up the Strategic Priorities Initiative and by organizing the Financing for Rural Development Program.

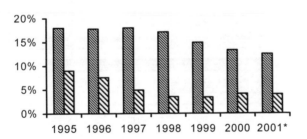

■ Employed in agriculture from total employment
■ The weight of agriculture products in GDP

Source: Yearly Report on Agriculture, Ministry of Agriculture of LR, 1999.

Figure 7.1 The weight of agriculture in total employment and GDP (*predicted)

Traditionally, agriculture has been the only business in rural parts of Latvia. However, during the last ten years, the importance of agricultural production as a percent of Gross Domestic Product (GDP) has decreased (see Figure 7.1). Examining Figure 7.1 more closely, we can see a slight increase in agriculture's share of GDP in 2000 and 2001. Although some observers view this development as hopeful for rural Latvia, the other trend revealed in Figure 7.1 dashes those hopes. The percentage of total employment in agriculture has fallen continuously and rapidly since 1997.

Comparing Latvia with selected European countries (Figure 7.2) with respect to the importance of agriculture for GDP and total employment, the problem becomes apparent. Latvia's agricultural share of GDP is not that different from the selected comparison countries, but its share of agricultural employment is comparatively large. This suggests that labour productivity in agriculture is relatively low and that, as productivity grows, increasing amounts of labour will be released from agriculture and available for other uses.

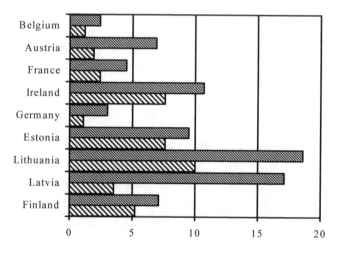

⬚ Employed in agriculture (% from total employment)
◩ Agriculture (% from total GDP)

Source: Yearly Report on Agriculture, Ministry of Agriculture of LR, 1999.

Figure 7.2 GDP and employment in agriculture as a percentage of the total: the Baltics and other selected European countries

The average farm sizes in the four regions of Latvia are – 28.9 ha in Vidzeme, 25.5 ha in Kurzeme, 23.3 ha in Zemgale, 20.9 ha in Latgale. In fact, it is 16.6 ha in the Rīga region, a sub region of Vidzeme. Finding smaller farms in the area around Rīga may not be surprising because of the type of agriculture that usually surrounds large cities. Although these average sizes suggest that the large collective and state farms have been privatized, they also suggest that there may be future farm consolidation. If so, it would be in search of greater productivity, which suggests again a reduction in the labor force in rural areas.

To offset the economic effect on rural areas of the decline in the importance of traditional agriculture, employment and productivity growth in new areas of agriculture, as well as in agribusiness, manufacturing and services, will be required. Such a transformation would require a strengthening of rural entrepreneurship.

Two government activities are focused on improving the rural economy. The Law on Agriculture in Latvia, in support of rationality, effectiveness and competitiveness, stipulates state support to rural enterprises (mostly agricultural) equalling to 3 percent of the central government budget – mainly in the form of subsidies.

The other quite successful support institution, the Regional Development Fund, is the main economic instrument for promotion of economic growth of the rural areas of Latvia. The biggest share belongs to traditional agriculture – both in terms of the number of the projects and funding. This sector was represented by 36 percent of the submitted projects to which 30 percent of Regional Fund financing were allocated (see Figure 7.3). The second position belongs to services (26 percent of total projects; 17 percent of financing). Services include such areas as household services, trade, public catering, maintenance of technical equipment, and agriculture related services. Almost 10 percent of total financing was given to the development of infrastructure and another 2 percent to other types of support to business activity. The recipients of this financing are local governments or their structural units. The projects submitted by local governments are mainly aimed at the development of the business environment. Typical projects include activities like the establishment of various information centres (businesses, tourism), infrastructure improvement and tourism promotion.

The following results were recognized by the local communities as being very important for the development of local business and overall promotion of the region:

- Business activity has increased partly because people feel encouraged by this support;
- Entrepreneurs have benefited from consultative support;

- Educational activities – training, seminars, consulting and exchange of experience – have encouraged networking;
- Business people have increased the use of state support;
- Improved cooperation between local governments and businesses has strengthened both institutions;
- Cooperation among businesses has been encouraged;
- Infrastructure improvements have gained support;
- Non-traditional agriculture and tourism have received support and are developing in rural areas.

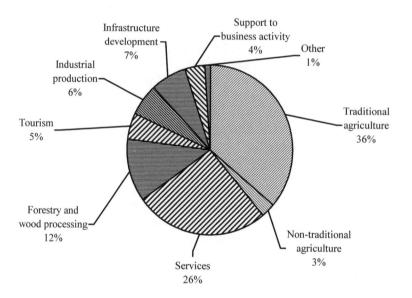

Source: Regional Development Annual Report (2001).

Figure 7.3 Regional distribution fund: projects by sectors, 1998–2001

In line with regulations of the European Council on the Community support to pre-accession activities in agriculture and rural development (SAPARD), Latvia in the pre-accession period benefited from EU support. Within the scope of this program, financing was given to such programs as improvement of rural infrastructure, investments into rural enterprises, diversification of rural economy, and environmentally friendly agricultural methods.

In the remainder of this chapter, we examine some of the scientific literature on rural entrepreneurship and entrepreneurship in general as a preliminary to developing a survey of rural entrepreneurship in Latvia. Then, we present some of the results of the survey, highlighting the responses relevant for rural entrepreneurship. With this in mind, we then use the Chi-square method to find associations between internal and external success factors and the characteristics of survey respondents.

7.2 BACKGROUND RESEARCH

Since 1988 EU legislation has defined small and medium-size enterprises (SMEs), which account for approximately 99 percent of all enterprises in EU, as enterprises that are not involved in agriculture, hunting, forestry or fishery and that have 250 or fewer employees and a small turnover. It would facilitate Latvian rural economic development if this implicit attitude toward farmers were changed, treating farmers not as peasants, but as *rural entrepreneurs.* Other EU countries, like the United Kingdom, have realized the importance of such a change in thinking (Performance and Innovation Unit, 1999).

To develop rural entrepreneurs, it is important to understand the scientific literature on entrepreneurship. Although such research has gone on for more than a century, the determinants of entrepreneurial success and failure have been studies mainly of entrepreneurship in general (Drucker and Flaherty, 1999). Many determinants have been identified: financial ratios (Thomas and Evanson, 1987), marketing strategy (Bhardwaj and Menon, 1993), credit management (Baker, 1992), management style (Aquino, 1990), manager or management competence and skills (Martin and Staines, 1994), managers' personal characteristics and motivation (Cragg and King, 1988), business planning (Baker et al., 1993) and entrepreneurs' gender (Everett and Watson, 1998; Fucini and Fucini, 1985). It is important to understand these, but it is also important to consider whether rural entrepreneurship has different determinants.

7.2.1 A Model of the Determinants of Enterprise Performance

Cragg and King in their article 'Organizational Characteristics and Small Firms' Performance Revisited' (1988) have developed an interesting model (see Figure 7.4), where the owner/manager of the firm is the person who initiates all the processes. His/her personal characteristics and personality, along with the firm's targets, managerial and financial skills, and the firm's environment, particularly its market, are the basic determinants of a firm's performance.

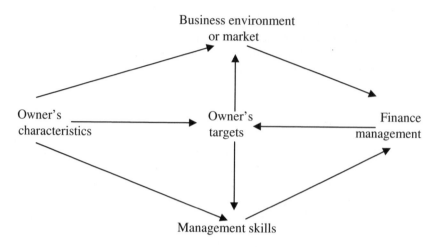

Source: Bhardwaj and Menon, 1993.

Figure 7.4 Factors influencing enterprise performance

Another model, which analyses many enterprises performance determinants, is quite useful in developing and applying these ideas to rural entrepreneurship (see Figure 7.5). The model divides the determinants of a firm's competitive strategy and thus its performance into internal and external ones.

This model provides a framework for analysing the entrepreneurial environment and for isolating important determinants of successful entrepreneurship. In some ways the internal determinants in Figure 7.5, which, following the model in Figure 7.4, can be grouped into the entrepreneur's characteristics (resources, skills, and possibilities) and targets (motivation and attitude), are important to successful entrepreneurship. One of the aspects of the characteristics is the ability to cooperate and network, and the possibility of doing so. I expect that this ability to cooperate and network will be a particularly important determinant of a successful rural Latvian entrepreneurship environment because most of the enterprises are quite small.

The external determinants are those that facilitate enterprise development or entrepreneurship from outside by supporting and nurturing. These determinants are emerging and improving in Latvia, but generally they are not as positive for *rural* entrepreneurship. I expect the most sensitive determinant of rural entrepreneurship to be access to financial resources because banks are seemingly unwilling to support rural businesses. One reason would certainly be the high risk associated with rural enterprises, particularly in agriculture.

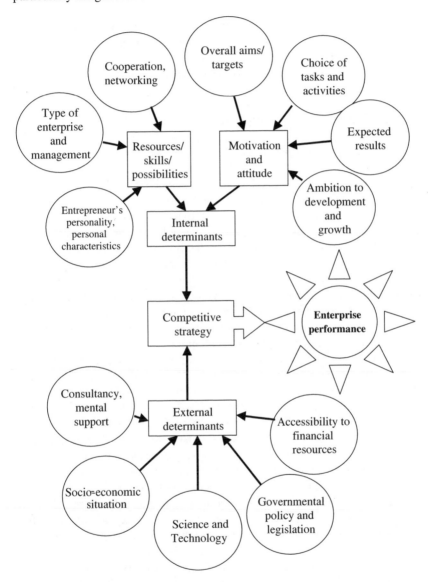

Figure 7.5 A model of the main determinants of enterprise success

Although this model could be discussed further, the purpose here is to isolate the parts of the model that might be influential in rural entrepreneurship in Latvia rather than entrepreneurship in general. Therefore, rather than a more detailed discussion of these models, the research was to use the models that I have briefly discussed to develop a questionnaire to study rural entrepreneurship. One isolated part of the model, however, merits additional attention, namely the one dealing with cooperation and networking.

7.2.2 Cooperatives and Economic Success

The specific type of cooperation to be discussed is the concept of a business cooperative. A business cooperative is owned by a group of users who organize it to overcome business problem perceived by the organizers. It might be that individual entrepreneurs and enterprises are not large enough to successfully market their product – perhaps a craft product or fresh vegetables – effectively. Alternatively, a single user might not be large enough to take advantage of the most effective farm machine. Almost any business problem – accounting, market projection, processing of raw materials, purchasing of materials – faced by a small enterprise might be handled through a cooperative. Individual entrepreneurs maintain ownership and control of their primary enterprise, be it a farm or a small manufacturing enterprise, but they essentially contract out certain business services to the cooperative. Because the individual entrepreneurs have joint ownership of the cooperative, they have a joint interest in it being operated efficiently. As owners, they share in the profits or losses. Even if the cooperative makes losses, individual entrepreneurs may obtain business services at a lower cost than if they provided the services themselves or went into the market for the services. Economies of scale may make the cost of the service, including the entrepreneurs' share of the losses, less than the cost of own-enterprise provision. Cooperatives, however, are not very popular in Latvia because of the recent history of forced collectivization and formation of state enterprises. It is obvious to local observers that cooperation of this type has failed. These state and collective farms, according to the propaganda, were the ideal production cooperatives, where the owner was everybody and nobody. It's no wonder that people are skeptical of these different forms of cooperation.

In addition to its economic shortcomings, the establishment of collective and state farms was connected with pain and robbery. Before occupation by the Former Soviet Union, the Latvian economy was well developed with normal entrepreneurship and well-functioning cooperative societies. Indeed, it was competing well with other European countries for the market. Alas, many of the successful entrepreneurs either emigrated, or were exiled as enemies to the soviet nation to the camps in Siberia, where many died prematurely because of dreadful conditions in the camps.

Cooperative societies, however, have survived and are flourishing in various parts of the world. They are aimed at the solving of common business problems by certain groups of entrepreneurs. The successful development of cooperative societies would help entrepreneurs and enterprises, and it would promote community and even regional development, because it helps to increase employment. Besides, any cooperative society is serving rural entrepreneurs also in other regions.

7.3 INTERNAL AND EXTERNAL DETERMINANTS OF ENTREPRENEURIAL AND ENTERPRISE SUCCESS

To determine success and failure factors, we used specially prepared questionnaires. These questionnaires were informed by the models outlined in Figures 7.4 and 7.5. They were sent to the satellite offices of the Latvian Agricultural Consultancy and Training Centers with a focus on rural entrepreneurs and owner-managers. The sample with 306 respondents came from the active clients of the Latvian Agricultural Consultancy and Training Center (Krastiņš, 1998). The first purpose of the questionnaires was to obtain qualitative information describing the important success determinants as seen by the respondents. In the next section, we used a filter question to identify respondents that thought of themselves as successful. Then, statistical grouping and testing was used to identify the respondent characteristics associated with success.

7.3.1 The Characteristics of the Respondents

Table 7.1 gives the percentage distribution of different indicators describing the respondents. An examination of the table helps to understand the nature of the sample and of entrepreneurship in rural Latvia. Seventy-one percent of the sample is aged between 30 and 50, which indicates that entrepreneurs are in their prime working years. Over one-third of the entrepreneurs are women, which suggests that women are economically active as entrepreneurs in rural areas. Over one-half of the respondents owned less than 50 ha of land, suggesting a preponderance of small farms and limited availability of land as a source of financial capital. The entrepreneurs in rural Latvia are well educated with more then 95 percent with at least a secondary education and 43 percent with a university education. A large percentage of the enterprises were founded as the old system broke down, but new enterprises continue to be formed. Finally most of the respondents are owners, most of the enterprises are farms, and they are quite small both in terms of employment and turnover.

Table 7.1 Characteristics of respondents

Indicators	Structure, %
Age	
Up to 30	8
30–40	32
40–50	39
50–60	15
60–70	6
Gender	
Women	37
Men	63
Land	
No land	2
Up to 10 ha	7
11–20 ha	21
21–50 ha	24
51–100 ha	21
Over 100 ha	25
Education	
Primary	2
Secondary	53
University	43
Other	2
Foundation year of enterprise	
1988–1990	8
1991–1993	49
1994–1996	24
1997–1999	15
2000–2001	4
Relationship to enterprise	
Owner	79
Co-owner	2
Manager	11
Other	8

Legal status of enterprise	
Farm	84
Limited Liabilities Company	1
Households	10
Individual Comersant	1
Statute company	1
Cooperative society	2
Research company	1
Number of employees	
None	23
1–2	53
3–5	18
5–10	3
10 and more	3
Turnover of the enterprise	
Less then 1000 LVL	14
1001–3000 LVL	24
3001–5000 LVL	15
5001–10 000 LVL	18
10 001–20 000 LVL	13
20 000 LVL and more	16

7.3.2 Internal Success Determinants

The internal success determinants identified by respondents are the following with the ones mentioned most frequently first.

Finance management

Basically respondents argue that they cannot grow as productively as they would like, because the production process is very expensive compared to income. They recognize that they need to be very successful to receive credit or other forms of investment, but without the credit, it is difficult to be successful. They also recognize that they need to develop their business-planning skills.

Management of enterprise

They are willing to change the type of production because most of them have used extensive methods of rural enterprise management. Some of them have declared that expansion is the only way to growth and prosperity. But almost all of them agree that agriculture is not the only business with potential in rural areas.

Raw materials, mechanics and premises
The lack of basic machines and technology leads rural entrepreneurs to use possibly obsolete farming techniques. Machine-rings, a form of cooperation, are not widespread.

Production process
Respondents acknowledge that they still use a lot of manual labor, which makes their products too expensive for consumers. Another problem raised is too many different products produced in one enterprise. They believe that the lack of specialization reduces efficiency.

Amounts offered in the market
The best perception is that for very small rural enterprises only cooperation can help to survive in the market economy – to fight for better prices for raw materials, services and products.

Personnel management
This is the first research where rural entrepreneurs in Latvia have identified a personnel selection problem. Young people try to leave rural parts of Latvia. Most of them move to the cities, where educational institutions are located, and never return to their native land. This inconveniences most of the potentially successful rural entrepreneurs, because they need employees – workers and managers – well equipped with knowledge and skills.

Marketing and sales
Respondents do not like to undertake the hard and time-consuming personal marketing and sales activities important for success, because they divert attention from the entrepreneur's main activity of producing. The problem is that economies of scale and scope in marketing make it inefficient for each entrepreneur to do his or her own. They conclude that it would be beneficial to recruit professionals to accomplish this service.

7.3.3 External Success Determinants

The main external success determinants were mentioned in following order:

State policy and government
Policy carried out by our government must fully support rural and agricultural development. The weakness of this determinant has formed some

obstacles in legislation and taxation. In addition, subsidies are not allocated in a satisfactory manner.

Market situation

There is a monopoly for some processes in Latvia, which influences the balancing of supply and demand. Marketing and sales systems for agricultural products must be established through forming of economic associations, strategic alliances, or cooperative societies among rural entrepreneurs.

Finances available

Most of the Latvian banks are not willing to give credits to entrepreneurs that come from rural Latvia or who have land as collateral. The management of debtors has been identified as a very important factor. And subsidies have been recognized as not supporting the development of rural entrepreneurship.

Information

The most important bits of information are market analysis, business activities in the region, and support and funding possibilities.

Infrastructure

Rural entrepreneurs are directly and indirectly isolated from centralized buying institutions. They have identified several important parts of infrastructure – normal motorways, easily accessible Internet connections and other communication services – that could be improved.

Raw materials

Basically respondents have identified the prices of fuel, fertilizers and herbicides as the main cost-raising factors. And some of them have mentioned the weather as another important determinant.

Respondents were also asked to answer where and what changes they would like to introduce – at the state level, at the local municipality level, and at the own enterprise level. Most of the changes were identified for the state level, a few for the enterprise, and almost none for the municipality. Although one might conclude that business support activities at the municipality level are functioning and in order, one would probably be wrong. The truth be told, the local municipality is perceived as so weak and incapable that government support must come from the state.

7.3.4 How Do the Respondents See Their Environment?

The respondents recognize that their entrepreneurial and management skills need further development. They see that they could improve the operation of their enterprise if they had access to better financing. But they also see that they must be flexible, adopt new techniques and perhaps new products, and they recognize that they could make effective use of specialists in planning, marketing and other business services. They also recognize that, as small as they are, they must figure out ways to cooperate in obtaining these services.

Similarly, they recognize certain external limits to their success. Again these limits relate to financing, infrastructure, information, access to government assistance and access to materials. Just as with the internal limitations, it would seem that some forms of cooperation could overcome some of the external factors. In the next section, I test hypotheses regarding the characteristic of entrepreneurs who regard themselves as successful.

7.4 INITIAL ANALYSIS OF SUCCESS FACTORS FOR RURAL ENTREPRENEURS

During the research process, we discovered that SME and rural entrepreneurship statistics, especially financial figures like profit, couldn't be obtained at the Central Statistical Bureau of Latvia. Clearly, to identify the factors that are associated with entrepreneurial success, it is necessary to identify successful entrepreneurs and enterprises. I did so by asking a filter question 'Do you consider your company successful?' Fifty-five percent answered that they consider their company successful, and 40 percent, unsuccessful. Only 5 percent did not answer this question.

The next part of analysis is to find coherence among respondents' indicators and their answers on the success determination question. The analysis is done using the Chi-square method. Three hypotheses were related to the respondents' personal characteristics: age, gender and education. Three hypotheses related to the size of the enterprise: turnover, amount of land owned, and number of employees. Three more hypotheses related to regional location with Latvia, the age of the enterprise, and whether the respondent was an owner or manager. The tenth hypothesis relates to the willingness of the entrepreneur to join a cooperative society. The results are shown in Table 7.2.

Table 7.2 Calculation results for 10 hypotheses, using the chi-square method

Hypothesis: There does not exist a relationship between respondents considering themselves successful and	Level of significance α	Degrees of freedom ν	Chi-square critical limit/ test χ^2			Conclusions: statistically significant relationship?
			χ^2_{calc}	χ^2_{crit}	$\chi^2_{calc} \geq \chi^2_{crit}$	
1. their belonging to the age group	0.05	4	5.01	9.49	<	No
2. the enterprise's turnover	0.01	5	51.67	15.09	>	Yes
3. the gender of the entrepreneur	0.01	1	1.91	3.84	<	No
4. the amount of land owned	0.05	4	28.34	9.49	>	Yes
5. the geographical placement in four regions of Latvia	0.05	3	15.95	7.81	>	Yes
6. the enterprise foundation year	0.05	3	1.57	7.81	<	No
7. the education of entrepreneurs	0.05	3	2.53	7.81	<	No
8. their ownership of the enterprise	0.05	2	0.97	5.99	<	No
9. the number of employees	0.01	6	7.95	16.81	<	No
10. the willingness to join a cooperative society	0.01	2	10.33	9.21	>	Yes

Each hypothesis is stated at the null hypothesis that there is no relationship between the category in which the respondents fall and whether the respondents believe they are successful. The analysis fails to rejects all of the null hypotheses regarding the entrepreneur's personal characteristics – age, gender, and education. They apparently make no difference. On the other hand, it fails to reject two of the three null hypotheses regarding the size of the enterprise. Both turnover and the amount of land make a difference. Enterprise age and ownership do not make a difference. Location within Latvia makes a difference. And finally, and interestingly, the successful entrepreneurs have different opinions with regard to the willingness to join a cooperative society. As the discussion below shows, the data indicate that self-styled successful entrepreneurs are associated with larger enterprises, location, and greater interest in cooperatives.

7.4.1 Size of Enterprise: Turnover

Figure 7.6 shows the data that support the conclusion that respondents, who have declared their enterprise as successful, are more likely to have higher turnover. The conclusion is that amount of turnover has impact on entrepreneurship performance and competitiveness.

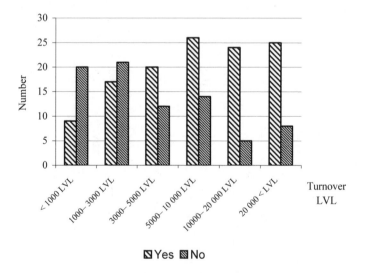

Figure 7.6 Respondents grouped by self-styled success and enterprise turnover

7.4.2 Size of Enterprise: Land Owned

Just as with turnover, respondents who view their enterprise as successful are more likely to own larger parcels of land (see Figure 7.7). This result reinforces the result with regard to turnover. In fact, there is a study increase in the number of respondents who consider themselves successful as the size of the enterprise in terms of land ownership increases. This same steady increase is not observed in terms of turnover. Although not conclusive, the two size results suggest that rural entrepreneurs with small enterprises are at a disadvantage, a disadvantage that cooperative societies might attenuate.

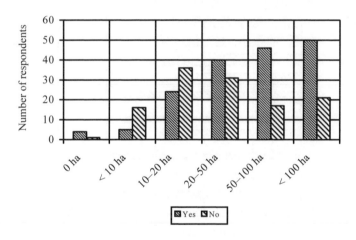

Figure 7.7 Respondents grouped by self-styled success and land owned

7.4.3 Enterprise Location

As we can see in Figure 7.8, in different regions people evaluate their entrepreneurship performance differently. Regions statistically are divided in the following order:

- LATGALE – Rēzekne, Preiļi, Ludza, Krāslava, Daugavpils and Balvi.
- VIDZEME – Valmiera, Valka, Rīga, Ogre, Limbaži, Gulbene, Cēsis, Aizkraukle, Alūksne;
- ZEMGALE – Tukums, Jēkabpils, Dobele, Bauska;
- KURZEME – Talsi, Saldus, Liepāja, Kuldīga

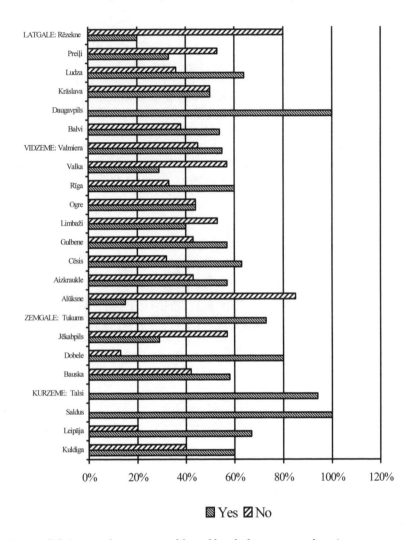

Figure 7.8 Respondents grouped by self-styled success and regions

We can see from Figure 7.8 that entrepreneurs in Kurzeme are more likely to consider themselves successful than those in other regions. In two cities in Kurzeme, no entrepreneurs considered themselves unsuccessful and in the other two cities about 65 and 75 percent considered themselves successful. In Latgale, on the other hand, only about 60 percent or less of the entrepreneurs in five of the region's six cities considered themselves successful. Results for the other two regions lie between the results for Latgale and Kurzeme.

7.4.4 Willingness to Join Cooperative Societies

This is a very important point in this analysis. Those entrepreneurs who consider their business as successful, have expressed great willingness to join cooperative societies. They see cooperatives as an institutional arrangement that can help solve the managerial problems identified in the survey. At the same time in answering the questionnaires they were more open. They concluded that by joining some of their activities with other entrepreneurs they could increase their power in the market competition.

7.5 CONCLUSION

The success and failure of rural entrepreneurs depends on a range of external and internal factors. The individual entrepreneur has little if any control of the external factors. Internal factors, on the other hand, can be influenced by the entrepreneur. We have identified a series of problems faced by rural entrepreneurs because they operate small enterprises and because the rural economic infrastructure (roads, markets, business services, and so on) is not well developed. One possible solution could be the consolidation of efforts to overcome these managerial problems. The presence of these problems presents entrepreneurs with opportunities. In fact, the existence of these problems and opportunities may be the defining characteristic that distinguishes rural entrepreneurship from entrepreneurship in general. The problem relates to the exploitation of new techniques, the organization of purchases and sales, and the reorganization of the ownership of equipment, machinery and production processes. This might be done, if entrepreneurs cooperate either informally or formally through such institutions as cooperatives.

Ten hypotheses were tested, using Chi square tests, to determine the most important characteristics of successful entrepreneurs. Four characteristics were identified. They have high turnover, more then 50 hectares of land property, live in a certain region and are willing to join a cooperative society.

Some successful entrepreneurs were unsure about joining cooperative societies. I believe that many of them really do not think about joining them because they think they are doing well on their own and do not realise the benefits of cooperation. The part of research discussed in this article for the present allows one to draw only tentative conclusions, but these conclusions should be helpful in pursuing additional research.

ACKNOWLEDGEMENTS

This research is part of my Doctoral Thesis and therefore analysis of data gained will be continued. Special thanks to Professor Baiba Rivza as my dissertation supervisor, to Nina Rakstina as the consultant–manager of the Department of Rural Development at Ministry of Agriculture and, particularly, to Kaspars Zurins as Managing Director of Latvian Agricultural Consultancy and Training Center.

REFERENCES

Aquino, N.R. (1990), 'Success secrets', *Business and Economic Review*, **36** (4), pp. 20–23.

Baker, C. (1992), 'Small business success factors', *Credit Management*, August, pp. 23 f.

Baker, W.H., H.L. Addams and B. Davis (1993), 'Business planning in successful small firms', *Long Range Planning*, **26** (6), pp. 82–8.

Bhardwaj, S.G. and A. Menon (1993), 'Determinants of success in service industries: a PIMS-based empirical investigation', *Journal of Service Marketing*, **7** (4), pp. 19–40.

Cragg, P.B. and M. King (1988), 'Organizational characteristics and small firms' performance revisited', *Entrepreneurship Theory and Practice*, Winter, pp. 49–64.

Drucker, P. and J.E. Flaherty (1999), 'Shaping the managerial mind', in P. Krass (ed.), *The Book of Entrepreneurships' Wisdom. Classic Writings by Legendary Entrepreneurs*, New York: John Wiley and Sons, Inc, pp. 1–11.

Everett, J. and J. Watson (1998), 'Small business failure and external risk factors', *Small Business Economics*, No.11, pp. 371–90.

Fucini, J.J. and S. Fucini (1985), *Entrepreneurs. The Men and Women behind Famous Brand Names and How They Made It*, Boston: G.K. Hall and Co.

Krass, P. (1999), *The Book of Entrepreneurships' Wisdom. Classic Writings by Legendary Entrepreneurs*, New York: John Wiley and Sons, Inc.

Krastiņš, O. (1998), *Statistika un ekonometrija* (Statistics and Econometry), Riga: Institute of Statistics of Latvia.

Martin, G. and H. Staines (1994), 'Managerial competences in small firms', *Journal of Management Development*, **13** (7), pp. 23–34.

Ministry of Agriculture of LR (1999), *Lauksaimniecības gada ziņojums* (Yearly Report on Agriculture), Riga, pp. 8–91.

Performance and Innovation Unit (1999), *Rural Economies*, Cabinet Office, London.

Thomas, J. and R.V. Evanson (1987), 'An empirical investigation of association between financial ratio use and small business success', *Journal of Business Finance and Accounting*, **14** (4), pp. 555–71.

Veinbergs, V. (2001), *Par kooperāciju* (About cooperation), Riga: Association of Agricultural Statute Companies of Latvia, pp. 5–7.

www.lursoft.lv/db (Lursoft legal databases).

8. The Role of Socioeconomic Factors in Entrepreneurship Development: A County Level Analysis

Eric A. Scorsone, Ronald A. Fleming, Margarita Somov and Victoria Burke

8.1 INTRODUCTION

Entrepreneurship has potential as an important regional economic development strategy. A definition of entrepreneurship, however, is elusive and difficult to formulate. Entrepreneurs are risk takers due to the inherent uncertainty through which they market and sell goods and services. In some cases, entrepreneurship has been associated with an individual or group of individuals creating a business with a new product or service. In other cases, entrepreneurship has been associated with decision makers in existing firms introducing new goods and services to the marketplace. The act of entrepreneurship from within an existing firm, however, is much more difficult to measure. For the purposes of this chapter, an entrepreneur is defined as a 'firm organizer' or one who starts a new firm in order to deliver a new or refined good or service to the marketplace (Baumol, 1988).

Regional economic development policies are partly driven by the likelihood that policy makers can affect business location decisions. One particularly important business decision, until recently largely ignored, is the decision to start a business in a particular place. Previous work on business location decisions and economic geography has concerned knowledge of where different types of businesses move based on transportation costs, labor market conditions and regional amenities. These models were particularly appropriate for business relocation decisions or branch plant location decisions. However, in the case of indigenous entrepreneurship, there is limited understanding of the processes that influence start-up decisions.

Business starts in the United States exhibit a wide range of geographic variation. According to the U.S. Small Business Administration, new firm start-up rates in 2002 varied from 18.3 percent in Colorado to a 6.1 percent in South Dakota (SBA, 2004). This variation is also noted in Europe and other countries and illustrates the importance of accounting for spatial variation in new firm start-up rates. The factors that influence this dispersion are likely different from those that affect business relocation or expansion decisions.

Data limitations have shaped the type and geographic level of empirical analysis in the field of regional entrepreneurship. It is very difficult to track 'entrepreneurship' among existing firms and doing so would require extensive in-person or mail surveys. Even with some form of survey analysis, there remains the difficulty of classifying entrepreneurial versus non-entrepreneurial behavior. There is even less research that describes and predicts the variation in regional or local business start-up rates. This lack of information hampers the efforts of state, provincial or local officials in crafting entrepreneurship policy. Finally, there is little agreement on a common measurement tool for depicting business start-up rates at the regional or local level.

Freshwater and Goetz (2001) and Acs and Armington (1999) represent major attempts to understand the variation in business starts across US states. In both models, business starts were regressed against a set of economic, demographic and education variables. Freshwater and Goetz suggested that the residual the analysis captured entrepreneurial culture or infrastructure in a state. These articles remain the pioneering attempts to understand subnational variation in business starts.

This research examines the casual factors driving retail and service related business start-ups at the sub-state or local level in the United States. Similar to variation at the state level, a wide range of business start-up rates exists at the local or county level. Based on previous research and theoretical expectations, economic, demographic, social and educational variables are included as potential explanatory factors. The focus of this research is the 120 counties that comprise the state of Kentucky in the United States. Restricting our focus to one state reduces the difficulties associated with obtaining comparative business start-up data for all US counties.

8.2 LITERATURE REVIEW

The literature regarding levels of entrepreneurship, entrepreneurial climate and start-up rates for new firms has expanded significantly over the last decade. New firm formation and existing small firms' contribution to economic development at both the local and national levels are discussed in the literature. Moreover, empirical evidence from different countries (Sweden, Great Britain, Italy, United States; Reynolds et al., 1994; Acs and

Armington, 2002) clearly reflects the contribution of small and new firms to economic development, as measured by new job growth. Small firm formation has become an important policy approach in addressing problems of uneven regional economic development in many countries.

A growing consensus has emerged concerning the variables that should be included in a macro or regional model that explains the variation in entrepreneurship. The likely determinants of new firm formation can be categorized into three main groups: demand-side variables, supply-side variables and policy variables. Variables associated with demand, including population growth, changes in household income and changes in real GDP, are hypothesized to increase firm creation rates. The supply-side variables that indicate the resource availability for firm start-ups include industry density structure, urbanization and agglomeration effects on entrepreneurial activities, availability of financial and human capital (educational levels and experience) and rates and changes in unemployment. The policy variables are hypothesized as having a positive effect on new firm formation include taxation, regulation and variations in laws related to business.

Micro level research, though theoretically weak, has provided appropriate explanatory variables of new firm formation. Evident throughout the literature is the hypothesis that variations in regional characteristics in these variables can explain a large part of the differences in start-up rates. Regional variations in start-up rates and small firm job creation have been analyzed for various countries including Italy (Garofoli, 1992), Republic of Ireland (Hart and Gudgin, 1994), France (Guesnier, 1994), United Kingdom (Keeble and Walker, 1994), Germany (Audretsch and Fritsch, 1994), United States of America (Goetz and Freshwater, 2001; Kilkenny et al., 1999; Reynolds et al., 1994), Finland (Kangasharju, 2000), Spain (Callejon and Segarra, 2001) and Turkey (Gaygisiz and Köksal, 2003).

Population growth can generate new firm formation. Increased population leads to a derived demand for goods and services, hypothesized to positively impact new firm start-ups. In general, migration will exhibit a positive or negative relationship depending on net out-migration or in-migration. Out-migration reduces the potential demand for new goods and services by entrepreneurs and also reduces the supply of potential entrepreneurial talent. Net in-migration is expected to boost the potential pool of entrepreneur talent and the demand for new goods and services.

Industrial density and industry structure have a supply-side influence by shaping the overall business environment in the region (Kangasharju, 2000). More firms in an area provide a greater source of business demand for new start-ups (Keeble and Walker, 1994). Urban regions, for example, have higher firm birth rates relative to their rural counterparts in many of the studied regions. Sweden's urban areas of Stockholm and Gothenburg, for instance, had the highest rates of start-ups compared to rural areas in Sweden (Davidsson et al., 1994). However, it is also hypothesized that the presence of large firms in an area, especially large manufacturing firms, will reduce the ability of new firms to enter the marketplace (Garofoli, 1992). Further, population structure, such as the percentage of young individuals is another factor of new firm formation. For instance, young individuals (between 24 and 44 years of age) have a higher probability of becoming entrepreneurs (Garofoli, 1994).

The role of human capital concerning firm start-ups is related to the degree of specialized labor. Results regarding education and entrepreneurship growth have been ambiguous. Guesnier found the propensity to create a new firm was positively correlated with adults with a bachelor degree (1994). However, Hart and Gudgin (1994) found an inverse relation between individuals with university degrees and rate of new firm formation. Generally, educational attainment is expected to influence the number of business start-ups. A better educated workforce will be able to identify a broader range of business opportunities and likely be exposed to a wider business environment. A low skilled workforce will be less likely to be able to identify potential entrepreneurial opportunities or be locked out of the financial capital market due to lack of collateral.

Household wealth and household prices are expected to positively influence entrepreneurial start-ups. Both of these variables measure the potential access to financial capital for a new business venture. Surprisingly, very few studies have used household wealth or personal income in measuring variations in business starts.

Unemployment rates have had an ambiguous impact on start-up rates across different regions (Audretsch and Fritsch, 1994; Acs and Armington, 2002). Regional variation may account for the differences in the impact of this variable on start-up rates. Hypothetically, unemployment rates are expected to be positively correlated with the number of start-up rates, as people are forced to search for new income. However, unemployed individuals can either start a new business or they can also start work as new employees in another firm. Unemployment may also be negatively correlated, especially over time, due to its dampening effect on the workers' motivation and stock of resources.

Government policies and several social variables have also indicated influence in new and small firm formation (Audretsch and Fritsch, 1994; Davidsson and Henrekson, 2000; Christy and Dassie, 2000). For this chapter, government regulation, legislation and taxation were excluded from the analysis because national or state government impacts are not expected to vary across a state landscape. Local government policies are excluded here as measures explaining start-up rate variation, because local government has fairly limited powers. Other regional variables, including household wealth and home prices, education, regional diversity in industry structure and in- and out-migration have all been used as explanatory factors expected to positively or sometimes negatively relate to the regional start-up rates.

In all cases, data availability has hampered efforts to properly measure some factors, resulting in the use of proxy variables. Much of the literature has relied on previous research and anecdotal evidence to build a case for including specific variables in the model. Different approaches have thus been used to examine the different factors and sectors, both in different periods and for different regions. There is an extensive literature that focuses specifically on regional characteristics (economic, social, political and environmental structures), as indicators of start-up rates for new firm growth. The most significant of the explanatory variables for disparities in the start-up rates at the local, regional and national levels included the following: measures of urbanization and agglomeration, demand and population change and unemployment and firm size structure.

8.3 THE MODEL

This study develops a spatial model to estimate the statistical relationship between new business start-ups and a set of economic, social and demographic variables. The data used in this study are aggregated to the county level for the 120 Kentucky counties. The state of Kentucky can be divided into numerous distinct regions based on similarities in geography, economic conditions, or other characteristics. In this study, we choose to group counties into three regions based largely on economic factors with some recognition of geography. The three regions are identified in this study as Eastern Kentucky, Central Kentucky and Western Kentucky.

Eastern Kentucky includes 40 counties in the mountainous portions of the state that are part of Appalachia. Central Kentucky includes 43 counties in the portion of the state commonly referred to as the Bluegrass and Northern Kentucky. Western Kentucky includes 36 counties that are largely dominated by agriculture. Note that Spencer County in the Central region did not have any start-up data for any of the years available, thus 119 counties were included for analysis.

Given the grouped, spatial nature of the data, it was anticipated that group-wise heteroscedasticity and (or) contemporaneous correlation would be an issue. Furthermore, model coefficients are likely to vary across regions. In light of potential spatial heterogeneity, a model similar to Seemingly Unrelated Regression is used to allow separate parameter estimates for each region.

Following Greene (1990) each region is treated as a separate regression equation. The data comprising the three regions is grouped and stacked by equation following Equation (8.1).

$$Y_1 = X_1 b_1 + 0 b_2 + 0 b_3 + \varepsilon_1$$
$$Y_2 = 0 b_1 + X_2 b_2 + 0 b_3 + \varepsilon_2 \qquad (8.1)$$
$$Y_3 = 0 b_1 + 0 b_2 + X_3 b_3 + \varepsilon_3$$

In (8.1) Y represents the dependent variable arranged in a column vector, X is a matrix comprised of a constant and relevant independent variables, b is a column vector of parameters or solution values and ε is the unknown error term. Stacked and converted to matrix form, (8.1) is expressed as Equation (8.2). The X matrix in (8.2) has a special 'block-diagonal' form. It is this form that allows estimation of separate parameter values for each region. Keeping track of the dimensions of this system is very important. As previously discussed, each region possesses a unique number of counties. This investigation also considers two time periods so there are 238 total observations (T). For each region K parameters are estimated for a total of KR parameters (R represents regions of which there are 3). Thus, Y and ε are T by 1, X is T by KR and b is KR by 1.

$$\begin{bmatrix} Y_1 \\ Y_2 \\ Y_3 \end{bmatrix} = \begin{bmatrix} X_1 & 0 & 0 \\ 0 & X_2 & 0 \\ 0 & 0 & X_3 \end{bmatrix} \begin{bmatrix} b_1 \\ b_2 \\ b_3 \end{bmatrix} + \begin{bmatrix} \varepsilon_1 \\ \varepsilon_2 \\ \varepsilon_3 \end{bmatrix} \qquad (8.2)$$
$$Y = Xb + \varepsilon$$

The difficult aspect of this investigation is that each region contains a unique set of counties, thus the regions represent unbalanced panel data. Let R_1 represent Eastern Kentucky (40 counties), R_2 Central Kentucky (43 counties), R_3 Western Kentucky (36 counties). Following Judge et al. (1988), matrices are partitioned to reflect shared observations (M) and remaining observations (N). The number of shared observations is equal to the number of observations in the smallest cross-section ($M = R_3 = 36$). It follows, then, that the number of remaining observations in each region is equal to the number of observations in the region less M (that is, $N_i = R_i - M$ for all $i = 1$ to 3). Note that $T = \Sigma_{i=1}^{R} R_i = R \cdot M + \Sigma_{i=1}^{R} N_i$ for all $i = 1$ to 3 and $R = 3$.

The spatial nature of the data is expected to give rise to contemporaneous correlation. Specifically, each region is hypothesized to possess a unique variance term (σ_{ii}) and covariance term (σ_{ij}) that is grouped in a matrix Σ (Equation (8.3)). Again, the form of Σ accounts only for contemporaneous correlation. The issue of spatial autocorrelation is left to further study. In the case of unbalanced panel data, derivation of Σ is difficult. Following Judge (1988), the variance and covariance terms in Σ are derived and then partitioned to reflect M and N. In Σ, I_M is an M by M identity matrix for the shared observations and I_{Ni} is an N_i by N_i identity matrix for the remaining observations in region $i = 1$ to 3. Note that Σ is a square T by T, symmetric, positive definite matrix. The mathematical definitions of the variance (σ_{ii}) and covariance terms (σ_{ij}) are also provided in (8.3). In the definitions, e^* is the residual vector for the shared observations.

$$\Sigma = \begin{bmatrix} \sigma_{11}I_M & 0 & \sigma_{12}I_M & 0 & \sigma_{13}I_M & 0 \\ 0 & \sigma_{11}I_{N_1} & 0 & 0 & 0 & 0 \\ \sigma_{21}I_M & 0 & \sigma_{22}I_M & 0 & \sigma_{23}I_M & 0 \\ 0 & 0 & 0 & \sigma_{22}I_{N_2} & 0 & 0 \\ \sigma_{31}I_M & 0 & \sigma_{32}I_M & 0 & \sigma_{33}I_M & 0 \\ 0 & 0 & 0 & 0 & 0 & \sigma_{33}I_{N_3} \end{bmatrix} \qquad (8.3)$$

$$\text{where } \sigma_{ii} = \frac{e_i e_i}{R_i} \text{ and } \sigma_{ij} = \frac{e_i^* e_j^*}{M}$$

Following Greene (1990) and given the definitions for σ_{ii} and σ_{ij} from (8.3), the presence of contemporaneous correlation is tested using the Lagrange multiplier statistic (Equation (8.4)). The null and alternative hypotheses for the Lagrange multiplier test are Ho: $\sigma_{21} = \sigma_{31} = \sigma_{32} = 0$ (that is, the disturbances of the regions are unrelated) and Ha: at least one covariance term is nonzero. Note that the Lagrange multiplier statistic utilizes only values of σ_{ij} from the lower triangle of Σ., λ is distributed asymptotically according to a chi-squared distribution with $R(R - 1)/2$ (or 3) degrees of freedom.

$$\lambda = T \cdot \sum_{i=1}^{R} \sum_{j=1}^{i-1} \frac{\sigma_{ij}^2}{\sigma_{ii}\sigma_{jj}} \Rightarrow \chi^2_{R(R-1)/2} \qquad (8.4)$$

If the outcome of the Lagrange multiplier is to reject Ho, then the solution values (or parameters) of (8.2) are determined using feasible generalized least squares (GLS; Equation (8.5)). Here b_{GLS} is more efficient than regression (OLS) equation by equation or regression using an alternative estimation technique like fixed or random effects. In general, the greater the correlation of the disturbances, the greater is the efficiency gain accruing to GLS. It is also important that the explanatory variables in each region not be the same across all observations. The presence of contemporaneous correlation and thus the appropriateness of this regression model, is demonstrated in subsequent results. In (8.5) Y is T by 1, X is T by KR and Σ is T by T, which yields the T by 1 solution vector b.

$$b_{GLS} = \left[X'\Sigma^{-1}X\right]X'\Sigma^{-1}Y \qquad (8.5)$$

8.4 DATA

The data used in this investigation were obtained from the US Census Bureau, County Business Patterns, the U.S. Bureau of Economic Analysis and the state unemployment insurance records (business start-up data). The model is estimated using data from the 1990 and 2000 Decennial Population Census. The variables are chosen based on the discussion in the introduction and literature review.

The main dependent variable is the business start-up rate in the retail and services sectors per 1 000 workers in the sectors (BSU_R&S). These sectors were chosen because of data availability and the expectation that similar factors would be involved in these sector start-ups versus other sectors such as manufacturing. Manufacturing and other industrial sectors are likely driven by a variety of regional and economic factors. Furthermore, many counties do not have manufacturing starts in any given year. For these reasons, the focus was placed on retail and business service firms where data availability is not an issue and there is likely to be a common set of independent variables that affect these types of businesses. At the same time, the parameters on these variables will likely vary across regions.

The independent variables included in this investigation can be grouped according to those that are related to economic factors, those related to the industrial base and those that are related to socio-demographic factors. The variables related to economic factors include percent of county eligible work force that was unemployed in 1990 or 2000 (u_rate), number of work places per 1 000 workers (EstDens) and the number of large manufacturing firms with at least 100 employees (LFM).

The variables related to the industrial base include percent of workers employed in the farm industry (PFE), percent of workers employed in the manufacturing industry (PME), percent of workers employed in the retail and services industry (PRSE), percent of workers employed in the government sector (PGE) and an index of economic diversity (ogive). The index of economic diversity, ogive is defined as $\Sigma\,(X_i - 1/N)^2/(1/N)$, where N is the number of sectors in the economy and X_i is the sectoral share of economic activity for the ith sector. This index is a 'goodness-of-fit' measure that is sensitive to the chosen N. It assumes that the more evenly economic activity is distributed among various sectors, the greater the 'diversity' of the local economy. The variable ogive can be interpreted as follows. When ogive is 0, then there is perfect diversity in the economy, or the share of employment in each sector is evenly distributed among the different sectors (Siegel et al., 1995). The higher the ogive is, the more unequal is the distribution of economic activity within a local area.

The variables related to sociological and (or) demographic factors include percent of people working outside of county of residence (commute), median household income (m_inc), gender gap in labor force participation rates (g_gap), population density (density), percent of the population with high school education or equivalent (hs_grad), percent of the population below the poverty threshold (pov), percent of the population between ages 25 and 44 (age), percent of workers in managerial occupations (PMO), median home value per $1 000 of value (MHV), percent of the population that own their house (own), county Beale code (beale) and a dichotomous (or dummy) variable that captures differences in the dependent variable due to census year (Yr00). The variable g_gap is measured as the difference between the percent of males in the labor force and the percent of females in the labor force. The Beale code is a measure developed by the United States Department of Agriculture to reflect the urban or rural geography of a county. It is based on a county's population and adjacency to a metropolitan area, as defined by the U.S. Office of Management and Budget. Beale codes ranging from 1 to 3 denote counties in metropolitan areas, while codes 4 through 9 signify nonmetro counties, with codes 8 and 9 denoting completely rural counties. The dummy variable Yr00 captures differences in the dependent variable that can be attributed to changes in the census year. It retains the value of 1 for census year 2000 and is 0 otherwise.

8.5 RESULTS

The 'Factor' procedure in SAS was used to determine the degree of collinearity between the 20 independent variables described above. Results of factor analysis indicate that the independent variables PMO, m_inc, hs_grad, pov, age, MHV, own and beale are highly correlated and 'act' as a group. This result is intuitive in that managers (PMO) tend to have higher salaries and thus higher incomes (m_inc). Higher incomes tend to be associated with a high school degree (hs_grad) and lower unemployment rates. People between 25 and 44 (age) tend to be gainfully employed; thus they have higher incomes. Lower incomes are associated with poverty (pov), rural areas (higher beale codes), lower valued homes (MHV) and lack of home ownership.

Factor analysis also indicates that EstDens, commute, density, PME, PFE, u_rate and beale act as a group. While the relationships between some of these variables are less obvious, plausible explanations are possible. For example, the greater is establishment density, manufacturing employment and population density, the smaller is the commuting percentage because people are more likely to be employed in urban areas with greater business and population densities. Manufacturing jobs also anchor people to their counties. A higher Beale code (indicating a rural county) is associated with an increased number of commuters because of a lack of employment opportunities. However it is also possible that the percentage of commuters is lower if the rural county is also located some distance from an employment center and roads are poor.

In the first grouping, factor analysis suggests that the variable median household income (m_inc) would best represent the group in a regression with business start-up rate as the dependent variable. Similarly, the variable commute best represents the second grouping. In the primary and secondary regressions the dichotomous variable indicating data for the 2000 census (Yr00) and the variable beale are included as independent variables.

The primary and two secondary models are expressed, respectively, as Equations (8.6), (8.7) and (8.8). In (8.6), (8.7) and (8.8) the subscript i ranges from 1 to $T = 238$, the total number of observations. The variable R_{ij} is a dummy variable that retains the value of 1 if the ith observation resides in region j and is 0 otherwise. Use of R_{ij} generates the stacked X matrix illustrated in Equation (8.2). It is important that the i observations in (8.6) be ordered by region. P_{ij} is the square root of the individual elements in Σ^{-1} (the inverse of Σ; Equation 8.3). Using P_{ij} the data are weighted to correct for contemporaneous correlation. Note that P_{ij} in (8.6) is different from P_{ij} in (8.7) or (8.8).

$$P_{ij} \cdot BSU\_R\&S_i = \sum_{j=1}^{R} P_{ij} \cdot \begin{pmatrix} b_{j0} + bm_{j1}\_inc_i + b_{j2}commute_i \\ + b_{j3}ogive_i + bg_{j4}\_gap_i \\ + b_{j5}LFM_i + b_{j6}PRSE_i \\ + b_{j7}PGE_1 + b_{j8}beale_i \\ + b_{j9}Yr00_i \end{pmatrix} \cdot R_{ij} \quad (8.6)$$

$$P_{ij} \cdot m\_inc_i = \sum_{j=1}^{R} P_{ij} \cdot \begin{pmatrix} \alpha_{j0} + \alpha_{j1}hs\_grad_i + \alpha_{j2}pov_i \\ + \alpha_{j3}age_i + \alpha_{j4}PMO_i + \alpha_{j5}MHV_i \\ + \alpha_{j6}own_i + \alpha_{j7}beale_i + \alpha_{j8}Yr00_i \end{pmatrix} \cdot R_{ij} \quad (8.7)$$

$$P_{ij} \cdot commute_i = \sum_{j=1}^{R} P_{ij} \cdot \begin{pmatrix} \gamma_{j0} + \gamma_{j1} \cdot EstDens_i + \gamma_{j2} \cdot density_i \\ + \gamma_{j3} \cdot PME_i + \gamma_{j4} \cdot PFE_i + \gamma_{j5} \cdot u\_rate_i \\ + \gamma_{j6} \cdot beale_i + \gamma_{j7} \cdot Yr00_i \end{pmatrix} \cdot R_{ij} \quad (8.8)$$

This analysis, using (8.6), (8.7) and (8.8), is conducted in two steps. First, parameter estimates are determined for the primary model (that is, (8.6)) that includes the independent variables that did not group and the representative variables from the two groups (m_inc and commute). Next, parameter estimates are determined for the two secondary regressions (that is, (8.7) and (8.8)). In the secondary regressions, the group representative is the dependent variable and the remaining group variables serve as the independent variables.

This structured estimation has two advantages. First, it breaks what would otherwise be severe multicollinearity within the primary model. Had all the variables been included in the primary model, few variables would have been associated with statistically significant parameter estimates. Second, this structured estimation allows for substitution of the independent variables in the secondary regressions into the primary regression. By substitution it is possible to establish the statistical relationship between the new firm start-up rate and the independent variables of the secondary models. Note, however, that substitution is valid only if the parameter estimate for the group representative in the primary model is statistically significant from zero.

Table 8.1 presents descriptive statistics for the variables in the primary and two secondary models for all 120 counties in 2002. Table 8.2 is similar, but reports the mean and standard deviation for each variable by region. A comparison of Tables 8.1 and 8.2 illustrates the regional diversity within Kentucky. Eastern Kentucky is far different from the other two regions. The mean values for poverty and unemployment are significantly higher in Eastern Kentucky, while the mean values for having completed high school, median household income and median home value are significantly lower. The data depict a region that is economically based in retail and government services with less commuting to other regions.

As indicated by Table 8.2, Central Kentucky is more urban (the Central Kentucky region included several suburbs of Cincinnati and the cities of Lexington and Louisville). This region has the highest mean values for median household income, housing values, commuting percentages, educational attainment and the lowest unemployment rate. Being the historical cornerstone of the racing horse industry, Central Kentucky is identified with great personal wealth. It is also in Central Kentucky that the owners of the mines and timber operations of Eastern Kentucky lived.

Table 8.1   Descriptive statistics for modeled variables: all 119 counties

Variable	Min.	Max.	Mean	S.D.
Primary Model (Equation (8.6))				
Business start-up rate in the retail and services sectors per 1 000 workers in the sectors: BSU_R&S	0.37	6.14	3.24	1.14
Median household income: m_inc	11.32	63.23	28.01	7.98
% working outside of county of residence: commute	3.66	71.42	35.01	16.20
Index of economic diversity: ogive	0.48	2.87	1.12	0.43
Gender gap in labor force participation rates: g_gap	–3.70	35.08	17.11	5.82
# of manufacturing firms with at least 100 employees: LFM	0.00	133.00	5.57	12.68
% employed in the retail and services industry: PRSE	13.07	55.30	35.20	8.46
% of workers employed in the government sector: PGE	5.86	52.71	15.18	6.81
County Beale code: beale	0.00	9.00	6.03	2.66
Data for census year 2000: Yr00	0.00	1.00	0.50	0.50
Secondary Model 1 (Equation (8.7))				
% of the population with high school education: hs_grad	18.86	46.90	34.39	5.17
% of the population below the poverty threshold: pov	4.10	52.13	21.19	8.97
% of the population between ages 25 and 44: age	24.60	37.88	29.60	2.10
% of workers in managerial occupations: PMO	9.20	40.40	20.81	5.66
Median home value per $1 000 of value: MHV	31.81	158.60	62.03	19.62
% of the population that own their house: own	53.01	86.92	75.07	6.07
Secondary Model 2 (Equation (8.8))				
# of work places per 1 000 workers: EstDens	19.28	73.50	39.91	10.63
Population density: density	2.12	180.12	10.34	19.81
% employed in the manufacturing industry: PME	0.00	55.63	15.43	9.86
% of workers employed in the farm industry: PFE	0.00	55.78	13.91	10.67
% of county work force that was unemployed: u_rate	1.60	15.70	6.23	2.80

The data for Western Kentucky lie between those reported for Central and Eastern Kentucky. Western Kentucky is more agrarian, thus rural, than the Central region, but includes some small metropolitan areas like Owensboro,

Hopkinsville, Bowling Green and Paducah. While rural like Eastern Kentucky, Western Kentucky is more accessible and blessed with highly productive agricultural land. Thus, it has not suffered the economic difficulties of Eastern Kentucky.

Table 8.2   Descriptive statistics for modelled variables by Kentucky region

	East		Central		West	
	Region 1		Region 2		Region 3	
Observations	80		86		72	
Variable	**Mean**	**S.D.**	**Mean**	**S.D.**	**Mean**	**S.D.**
Primary Model						
Business start-up rate in retail and services per 1,000: BSU_R&S	3.37	1.24	3.14	1.08	3.24	1.10
Median household income: m_inc	20.78	4.07	34.27	7.58	28.57	4.31
% working outside resident county: commute	30.83	13.23	42.55	17.06	30.64	15.00
Index of economic diversity: ogive	1.06	0.37	1.03	0.33	1.28	0.54
Gender gap in labor force: g_gap	16.22	7.26	17.06	4.46	18.15	5.34
# of large manufacturing firms (at least 100 employees): LFM	2.04	2.45	9.08	19.74	5.29	5.85
% employed in retail and services: PRSE	37.67	8.23	34.38	7.83	33.44	8.91
% employed in the government: PGE	17.13	4.74	13.83	7.25	14.62	7.75
County Beale code: beale	7.43	1.78	4.30	2.82	6.54	2.10
Data for census year 2000: Yr00	0.50	0.50	0.50	0.50	0.50	0.50
Secondary Model 1						
% with high school education:hs_grad	30.59	4.09	36.14	4.93	36.51	4.11
% below the poverty threshold:pov	30.72	7.27	15.04	5.24	17.96	4.24
% between ages 25 and 44: age	29.40	1.61	30.73	2.13	28.47	1.87
% in managerial occupations: PMO	20.44	4.71	22.22	6.60	19.53	5.10
Median home value per $1 000: MHV	50.00	10.44	76.70	21.26	57.89	13.45
% that own their house: own	76.53	3.73	72.86	6.78	76.09	6.57
Secondary Model 2						
# of work places per 1 000 workers: EstDens	41.50	12.66	37.20	8.55	41.37	9.86
Population density: density	6.31	4.78	17.56	31.15	6.19	4.94
% employed in manufacturing: PME	11.39	8.74	15.66	8.58	19.65	10.73
% employed in the farm industry: PFE	11.37	10.47	16.46	11.94	13.68	8.47
% of county work force unemployed: u_rate	8.10	2.94	4.44	1.90	6.30	2.10

First round OLS estimation of the regional models was conducted separately, by region, to test for data issues including infinite error variance (IEV), heteroscedasticity and autocorrelation. Data issues related to IEV and FOA were not detected in the primary or two secondary models. Within the cross-section, heteroscedasticity was detected in two regions (Central and Western), but the data were not corrected because the weighting procedure exacerbated estimation issues related to multicollinearity. Specifically, the use of weighted data in the final estimation resulted in parameter estimates for all variables that were not different from zero. Thus, in this case, bias in the variance estimates was accepted in order to improve efficiency.

The next step in estimating the regional model involved testing for contemporaneous correlation. Results of the Lagrange multiplier test for contemporaneous correlation (Equation (8.4)) indicated rejection of the null hypothesis that the disturbances across the regions are uncorrelated for (8.6), (8.7) and (8.8). Thus, GLS estimation of (8.6), (8.7) and (8.8) is more efficient than OLS estimation equation by equation or estimation using an alternative regression technique.

Results of the primary and two secondary estimations for the regional model are reported by region, in Tables 8.3, 8.4 and 8.5. The primary estimation of the regional model explains 96.5 percent of the variation in the dependent variable (Table 8.3), while the secondary models 1 and 2 explain 99.5 percent and 91.1 percent of the variation, respectively (Tables 8.4 and 8.5). For all three models, at least one of the independent variables contributes to our understanding of the dependent variable with 95 percent (or better) confidence.

The model allows for regional differences in the value of the intercept term and the value of the parameter coefficients. Nevertheless, if the parameter coefficient for a variable shares the same sign and is statistically different from 0 across the three regions, then this variable has a consistent, predictable relationship with retail and service firm start-up rate. Similarly, if the parameter coefficient for a variable is not statistically different from 0 across the three regions, then this variable is consistent, but there is no relationship with firm start-up rate. Variables where the associated parameter estimate is statistically different from 0, but not of the same sign, or statistically different in some regions, but not in others (with or without the same sign) are indicative of inconsistent results. It is this latter category where the relationship between one of the independent variables and firm start-up rate cannot be determined indicating differences in socio-demographic phenomena across distinct regions (that is, the correlation between an independent variable and firm start-up rate depends on region-specific characteristics).

*Table 8.3   Parameter estimates and standard errors for the primary
equation (Equation (8.6)) of the regional model*

Variable	East	Central	West
Dependent variable is business start-up rate in the retail and services sectors per 1 000 workers in the sectors.			
Intercept: b_0	-2.843 (1.776)	6.005^a (1.171)	3.659^b (1.850)
Median household income: b_1	0.100^a (0.039)	0.0309^b (0.015)	0.008 (0.035)
% working outside of county of residence: b_2	-0.026^a (0.009)	-0.047^a (0.006)	-0.038^a (0.010)
Index of economic diversity: b_3	0.593^b (0.286)	-0.706^a (0.005)	-0.088 (0.295)
Gender gap in labor force participation rates: b_4	0.030 (0.019)	-0.023 (0.022)	0.000 (0.022)
# of manufact. firms with at least 100 employees: b_5	0.054 (0.046)	-0.008^c (0.005)	-0.024 (0.027)
% employed in the retail and services industry: b_6	0.074^a (0.017)	-0.001 (0.013)	0.041^b (0.018)
% of workers employed in the government sector: b_7	0.082^a (0.024)	-0.013 (0.011)	0.019 (0.017)
County Beale code: b_8	0.007 (0.085)	0.014 (0.038)	-0.065 (0.067)
Data for census year 2000: b_9	-1.076^a (0.305)	-1.130^a (0.195)	-0.894^a (0.276)

Notes:
Bold text indicates a parameter estimate that is statistically different from 0.
Superscripts indicate level of statistical significance.
[a] Statistically different from 0 at the 0.01 level of significance or better.
[b] Statistically different from 0 at t the 0.05 level of significance or better.
[c] Statistically different from 0 at the 0.10 level of significance or better.
Adjusted R^2 = 0.965

Given the systematic method used to estimate the regional model, the parameter estimates for the median household income and commute need to be statistically different from 0 if the variables of the secondary equations are to be substituted into the primary model. Only by substitution are the effects of the secondary variables on service and retail firm start-up rate able to be determined. Fortunately, the parameter estimates for percent working outside the county (commute) are statistically different from 0 across the three regions (and of the same sign; Table 8.3). This is not the case for median household income. Its coefficient is statistically different from 0 in the East and Central regions, but not in the West region. This result cannot be explained. However, given that the sign of the estimate is consistent across the three regions, complications due to the insignificant parameter for median household income in the Western region are set aside and the variables of the secondary equation related to median household income are included for analysis. Finally, the parameter estimates for median household income are positive; thus the (statistically significant) substituted values from secondary model for median income (Table 8.4) are of the correct sign. The parameter estimates for percent working outside the county (commute) are negative (Table 8.5); thus the (statistically significant) substituted values from this secondary model must be multiplied by –1.

Table 8.4   Parameter estimates and standard errors for the first secondary equation (Equation (8.7)) of the regional mode

Variable	East	Central	West
Dependent variable is median household income (m_inc)			
Intercept: α_0	**14.444**[b]	7.266	**27.131**[a]
	(7.327)	(4.784)	**(9.090)**
% of the population with high school education: α_1	0.058	0.017	**0.350**[a]
	(0.092)	(0.052)	**(0.096)**
% of the population below the poverty threshold: α_2	**–0.330**[a]	**–0.531**[a]	**–0.447**[a]
	(0.051)	**(0.058)**	**(0.095)**
% of the population between ages 25 and 44: α_3	0.093	0.076	–0.122
	(0.125)	(0.103)	(0.163)
% of workers in managerial occupations: α_4	**0.125**[c]	0.078	–0.0385
	(0.070)	(0.054)	(0.104)
Median home value per $1 000 of value: α_5	**0.088**[a]	**0.239**[a]	**0.145**[a]
	(0.029)	**(0.019)**	**(0.035)**
% of the population that own their house: α_6	**0.128**[b]	**0.180**[a]	–0.080
	(0.060)	**(0.025)**	(0.055)
County Beale code: α_7	**–0.551**[a]	–0.007	–0.169
	(0.154)	(0.072)	(0.158)
Data for census year 2000: α_8	–1.366	**–2.158**[a]	–0.633
	(0.860)	**(0.606)**	(0.968)

Notes:
Bold text indicates a parameter estimate that is statistically different from 0.
Superscripts indicate level of statistical significance.
[a] Statistically different from 0 at the 0.01 level of significance or better.
[b] Statistically different from 0 at the 0.05 level of significance or better.
[c] Statistically different from 0 at the 0.10 level of significance or better.
Adjusted $R^2 = 0.995$

Table 8.5 Parameter estimates and standard errors for the second secondary equation (Equation 8.8) of the regional model

Variable	East	Central	West
Dependent variable is the % working outside of county of residence (commute)			
Intercept: γ_0	**78.464^a**	**107.446^a**	**58.649^a**
	(11.377)	**(7.072)**	**(12.965)**
# of work places per 1 000 workers: γ_1	**−0.888^a**	**−1.252^a**	**−0.452^a**
	(0.136)	**(0.140)**	**(0.180)**
Population density: γ_2	0.160	**−0.157^a**	**−1.165^a**
	(0.393)	**(0.0372)**	**(0.349)**
% employed in the manufacturing industry: γ_3	**−0.502^a**	**−0.382^a**	**−0.589^a**
	(0.150)	**(0.129)**	**(0.122)**
% of workers employed in the farm industry: γ_4	0.094	0.073	0.256
	(0.149)	(0.140)	(0.246)
% of county work force that was unemployed: γ_5	0.199	−0.820	0.466
	(0.473)	(0.579)	(0.700)
County Beale code: γ_6	−1.254	**−1.443^a**	0.396
	(0.878)	**(0.451)**	(0.761)
Data for census year 2000: γ_7	1.132	−1.949	0.896
	(2.556)	(1.965)	(2.884)

Notes:
Bold text indicates a parameter estimate that is statistically different from 0.
Superscripts indicate level of statistical significance.
^{a} Statistically different from 0 at the 0.01 level of significance or better.
^{b} Statistically different from 0 at the 0.05 level of significance or better.
^{c} Statistically different from 0 at the 0.10 level of significance or better.
Adjusted $R^2 = 0.911$

The coefficients of the variables measuring median household income, percent working outside the county, poverty, median home value, establishment density, (number of workplaces per 1 000 workers) and percent employed in manufacturing are consistently different from 0 and of the same sign across the three regions (Tables 8.3, 8.4 and 8.5; note the exception for median household income discussed above). The results of this investigation indicate that a one unit increase in median household income, median home value per $1 000 of value, number of work places per 1,000 workers and percent of workers employed in the manufacturing industry are associated with an increase in the retail and service firm start-up rate. Additionally, the results of this investigation indicate that a one unit increase in the percent of workers working outside the county of residence and the percent of population below the poverty threshold are associated with a decrease in the retail and service firm start-up rate.

The positive relationship is expected for median household income and is consistent with findings from the literature. Greater wealth or income gives potential entrepreneurs more resources and allows them to better handle risk in starting up a new enterprise. The negative implications of these results are that poor or low-income regions face significant difficulties in generating more business starts in their region holding other factors constant.

The negative relationship between the retail and service firm start-up rate and the percent of workers working outside the county of residence is not surprising. People that have jobs outside of the county would be less tied to their community, would tend to have less time and would mostly shop or use services outside of their county. People may commute out of the county because the jobs are better paid in the neighboring counties, or they may commute out of necessity or lack of jobs in their county of residence. It is possible that people may eventually be 'pushed' into entrepreneurship as a way to break out of the commuting tradition and save on travel time.

Several parameter estimates, including those on the variables gender gap in labor force participation rate, number of manufacturing firms with at least 100 employees, percent of the population between ages 25 and 44, percent of workers employed in the farm industry and percent of county work force that was unemployed, are consistently 0 across the three regions (Tables 8.3, 8.4 and 8.5). In all cases, results indicate that there is no statistical relationship between these variables and retail and service firm start-up rate.

The gender gap variable does not play a large role in the literature, as gender issues have entered the field of entrepreneurship only recently. In Kentucky, there appears to be little difference in county gender gap across the regions (Table 8.2) and it is not an important factor within a region. Similarly, the literature is ambivalent about the final effects of unemployment on firm start-up rates due to the possibilities of it being both a 'pull' and a 'push' factor for the entrepreneurial spirit.

The majority of variables is inconsistent in that some regions are associated with non-zero parameters while others are not, or the parameter estimates are statistically different from 0, but have opposite signs. Only for the index of economic diversity (ogive) were parameter estimates in two regions statistically different from 0, but with opposite signs (Table 8.3). In all other cases (six cases excluding the variables beale and yr2000), one or two regions were associated with parameter estimates that were different from 0 and when two regions, the regions shared the same sign. Interestingly, all six variables that fit the proceeding description were positive when statistically different from 0 within a region.

Variables that are largely consistent, defined as the case where parameter estimates in two regions are statistically different from 0, include percent of the population employed in the retail and services industry, population density and percent of the population that own their home. Home ownership has been used as a proxy for household wealth. Many new entrepreneurs finance their business using personal resources such as home equity loans. Therefore, this result matches prior expectations. Population density is a signal of potential demand for retail and service business establishments and we would expect a positive relationship as indicated by these results.

Variables that are indicative, defined as the case where a parameter estimate is statistically different from 0 in only one region, include percent of the population employed in the government sector, percent of the population with a high school education and percent of workers working in managerial occupations. Employment in the government sector would likely reduce the potential entrants into new business entries. High school attainment was expected to exhibit a positive relationship towards start-up rates. Previous research has shown that entrepreneurs tend to be better educated than the general population. Further, people in managerial professions will be more likely to have the resources and skills and thus be more likely to start their own business holding other factors constant. The fact that these variables are significantly in only one region indicates that these prior hypotheses are only weakly supported given the existing evidence.

Finally, two variables were included in all three regional models to capture variation in retail and service firm start-up rates due to time (the census year) and county type as defined by the Beale classification system. The dummy variable representing census year 2000 is consistently negative across the regions in the primary model. Apparently, economic conditions in 2000 relative to 1990 were such that there were fewer firm start-ups in 2000. In one secondary model census year was indicative (statistically different from 0 and negative in the Central region; Table 8.4) and in the other secondary model it was consistently 0 (Table 8.5).

The coefficient of the Beale code is consistently 0 across the regions in the primary model (Table 8.3). This finding is not surprising given that the regions of the state loosely break out according to Beale code. In the secondary models, its coefficient is indicative (statistically different from 0 in only one region; see Tables 8.4 and 8.5). However, the results are not consistent. In one secondary model, its parameter coefficient is statistically different from 0 and negative in the Eastern region. In the other secondary model, its parameter coefficient is statistically different from 0 and positive in the Eastern region. Note, however, that for both census year and Beale code, the focus is on the results of the primary model where there is no impact on firm start-up rate due to Beale code and firm start-up rates are lower in 2000.

6. CONCLUSIONS

The goal of this chapter was to determine the factors that influence entrepreneurship, defined as the number of business start-ups, in a county over time. While research has been conducted at the national level on differences in business starts across provinces, regions or states, no one has conducted empirical analysis on differences across counties or at the local level. This research was focused on variations in business starts across the state of Kentucky. A single state was chosen due to the limited availability of comparable business start data across US counties.

Potential influences on business starts can be defined as demand-side variables, supply-side variables and policy variables. Based on an extensive literature review, it was expected that demand side factors such as population growth, population density and per capita income would lead to higher levels of business start-ups. On the supply side, it was expected that a positive relationship would exist between housing prices, educational attainment, a more diversified industry structure, urbanization and the county level business starts. Policy variables were not directly included in the study, such as local tax rates, due to the difficulty of obtaining data and the limited variability of taxes across Kentucky counties.

The results confirm most of the predictions about the signs of the economic and socio-demographic variables. The variable that seems to be strongly significant and negative with respect to the start-up rate is the share of people commuting to work out of the county of residence. Other variables negatively correlated with start-up rates include employment share in the farm sector, the degree of rurality (Beale code) and poverty. Thus, local policymakers may need to focus on how to provide employment opportunities in addition to incentives for entrepreneurs to try and retain the labor force in the county. As expected, rural, agriculturally dependent counties, especially in the Eastern Kentucky region and to some extent in the West, had the lowest predicted start-up rates and the highest poverty rates. Variables with favorable effects on the start-up rate include median income, existing establishment density, population density, industry diversity, employment shares in the manufacturing industry, retail, services and government, as well as many socio-demographic variables such as home values and share of workers in the managerial occupations.

These findings may lead to the conclusion that policies that in general focus on improving the quality of the labor force as well as raising the general wealth of the county through agricultural diversification along with manufacturing firms' recruitment may lead to higher levels of entrepreneurship. Counties with higher existing establishment density are also likely to have higher start-up rates. Therefore, there is an indication of vicious and virtuous cycles in the patterns of development in Kentucky counties. Central Kentucky counties, which have historically led the state in income and job-generating capabilities, are also more entrepreneurial. Eastern Kentucky lags behind in many parameters and still needs to find a way to overcome the geographic barriers through development from the 'inside', which local entrepreneurship may provide. Western Kentucky is almost in the middle of the spectrum of development and may be characterized as well on its way into the virtuous cycle of new firm start-ups. Although it remains dependent on agriculture and large manufacturing firms for most of its income, it also has a quite high existing establishment density.

Future research may focus on regional differences among all US counties; in which case, regions may not necessarily be defined along the state lines, but rather based on common income ranges, industry structure and geography. Finding consistent data is a challenge, but the assistance of Small Business Administration and the continuing efforts of many agencies and individuals may result in new and better measures of entrepreneurship available for a wider set of counties. As evidenced by the problems of multicollinearity in this study, future research should focus on solving the problems of collinearity and endogeneity through a simultaneous estimation of entrepreneurship variable with income and industrial diversity variables, since these seem to be jointly determined by the particular policy course chosen by the county officials. Incorporating local policy differences would have aided the analysis as well, but, unfortunately, most of the entrepreneurship support structures and incentives are provided at the state or national levels, with local areas serving mostly in the role of recipients of aid, resources and information as opposed to being initiators of entrepreneurial culture and ideas.

REFERENCES

Acs, Z.J. and C. Armington (1999), 'Longitudinal establishment and enterprise mandata (LEEM) documentation', CES 98-9 Center for Economic Studies, Washington DC: US Bureau of the Census.

Acs, Z.J. and C. Armington (2002), 'The determinants of regional variation in new firm formation', *Regional Studies*, **36** (1), pp. 33–45.

Audretsch, D.B. and M. Fritsch (1994), 'The geography of firm births in Germany', *Regional Studies*, **28** (4), pp. 359–65.

Baumol, W. (1988), 'Entrepreneurship: productive, unproductive and imitative: or the rule of the rules of the game', Manuscript, New York: New York Univ.

Callejón, M. and A. Segarra (2001), 'Geographical determinants of the creation of manufacturing firms: the regions of Spain', http://www.ub.es/div2/recerca/documents/papers/68.pdf.

Christy, R. and W. Dassie (2000), 'Entrepreneurship-centered economic development: an analysis of African–American entrepreneurship in the Southern black belt', *TVA Rural Studies Contractor Paper* 00-10, July (www.rural.org).

Davidsson, P. and M. Henrekson (2002), 'Determinants of the prevalence of start-ups and high-growth firms', *Small Business Economics*, **19**, pp. 81–104.

Davidsson, P., L. Lindmark and C. Olofsson (1994), 'New firm formation and regional development in Sweden', *Regional Studies*, **1** (28.4), pp. 395–410.

Freshwater, D. and S. Goetz (2001), 'State level determinants of entrepreneurship and a preliminary measure of entrepreneurial climate',. *Economic Development Quarterly*, **15** (1), pp. 58–70.

Garofoli, G. (1992), 'New firm formation and local development: the Italian experience', *Entrepreneurship and Regional Development*, **4**, pp. 101–25.

Garofoli, G. (1994), 'New firm formation and regional development in Italy'. *Regional Studies*, **28** (4), pp. 381–93.

Gaygisiz, E. and M. Y Köksal (2003), 'Regional variation in new firm formation in Turkey: cross section and panel data evidence',. Economic Research Center Working Papers in Economics, no. 308.

Goetz, S. J. and D. Freshwater (2001), 'State-level determinants of entrepreneurship and a preliminary measure of entrepreneurial climate', *Economic Development Quarterly*, **15** (1), pp. 58–70.

Greene, W. (1990), *Econometric Analysis*, New York: Macmillan Publishing.

Guesnier, B. (1994), 'Regional variations in new firm formation in France',. *Regional Studies*, **28** (4), pp. 347–58.

Hart, M. and G. Gudgin (1994), 'Spatial variations in new firm formation in the Republic of Ireland 1980–1990', *Regional Studies*, **28** (4), pp. 367–80.

Judge, G. (1988), 'An Introduction to the Theory and Practice of Economics', New York: John Wiley and Sons.

Kangasharju, A. (2000), 'Regional variations in firm formation: panel and cross-section data evidence from Finland', *Regional Studies*, **79**, pp. 355–73.

Keeble, D. and S. Walker (1994), 'New firms, small firms and dead firms: spatial patterns and determinants in the United Kingdom', *Regional Studies,* **28** (4), pp. 411–27.

Kilkenny, M., L. Nalbarte and T. Besser (1999), 'Reciprocated community support and small town, small business success', *Entrepreneurship & Regional Development*, **11** (3), pp. 231–46.

Reynolds, P., D. J. Storey and P. Westhead (1994), 'Cross-national comparisons of the variation in new firm formation rates', *Regional Studies*, **28** (4), pp. 443–56.

Siegel, P. B., T. G. Johnson and G. Alwang (1995), 'Regional economic diversity and diversification,' *Growth and Change*, **26** (2), pp. 261–84.

U.S. Small Business Administration (2004), Office of Advocacy. Statistics of U.S, Employers and Nonemployer Statistics.

PART IV

REGIONAL SPILLOVERS

9. SMEs and Territorial Networks: The Emerging Framework in Romania

Daniela Luminita Constantin

9.1 INTRODUCTION

The regional dimension of the transformation processes undertaken in East European countries is an important field of research and one of the sources of 'new combinations' in regional science (Geenhuizen and Nijkamp, 1995). The elements of the structural reform (namely, the institutional and legislative framework for the market economy, the reform of enterprise structures, the physical structure for a competitive economy, human capital and attitudes) entail specific concerns at the regional level including restructuring regional economies, regional policy instruments in an era of limited financial means, regional institutional framework in an environment of decentralisation, the impact of European integration and the new role of local communities.

As many researchers have noticed, the experience of former socialist countries shows that transition deepens regional disparities because market forces that are gradually freed up replace the factors that previously controlled the economy. The speed of reform is ultimately responsible for a slower or a faster increase in regional disparities. In the case of Romania the pace of reform was rather slow in the first six to seven years (Romanian Government, Green Paper, 1997). But the basic question is whether after a period of growing interregional disparities a process of spatial economic convergence will start in the longer run. This means that the regional question is not simply a static allocation problem, but also one referring to dynamic long-range qualitative convergence. As long as a convergence trajectory will not be automatically followed, an active regional policy is necessary. This policy must be integrated in a complex outlook, which combines the need for local identity, self-reliance, and development with the challenges and opportunities of globalisation processes seen at both national and international levels in the context of future integration into the European Union (EU) (Constantin, 1999).

A major issue in this general framework is applying regional policy in a decentralised context that focuses on regional (local) efforts to foster socio-economic development: in other words, on endogenous development. The main idea in this view is that regional development is above all a local matter:

> The success of a region will in the end depend upon on its autonomous capacity to take matters in hand, to organise various actors around common goals, to adapt and to successfully adjust to outside pressures. Ultimately, the sources of development lie in the region itself, in its people, its institutions, its sense of community, and, perhaps, most important of all, in the spirit of innovation and entrepreneurship of its population (Polèse, 1998, pp. 13–14).

Directly related to this approach, the question of small and medium enterprises (SMEs) is a basic one. As demonstrated for more than 20 years by the experience of Western countries, SMEs represent an important source of local and regional dynamism. Economic recession and the accompanying changes in production organization revealed the vulnerability and deficiencies of the large company, proving that it is no longer the only engine of development (Maillat, 1990). From a positive perspective the economic reform occurring in Central and East European countries emphasizes the role of SMEs: this sector is considered to have a key role in restructuring the old centralized economies and maintaining economic dynamism. SMEs should be able to create a significant number of new jobs, to improve industrial relations by providing a superior working environment for employees, to create a diversified and flexible industrial base by creating a pool of entrepreneurs willing and able to take risks, to stimulate competition for small and large firms alike leading to an energetic enterprise culture, and to stimulate innovation (Armstrong and Taylor, 1993).

From a regional viewpoint the main question is whether SMEs have a similar effect in each region. The answer is negative:

> The presence of SMEs in a region does not necessarily mean development or revitalization. The arrival of SMEs in a region may be the result of the corporate strategy of large companies (for example, vertical dis-integration). Because SMEs depend on outside entities, in this case they do not help to generate 'autonomous' local dynamism. Nor is the existence or emergence of independent or local SMEs in a region necessarily the sign of a specific regional dynamic. True, these SMEs provide jobs, but they do not provide the region with the chance to control its development. Indeed, if local dynamism based on SMEs is to manifest itself, one condition has to be met: SMEs have to belong to a territorialized network. (Maillat, 1990, p. 347)

If the cluster typology based on relations between firms within the cluster is considered, territorial networks represent a step forward compared with pure agglomeration and the industrial complex. Whereas these two types are localization-oriented, territorial networks are organizationally oriented, leading to creation of a local business environment of confidence, risk-taking and co-operation (McCann, 2001; Cappellin and Steiner, 2002). The most comprehensive definition refers to territorial (regional) networks as

cooperation between (small and medium-sized) businesses, government agencies, educational and research institutions, intermediary institutions and other groups. Inter-firm networks and networks of public and other institutions are, therefore, integral components of the whole system of "regional networks", which is the structure of relations between all private and public sector and other participants. (Sprenger, 2001, p. 12)

A series of economic, social, and ecological benefits are expected by the actors involved in network cooperation and the region itself, including increasing the use of synergetic effects through cooperative planning; reducing the time of reaction to regional structural problems; development of new services and products; improving the integration of the environmental dimension into regional development by ex-ante assessment, indicators and choice of projects; and greater support for regional initiatives, creativity and cultural identity (Sprenger, 2001).

A very successful model of integrating SMEs in territorial networks is that of local production systems in North-East and Central Italy (NEC) where the model has flourished. It implies a dense network of interdependencies between enterprises (usually but not always specialized in a particular sector) as well as links, relations, exchanges between them and other agents acting in the region (like banks, higher education institutions, research institutions, training centres, consulting firms, sectoral associations of producers, chambers of commerce, local public administration, and so on). At the same time, the growing regional awareness and the growing efforts to shape regionally based alliances, networks and neighbourhood cooperation (Funck and Kowalski, 1993), together with changes in the competitive scenario of the international economy lay the foundations for further development of SMEs into interregional and international networks.

Starting from these overall considerations, this chapter aims to explore the main features and the significance of the SME sector development for addressing the regional question in Romania during the transition period and to identify the emerging evidence and the perspectives of SME territorial networking phenomenon. It also aims at analysing the usefulness and the relevance of this concept and those directly related to it (local entrepreneurship, local milieu) for regional policy purposes in the new context created by European integration.

9.2   THE ACTUAL STATE OF THE SME SECTOR IN ROMANIA

The role and results of SME sector development since 1990 should be evaluated and understood in the general context of the Romanian transition, with its specific features. The political turmoil in the first ten years after December 1989 made reform very difficult. Romania was severely criticized by the EU and international financial institutions for slow restructuring and privatization,[1] the incapacity to eliminate losses within the economy, and the lack of real changes in public administration. Three sub-periods can be identified within this decade, namely: 1990–1992 (the beginning of transition), when the GDP recorded a serious drop; 1993–1996, when a macrostabilization programme was applied with positive consequences for economic growth, unemployment and the inflation rate; 1997–2000, when the economic decline (until 1999) represented the first result of the massive restructuring and privatization process (too much delayed in Romania) undertaken in this period, being followed by a slow recovery starting in 2000.

Within this general context the evolution of the Romanian sector of SMEs results from a variety of conditions and causes, the following being the most relevant (CRIMM, 1998): the absence of such a sector before 1990, an initially legal framework for setting up this kind of enterprise, the incentives provided at the beginning of the process, and the speed of restructuring and privatization of the state firms.

Thus, unlike other former socialist countries, where some private activities had developed in the centralized economy, private initiative development in Romania started in fact in March 1990, when the first act in this direction was issued.

In general terms the support offered to SMEs up to the present has focused on several categories, including the stimulation of new firms, the development of the existing ones, and the provision of consultancy services. Assistance in these categories is both financial and non-financial. Some of these *measures supportive* of the SME sector include

- provision of loans (from the unemployment fund) with subsidized interest to SMEs hiring unemployed workers;
- a programme of subsidized credits carried out through the former Romanian Agency for Development;
- guarantees for private entrepreneurs;
- projects financed by the Romanian Fund for Social Development;
- investment grants offered by Phare via the Economic and Social Cohesion component;

- subsidies provided by the EU within the RICOP programme for industrial restructuring and professional reconversion and grants via the FIDEL programme (Local Initiatives for Economic Development Fund);
- loans on a commercial basis initiated by international financial institutions (the World Bank for exports and investments in food industry and the ERDB also for exports);
- the Romanian–American Fund for supporting private initiative, with capital investments as the main focus;
- business incubators;
- consulting centres which have been created using both internal and foreign funds and assistance (from UNDP, Phare, USAID, Know-How Fund of the British government, German, French, Dutch governments, and so on);
- encouraging the cross-national links between SMEs, universities, and research institutes with the support of the Framework Programme Five of the EU, and so on.

The importance of this sector for revitalizing the Romanian economy was recognized in the latter part of 2000 by the establishment of the Ministry for SMEs, which in June 2003 was transformed into a national governmental agency. It has developed a series of financing programmes for the SME sector (with the state budget as the main source), following the national and regional objectives of the National Development Plan for 2002–2005. These programmes refer to (Florescu, 2002):

- support for investment in newly established SMEs as well as in existing ones;
- creation of the National Fund for SME Credit Guarantee;
- supporting SMEs' access to training and consulting services;
- spreading knowledge about successful business experiences in the SME sector;
- creation of the national network of consulting centers;
- support for SME export activities;
- setting up and developing new business incubators.

As a result of these concrete measures and actions, the SME sector has recorded significant dynamism. In the year 2000 the total number of SMEs (fewer than 250 employees in Romania) was 781 327, representing 99.6 percent of total active enterprises and accounting for approximately 46.9 percent of total employment and 55.9 percent of turnover (NAED, 2000). With regard to capital ownership, 97.4 percent of total SMEs is private, 0.3

percent is state-owned and 2.3 percent is mixed. In general terms, the private sector contributes 65.5 percent to GDP, 65.7 percent to exports and 70 percent to imports (NIS, 2002). As regards the SME distribution by size, 92.9 percent are micro-firms (up to 9 employees), 5.8 percent are small (10–49 employees) and 1.3 percent are medium firms (50–249 employees). Small and medium firms hold approximately 60 percent of total SME turnover.

The structure of private sector by activity is also pertinent:

- one in ten firms mainly performs an industrial activity;
- every eight commercial firms correspond to one in industry and every 34 to one in the construction sector;
- 88 percent of micro-firms belong to the commerce and service sector, while 59.5 percent of medium-sized firms belong to industry and construction; the share of industrial medium-sized firms is increasing;
- within industrial SMEs those belonging to food, light, and the wood industry prevail (more than 57 percent of total industrial SME number); still, chemistry and machine building have recorded significant growth in recent years.

Related to these facts it is useful to explore the opinion of SME owners and investors with regard to the obstacles they have had to face in their development (see, for example, CRIMM, 1998; NAED, 2000; Nicolescu et al., 2003). The obstacles include:

- the uncertainty of the political framework;
- the incomplete, immature and continuously changing legal and institutional framework;
- the adverse macroeconomic framework: a high rate of inflation, price instability, and a low level of demand;
- financial aspects: a high tax level and difficulties with access to financial sources (high interest rates to bank credits);
- infrastructure aspects (including lack of premises), relationships with governmental organizations, and access to new technologies;
- human capital quality-related problems;
- insufficiency of agreements with foreign entrepreneurs and business firms.

The international experience shows that, in order to improve the existing situation, governments establish objectives and plans applicable to the whole business sector, regardless of firm size. Sometimes policies and programmes specific to SMEs can be added to these general measures. The overall objectives, however, take priority; in the majority of cases these general measures also are essential for SME development. They focus on:

- ensuring a stable fiscal and monetary framework, including reasonable levels of interest rate, with inflation under control;
- the development of a financial market system able to stimulate saving process and to offer mechanisms for transforming savings into investment;
- applying adequate policies for competition protection;
- human capital development;
- ensuring a favourable climate for new firm formation and the development of the existing ones;
- encouraging co-operation and partnership between firms;
- applying clear rules with regard to ownership and contract discipline.

In addition to the overall economic policy, the Romanian government had adopted by the beginning of 2001 special measures to stimulate the SME sector, such as: exemption from paying custom tariffs for equipment and know-how, exemption from paying the profit tax provided that profit is reinvested, reducing the bureaucratic chain, and so on. Questions have been raised, however, about whether these measures are appropriate and whether their implementation has been effective. In conclusion, the most important action for supporting the SME sector consists in encouraging business environment and overall economic development, accompanied, when necessary, by measures able to respond to objective requirements specific to SMEs.

9.3 TERRITORIAL DISTRIBUTION OF SMEs AND THEIR ROLE IN TERRITORIAL DEVELOPMENT AND NETWORKING

To grasp the facts revealed by the territorial distribution of SMES, it is necessary to describe Romania's administrative-territorial structure.   It comprises one regional level – the counties, named 'judete', corresponding to the NUTS 3 level of the EUROSAT (there are 41 counties plus the Bucharest municipality) and one local level (cities, towns, communes). Also, according to the Regional Development Act 151/1998, eight development regions, corresponding to the NUTS 2 level, have been established on a voluntary basis (without being administrative units) to a framework for regional development policy elaboration and implementation. Each region comprises between four and seven counties (except the Bucharest-Ilfov region).

The territorial distribution of SMEs generally reflects the discrepancies in terms of county size and county economic development, but it also reveals additional information about SME sector development (CRIMM, 1998; NAED, 2000; Nicolescu et al., 2003).[2]

More than 20 percent of all SMEs are concentrated in Bucharest. The same city holds an even higher share in construction and services (26.2 percent and 26.3 percent respectively), but its share is under 20 percent in commerce and only 16.1 percent in industry.

The number of SMEs is directly correlated with county size (in terms of population) and economic development. Eight counties, which have – each of them – more than 3 percent of total number of SMEs, have 28.4 percent of the total SMEs (Bihor, Brasov, Cluj, Constanta, Dolj, Iasi, Prahova, Timis). Most of them are big and well developed counties. The same eight counties have 21.1 percent of industrial SMEs, 33 percent of construction SMEs and 29 percent of service ones. At the opposite pole eight less developed counties (Ialomita, Mehedinti, Tulcea, Salaj, Teleorman, Vaslui, Calarasi, Giurgiu) account for less than 5 percent of industrial SMEs, which represent less than 1 percent in each of these counties. This fact demonstrates a high polarization of SME sector in industry and construction. The distribution by county of commercial SMEs is more homogenous, with the share varying between 0.7 percent (Salaj) and 4.1 percent (Cluj).

An examination of the sectoral distribution of SMEs at the county level shows that this distribution differs across space. Specifically, in Bucharest the commercial and service SMEs prevail (61.2 percent and 22 percent respectively). The share of industrial SMEs is only 6.8 percent, compared to 9 percent at national level. In respect to the SME sectoral structure at the county level, it is important to point out that the share of industrial SMEs within the sectoral distribution of SMEs is conditioned neither by the county nor economic development. Data suggest that the available resources of each county influence the industrial SME share. This confirms the orientation towards those SMEs able to turn to good account the natural advantages of local economies, in accordance with endogenous development principles. Thus, some counties which are not among the most developed ones have a higher share of industrial SMEs compared to the national average due to the wood industry (Covasna, Harghita, Maramures), light industry (Arad, Neamt, Satu Mare), and the food industry (Alba, Bistrita-Nasaud, Sibiu), which have found there favourable conditions for their development in these counties.

Considering the circumstances specific to the transition period, the commercial SMEs are predominant in all counties. A negative correlation exists between the share of commercial SMEs and SMEs in the service sector. These structures can experience significant changes only in so far as the private sector of SMEs is consolidated within a sustained restructuring process. Territorial networking is crucial for the development of a significant SME sector. Even though studies especially devoted to this phenomenon have not been undertaken as yet, a series of clues about the actual state of SME territorial networking in Romania can be drawn from various *indirect sources*. The most suggestive are two surveys organised by the Romanian Centre for SMEs: one of them is a special study regarding the barriers to SME sector development, and the other one concentrates on barriers to SME sector exports (CRIMM, 1998). Updated – even though fragmented, partial – evidence is presented in the monthly Entrepreneurial Barometer run by the National Council of Romanian SMEs and *Revista I.M.M.* (SME Journal). Another useful source of information is the research study undertaken within the International Centre for Entrepreneurial Studies in Bucharest in 1998. This study identifies a couple of emerging industrial clusters in Romania and proposes policies, such as, growth poles and a triangle pattern of development, to support their development (Manea, 1999).

The analysis of the information provided by these sources has revealed that the SME territorial networking phenomenon has already appeared in Romania, although it is still in an incipient stage. The geographical distribution of supply and delivery markets and other additional facts suggest the creation of an overall framework for networking not only at the regional (county) level, but also at the interregional and international levels. Within these networks SMEs interact mainly with other firms of the same sector and size, but at times also with big state firms. Empirical observations demonstrate that SMEs have focused on those products and services favourable for creating a competitive advantage. So far there is not enough information to measure the scope and the extension of the process of parallel outsourcing of functions, which perhaps could be better performed by specialized suppliers within indirect vertical integration through the creation of networks of local subcontractors, It has also not been possible to measure the creation of spin-offs and new firms in related sectors. These still remain subjects for further study.

Although industry represents a major factor able to mobilize local economies, construction, commerce and services play an active role as well, according to the special features of transition and new developments in local production systems. For example, production services such as wholesale trade, logistic activities, banking and insurance, and so on have been more and more integrated into territorial networks.

Following endogenous development models, encouraging signs of networking have also appeared between firms and universities, modern consulting services, training centres, sectoral associations of producers, local public administration and chambers of commerce. Counties with longstanding industrial traditions, where higher education institutions are also located, are particularly active in innovation process and promotion of new entrepreneurial skills. Unfortunately innovation support has lower priority in public policy. Not only in Romania, but in all former socialist countries 'there is a strong danger that the old R&D infrastructure, much of which could still provide a basis on which to build, is being weakened by funding cuts which took place after the transformation to a market system began' (Funck and Kowalski, 1997, p.413). That is why universities are more involved in promoting R&D at the local level than the old research establishments belonging to the National Academy of Science or ministries.

On the other hand privatization of state enterprises and the establishment of a quite large number of SMEs is gradually transforming the economic behaviour of economic actors. These private firms are well financed and compete against each other, being motivated to create new products, introduce new technologies, produce more cheaply, and sell more efficiently.

As analysis has demonstrated, the participation of foreign capital in Romanian SMEs[3] also influences the innovation mechanisms and innovative behaviour. Foreign partners contribute to the diffusion of new technologies, but importantly also bring about new ways of behaviour, new business routines, and new mentalities that are essential for the success of transition to the market economy.

From the networking perspective, SMEs can perform a role in an international framework when they are closely integrated with other firms in foreign countries. One of the characteristic phenomena from this viewpoint in Eastern Europe, including Romania, is subcontracting agreements between foreign SMEs and domestic ones within a process of outsourcing some parts of production by the former.

Another interesting phenomenon presented in studies devoted to the internalization process of SMEs is the increased activity in the same foreign countries of many small entrepreneurs originating from the same region (Cappellin, 1998). A relevant example is the activity of the Italian Veneto region's entrepreneurs in Romania. They are mostly interested in the South-West and Western regions of Romania due to the advantages in terms of infrastructure (especially transportation infrastructure: airports with direct flights to and from Italy and good rail and road networks) and traditional relationships in some industries (textile, leather, wood and furniture).

There are also numerous projects of SME development included in the transborder co-operation programmes (for example, those financed by Phare). Various examples of microintegration can be found not only in traditional industries like leather, clothing, metalworking, furniture, chemistry, car industry and electric appliances but also in advanced ones such as computer peripherals, software and electronic goods. The better the economic situation in a country, the more numerous the firms in the latter category (Török, 2001).

In general terms the measures aimed at encouraging a healthy business environment and overall economic development can contribute to supporting the expansion of the SME sector, with all entailed advantages for the local and regional dynamism. Of course, specific measures are also required and should be integrated in active regional policies promoting SME development and networking within the endogenous development model.

9.4 SMEs AND REGIONAL POLICY

Integrated in the process of reform required by the transition to the market economy, Romanian regional policy suffers a series of influences induced by the difficulties of this period, the clear tendency to decentralization, and increasing territorial competition. Under these circumstances one of the major options focuses on turning to good account the natural advantages of local economies in accordance with endogenous development objectives. The modern outlook of this model is centred on local production systems that are not seen just as a territorial concentration of specific firms working in the same sector or in closely related sectors, but also as a specific form of organization of the close relationships among all local actors. It seems that the NEC type of local production systems, based on intense SME networking, can serve as a model for the regional policies aimed at supporting SME development in the countries in transition, including, of course, Romania.

In general terms the importance of the SME sector to regional policy derives from the SMEs ability to innovate, their contribution to the performance of less developed regions, and their role in the revitalization of certain industrial regions. In the case of countries in transition, the SME sector has a specific relevance and a series of particular advantages such as (Dragusin, 1998):

- a source of intensifying competitiveness with SMEs acting as an engine of structural changes and economic revitalization following decentralization;
- the absorption of a part of the unemployment resulted from a radical restructuring of industrial giants;
- the facilitation of the transfer of economic resources from declining sectors to the prosperous ones;

- a contribution to the increase in the number of entrepreneurs and, thus, the creation of a new social category, important to setting the social basis of transition;
- the attenuation of the adverse consequences of privatization and/or restructuring on regional development;
- the reestablishment of macroeconomic equilibrium and movement towards relative stability.

These potential advantages have resulted in a special concern with SME development in Romania's National Development plan and corresponding sectorally and regionally oriented programmes. Without neglecting the importance of large firms for restructuring the production systems, the SME sector has been particularly focused by programmes aiming at reconstructing the regional economies in accordance with the specific problems of various areas (for example, disadvantaged areas, growth potential areas, border areas, and so on).

Nevertheless, as previously discussed, the basic requirement for making SMEs a true factor of local dynamism is integration into territorialized networks. Up to now this objective has not received adequate attention as a primary objective. This chapter makes suggestions based on the analysis of the international experience and literature devoted to territorial networks for consideration by Romanian regional policymakers in forthcoming years.

To meet the condition of creating and enhancing territorial networks, regional policy has several complementary solutions that have to be applied keeping in mind the stage of development of the SME sector and the perspective of the completion of transition.

First, an appropriate, comprehensive institutional and legal framework must be established, as a pre-condition for the success of any policy measure. The reform of public administration should have in view the replacement of the so-called 'prescriptive approach', based on dirigisme or top-down planning and characteristic of the centrally-planned economy, by a 'transactional approach' where both national and local government define general norms ('rules of the game'). This approach 'aims to remove the obstacles to a greater and more flexible integration among various economic actors through the provision of "public goods", such as information, infrastructure, services, and strategic initiatives based on public–private cooperation' (Cappellin, 1998).

In this framework the policies of territorial organization can be combined with the traditional instruments of local development policies, such as financial incentives and provision of specialized producer services to promote regional economic development. Such a framework can contribute to a gradual transition from the traditional model of industrialization, supporting production systems based on economies of scale, to the networking model, based on partnership, locally bounded spillovers, flexibility and knowledge and able to create and nurture a 'sense of belonging' (Cappellin and Steiner, 2002).

Taking into account the situation before 1990, special emphasis should be put on developing entrepreneurship, and the important role that SMEs can play in that development. It is often stated that a region can regain its dynamism if it regains its entrepreneurs (Coffey and Polèse, 1985). Of course, in the case of Romania the problem is not to regain, but to create, a generation of true entrepreneurs, characterized by qualities of responsibility, spontaneity, imagination, capacity to predict and to adapt to change by detecting new opportunities, development strategies, identifying new resources, and relational know-how with people and the environment.

In order to stimulate the spirit of enterprise, regional policies have to consider each region's particularities: structural (nature of industries, size of firms), socio-cultural (occupational profile of the local population) and economic (local availability of factors of production, such as premises or capital, and demand for new firm product from particular geographical markets) (Maillat, 1990).

Another aspect that has not been paid sufficient attention is strengthening SME research and innovation. It has been argued (Funck and Kowalski, 1997) that even with limited financial resources, such as found in countries in transition, the formulation and implementation of this policy is possible and necessary. The elements of such policies should encompass: promotion of development of small technology-oriented companies, assistance in the restructuring of applied research institutes, promotion of interaction between SMEs and technology organizations, provision of training in activities related to the innovation process, and creation of national and regional transfer channels and policy that can support the networks based on co-operation and learning as infrastructure for innovation (Cappellin and Steiner, 2002).

The integration of SME activity into complex networking at the regional, interregional and international level requires intense efforts for implementing large-scale infrastructure projects. So far infrastructure is a major problem in Romania and is considered a serious bottleneck in economic development.[4]

Without being exhaustive the exposure of some priorities of regional/local policies centred on SME sector development stresses an important idea: local dynamism does not result from the action of separate firms but from their overall behaviour. This phenomenon is illustrated by the notion of a milieu or local environment-based approach that is concerned with understanding the firm in its local and regional context. As described by Aydalot and Keeble the firm, and the innovating firm, are not viewed as pre-existing in or separate from the local environment, but as being a product of it. Local milieus are regarded the nurseries, the incubators of innovation and innovative firms. ... The historical evolution and characteristics of particular areas, their economic and social organization, their collective behaviour, the degree of consensus or conflict which characterizes local society and economy, these are major components of innovative behaviour. ... This approach implies that innovative behaviour is as much dependent on variables defined at the local and regional level as on national scale influences. Access to technological know-how, the availability of local industrial linkages and inputs, the impact of close market proximity, the existence of a pool of qualified labour – these are the innovation factors which will determine areas of greater or lesser innovative activity within the national space. (1988, quoted by Maillat, 1990, p. 345)

The milieu is composed of material and non-material elements, connected with hard and soft location factors acting within a given territory (Kowalski and Rottengather, 1998). The material elements are organized around the territorial production system, the local labour market and the territorial scientific system, closely interrelated. The non-material elements refer especially to the technical culture, but other aspects like the creative climate, the identification of local citizens with their location – city or region – based on historical and cultural motivation and future aspirations (Funck and Kowalski, 1996) should also be considered.[5]

In conclusion, the policy measures meant to improve the institutional framework for SMEs and for overall regional development should constitute a coherent 'package' including economic, legal, infrastructure, cultural and socio-political elements. 'The aim of the package must be the definition of a "regional profile", stressing and taking advantage of specific feature of each local area' (Funck and Kowalski, 1997). This conclusion brings about a new perspective on regional competition as well, especially for Central and East European countries, confronted with the EU accession requirements. As pointed out by international experience, in an increasing regional competition there will be always winners and losers, but 'it is important to recognize the difference between absolute and relative winners (and losers)' (Nijkamp, 1997, p.3). This requires bringing the SMEs and territorial networking question up as a crucial issue in the debates about current regional policies in the countries in transition: the regional development process in these countries follows the same rules as in the developed ones. Certain preconditions and institutional settings are required for ensuring promising regional development and competitiveness. Clusters and networks are one of these prerequisites: they do not represent only technical linkages between firms and development bodies within a region or institutions able to internalize external effects, but also require a certain institutional environment to function properly. Consequently, regional policy for new market economies and transition countries still requires 'starting a learning process for the establishment of local clusters and networks' (Steiner, 2002, p. 220).

9.5 CONCLUSIONS

The SME sector represents an important source of local and regional dynamism. Big firms, of course, remain a key factor in restructuring the productive system. From a regional viewpoint, however, SME activity appears as strategic for each region's economic reconstruction, provided SMEs are placed in a well-structured environment, in a coherent territorial network, involving links, relations, exchanges between them and other economic agents (like banks, higher education institutes, training centres, consulting firms, chambers of commerce, local public administration).

In order to capitalize on the development potential of the Romanian SMEs, stronger support should be offered to this sector within the overall economic policy, This support should concentrate on three aggregate objectives: the removal of any administrative, financial, legal and other barriers that hinder SME start-ups and development; the provision of assistance and information to SMEs; and the encouragement of cooperation and partnership between firms.

The analysis undertaken in this chapter has revealed that some of the overall co-ordinates for networking not only at regional level but also at an interregional and international level have been created. So far there is not enough information to measure the scope of this phenomenon. The extension of the process of parallel outsourcing of functions that could be better performed by specialized suppliers within indirect vertical integration through the creation of networks of local subcontractors, the creation of spin-offs and new firms in related sectors, the relations between firms and other actors acting within regions, and so on remain subjects for further studies in this field. At the same time, regional policy should focus explicitly on the objective of supporting the creation network creation within a well-organized learning process.

NOTES

1. An article in *Wall Street Journal Europe* (2002) entitled 'Romania worries IMF' considers that the 'state-owned sector is still cumbersome and government recorded slow progress in dismantling it'.
2. This chapter concentrates on comparisons at county level, the regions being more homogenous in terms of main economic and social indicators.

3. In general terms the regional distribution of new firms with private foreign capital is characterized by a high concentration in the city of Bucharest, and the West and North-West regions as well as south-east counties bordering the Black Sea, revealing the importance of the economies of scale and, respectively, of proximity to international connections (Traistaru, 2001).

4. A KPMG survey reveals that the main barriers perceived by foreign investors in Romania are stifling bureaucracy (71 percent), poor infrastructure (60 percent) and corruption (55 percent).

5. Such a background can create the basis for expanding a new, recent approach to business networks – *netwinning* – which brings together concepts related to territory, networks and businesses and the links between them. It has been developed within a project funded by the EC's Directorate-General for Regional Policy under the Recite II programme, aiming at examining how partnerships between companies in the same geographic zone could be developed to enhance innovation and competitiveness (EC, *Innovation and Technology Transfer*, 2002).

REFERENCES

Armstrong, H. and J. Taylor (1993), *Regional Economics and Policy*, second edition, New York, London: Harvester Wheatsheaf.

Aydalot, P. and D. Keeble (1988), *High Technology Industry and Innovative Environments*, New York, London: Routledge.

Cappellin, R. (1998), 'The transformation of local production systems: international networking and territorial competitiveness', in M. Steiner (ed.), *Clusters and Regional Specialization*, London: Pion, pp. 57–80.

Cappellin, R. and M. Steiner (2002), 'Enlarging the scale of knowledge in innovation networks: theoretical perspectives and policy issues', 42nd Congress of the European Regional Science Association (ERSA), Dortmund, Germany, August 2002

Constantin, D.L. (1999), 'Regional competition in Romania: determinants and policies', 39th Congress of the ERSA, Dublin, Ireland, August 1999

Coffey, W. and M. Polèse (1985), 'Local development, conceptual bases and policy implications', *Regional Studies*, **2**, pp. 85–94.

CRIMM (The Romanian Centre for SMEs) (1998), *Annual Report on the SME Private Sector Development in Romania* (in Romanian), Bucharest.

Dragusin, M. (1998), 'Contributions to the development of the commercial SME management' (in Romanian), PhD thesis, Academy of Economic Studies of Bucharest.

European Commission, Innovation/SMEs Programme (2002), 'Netwinning combination', *Innovation and Technology Transfer*, **5**, p. 27f.

Florescu, R. (2002), 'Financing programmes for SMEs' (in Romanian), *Revista I.M.M.* 30–31, May 2002, p. 56f.

Funck, R.H. and J.S. Kowalski (1993), 'Transnational networks and cooperation in the New Europe: experience and prospects in the Upper Rhine area and recommendations for Eastern Europe', in R. Cappellin and P.W.J. Batey (eds), *European Research in Regional Science 3. Regional Networks, Border Regions and European Integration*, London: Pion, pp. 205–14.

Funck, R.H. and J.S. Kowalski (1996), 'Management policies for Central European countries: How to induce research and development activities and innovative behaviour', in M. Chatterji and R. Domanski (eds), *Urban and Regional*

Management in Countries in Transition, Warsaw: Polish Academy of Sciences, Committee for Space Economy and Regional Planning, pp. 201–20.

Funck, R.H. and J.S. Kowalski (1997), 'Innovative behaviour, R&D development activities and technology policies in countries in transition: the case of Central Europe', in C.S. Bertuglia, S. Lombardo and P. Nijkamp (eds), *Innovative Behaviour in Space and Time*, Berlin-Heidelberg: Springer-Verlag, pp. 408–30.

Geenhuizen, M. van and P. Nijkamp (1995), *The Dynamics of Regional Science*, Tinbergen Institute Discussion Paper 43.

Kowalski, J. and W. Rottengather (1998), 'Introduction to soft factors in spatial dynamics', Scientific Seminar in Honour of Rolf Funck, University of Karlsruhe, Germany, February 1998.

Maillat, D. (1990), 'SMEs, innovation and territorial development', in R. Cappellin and P. Nijkamp (eds), *The Spatial Context of Technological Development*, Aldershot: Avebury, pp. 331–50.

Manea, Gh. (1999), 'Cluster-type development strategies' (in Romanian), Tribuna Economica, 15, pp. 41ff.

McCann, P. (2001), *Regional and Urban Economics*, Oxford: Oxford University Press.

NAED (National Agency for Economic Development) (2000), *Report on Private SME Sector in Romania* (in Romanian), Bucharest.

Nicolescu, O., A. Isaic-Maniu and I. Isaic-Maniu (2003), White Paper of SMEs in Romania (in Romanian), Bucharest: Arvin Press.

NIS (National Institute for Statistics) (2002), *Statistical Yearbook of Romania. 2001*, Bucharest: The National Institute for Statistics.

Nijkamp, P. (1997), 'Northern Poland regional development initiative and project. Some theoretical and policy perspectives', Department of Spatial Economics, Free University of Amsterdam, mimeo.

Polèse, M. (1998), 'From regional development to local development: on the life, death and rebirth of regional science as a policy relevant science', Address to the 5th Annual Meeting of the Associacao Portuguesa para o Desenvolvimento Regional (APDR), Coimbra, June 1998.

Romanian Government and European Commission, PHARE Programme (1997), 'Regional Policy in Romania', Green Paper.

Sprenger, R.U. (2001), *Inter-firm Networks and Regional Networks*, Bonn: NSS ADAPT.

Steiner, M. (2002), 'Clusters and networks: institutional settings and strategic perspectives', in P. McCann (ed.), Industrial Location Economics, Cheltenham, UK and Northampton, MA, USA: Edward Elgar, pp. 207–21.

Török, A (2001), 'Industry and regional networks', contribution to the European Policy Dialogue, Annual Meeting of the Austrian Economic Association (NoeG2001), Graz, May 2001.

Traistaru, I. (2001), 'Regional patterns of private enterprise development in Romania', 41st Congress of the ERSA, Zagreb, Croatia, August 2001.

Wall Street Journal Europe (2002), 'Romania Worries IMF', July 29, 2002.

10. Research and Development, Knowledge Spillovers and Regional Growth in Europe

Seyit Köse and Ronald L. Moomaw

10.1 INTRODUCTION

Regional knowledge accumulation and knowledge spillovers among regions have the potential to significantly affect regional growth and development. To evaluate their importance, this chapter investigates their effects on regional growth in three countries – France, Italy and Spain. The issue is important because attempts to institute policies that reduce regional disparities require an understanding of the role of knowledge accumulation in a regional context. To further that understanding, this chapter estimates the size, significance and nature of research and development (R&D) activity and R&D regional spillovers on growth in regional productivity.

We have chosen to focus on R&D intensity and spillovers because we want to gain insight into the mechanisms underlying knowledge intensity (accumulation) and spillovers. We recognize that knowledge effects can occur through other variables and control that possibility. Our approach is to adapt Romer's (1989) model of economic growth to a regional context. Others (including Badinger and Tondl, 2002; Cheshire and Carbonaro, 1996; Cheshire and Magrini, 2000; Keilbach, 2000; and Paci and Pigliaru, 2002) have drawn on endogenous growth models to study spatial spillovers. Like Badinger and Tondl, we specify our econometric model in a growth accounting framework that allows for Romer's endogenous growth. In fact, our econometric model is a modified version of Romer's (1989) model.

This chapter provides new information on R&D intensity and R&D spillovers by using panel data and panel estimators. We examine spillovers under the assumption that they are two-way, that is that they flow into and out of all regions and under the assumption that the spillovers are from R&D-intensive regions to regions that are less R&D-intensive and thus measure an R&D gap. It is one of the first to distinguish between the regional effects of private and public research and development, finding that they play similar and complementary roles. Moreover, the chapter also finds that a region's research intensity, perhaps a measure of its research capability, enhances the effects of regional spillovers and that spillovers enhance the effects of intensity, a virtuous cycle if you will.

In the next section, we develop our empirical model based on a model developed by Romer and adapted by regional economists. Next, empirical results with a neoclassical flavor are presented, including results comparing the effects of private and public R&D activity. Both regional research intensity and regional spillovers are significant in the regional growth process. Then, we estimate models with an endogenous or Romer flavor, again finding both research intensity and spillover affecting regional growth. In the process, we report evidence that a region's research capability enhances the effects of spillovers and vice versa.

10.2 SPECIFYING THE ECONOMETRIC MODEL

Romer's (1993) endogenous growth model assumes that the economy has two sectors: an object sector and an idea sector. The object sector is the final output sector where, following his notation and presentation, output (Q) is determined by technology or, in Romer's terms, the stock of knowledge (A), human capital employed in final goods production (H_q), labor quantity (L), and capital stock (K). Let

$$Q = A\, H_q{}^{\alpha}\, L^{\beta}\, K^{1-\alpha-\beta}. \qquad (10.1)$$

This production function has constant returns to scale in human capital, labor and physical capital with A, the stock of knowledge, fixed.

With Romer's approach an increase in the stock of knowledge does not immediately result in an increase in output. Rather, it increases the marginal product of capital, which increases output and may increase the investment rate. Ultimately, the increase in the stock of knowledge is associated with an increase in the capital stock and the marginal product of capital returns to its original value.

The capital stock is embodied in a potentially infinite variety of producer durables that are created in the monopolistically competitive idea or design sector. Although Romer (1990) assumes that knowledge or technology is inherently a nonrival, nonexclusive good, by using the Dixit–Stiglitz model of monopolistic competition to complete his general equilibrium model, he shows that it can be produced in the private sector. For this to happen, property rights (patents) and/or secrecy must make knowledge exclusive, allowing knowledge producers to charge for their product.

In Romer's economy, knowledge or technology is available to everyone at the same price, allowing swift diffusion throughout the economy. Romer sees the knowledge created as general knowledge, that is knowledge that can be transferred from one individual to another at zero marginal cost (Jensen and Meckling, 1992). If knowledge is specific, that is knowledge that can be transferred from one individual to another only by incurring transfer costs (Jensen and Meckling, 1992), even in the absence of intellectual property rights it may diffuse slowly over time and space. Or, if property rights are incomplete and unable to completely prevent transfer, its diffusion will take time and resources. In a spatial context, the diffusion of specific knowledge or imperfectly protected general knowledge from one region to another is likely to be impeded by distance. Thus, knowledge or technology can spill over from one region to another, and it may not be equally available to all regions.

Romer shows that the relationship between total capital stock and the variety of producer durables is

$$K = \eta A x \quad or \quad x = K / \eta A \ or \ A = K / \eta x \qquad (10.2)$$

where x implies an equal amount of each producer durable and η is the constant unit of foregone consumption necessary to produce one unit of the producer durable. Under this assumption, producer durables can be fragmented into two pieces, physical capital stock (K) and knowledge stock (A) as given in equation (10.2).

Romer's assumptions lead to a stationary state that results in the production function becoming

$$Q = H_q{}^\alpha L^\beta A x^{1-\alpha-\beta}. \qquad (10.3)$$

Substituting equation (10.2) into equation (10.3) gives

$$Q = H_q{}^\alpha L^\beta K^{1-\alpha-\beta} A^{\alpha+\beta} \eta^{\alpha+\beta-1}. \qquad (10.4)$$

This production function looks like the neoclassical one with technological change. Indeed, it can be interpreted as a neoclassical production function with human capital and labor augmented technological change by assuming that A is a constant. The essential difference between the neoclassical model and Romer's model arises from the assumption about technology or knowledge. In the neoclassical model, technological progress is assumed constant, while in this endogenous growth model it is a variable over time and across economic units. In the endogenous model it is produced in a specific sector of the general equilibrium. In the neoclassical model it is a *deux ex machina.*

According to the theory, which is summarized in equations (10.2)–(10.4), constant returns to scale in L, H_q and x holds, given that A is a constant number of diversified capital goods at any point of time (equation (10.2)). After adjustment is completed, an equal amount x of each variety x_i from A number of capital goods is employed in the production process in the steady state. The relative contribution of the aggregate amount of producer durables, Ax, to output is $(1 - \alpha - \beta)$. The producer durables are produced by combining ideas and raw capital units in the intermediate sector, and the sector is compensated for cost of knowledge production and of raw capital by the share of output received by Ax.

The production process is constant returns to scale in L, H_q and K in equation (10.4) if growth in A is constant, as in a neoclassical model. A, however, is a variable in the Romer model and, as seen by inspecting equation (10.4), the production function has increasing returns to scale of $1 + (\alpha + \beta)$ in L, H_q, K and A.

In Romer's model, the knowledge stock variable A has two effects on output growth. One is direct through technical change arising from knowledge stock A, which increases productivity of the traditional production factors without any cost and compensation. The other is indirect through a finer division of physical capital in the production of new intermediate goods. By increasing the marginal product of capital, this increases the value of aggregate fixed capital in a closed economy or causes aggregate capital accumulation in an open economy.

As Romer shows, the growth accounting decomposition of regional growth based on equation (10.4) is

$$Q'' = \varepsilon_H H_q'' + \varepsilon_L L'' + \varepsilon_K K'' + \varepsilon_A A'' \qquad (10.5)$$

where VAR'' is the derivative of natural logarithm of any variable (VAR) with respect to time: $VAR'' = d(\ln VAR)/dt$ and $\varepsilon_{VAR} = \partial(\ln Q)/\partial(\ln VAR)$ is the elasticity of output with respect to that variable. It follows that $\varepsilon_H = \alpha$; $\varepsilon_L = \beta$; $\varepsilon_K = 1 - \alpha - \beta$; and $\varepsilon_A = \alpha + \beta$.

Output growth is decomposed into that due to growth in human capital, in labor, in capital and in knowledge. Because panel capital data over European regions are not available to us, we follow Romer (1989) and estimate the equation using the investment's share of output (I/Q). In particular, capital growth is replaced by $(\partial Q/\partial K)(I/Q) - \varepsilon_K \lambda$ (where λ is the constant depreciation rate) giving

$$Q'' = \varepsilon_H H_q'' + \varepsilon_L L'' + (\partial Q/\partial K)(I/Q) - \varepsilon_K \lambda + \varepsilon_A A$$
$$= \varepsilon_H H_q'' + \varepsilon_L L'' + \kappa(I/Q) - \varepsilon_K \lambda + \varepsilon_A A'' \qquad (10.6)$$

where $\kappa = \partial Q/\partial K$ is the marginal product of capital.

Defining output per unit of labor as $q = Q/L$ and given constant returns to scale in H_q, L and K (that is, $\varepsilon_H + \varepsilon_L + \varepsilon_K = 1$) the growth equation is

$$q'' = -\varepsilon_K L'' + \varepsilon_H (H_q/L)'' + \kappa(I/Q) - \varepsilon_K \lambda + \varepsilon_A A'' \qquad (10.7)$$

This specification can be used to estimate a neoclassical growth equation or a Romer-type equation. In the neoclassical version, A'', strictly speaking, is exogenous. It may, however, differ exogenously among regions (countries). For this to happen, we must drop the neoclassical assumption that knowledge or technology is a public good. In the Romer version, A'' is endogenous because R&D efforts are endogenous in the model.

Both Magrini (1997) and Caniels (2000) assume that knowledge gradually spills over spatial economic units. The extent of the spillovers' influence on a particular economy decays with physical distance and is affected by the economy's characteristics. In a full specification of Romer's theoretical model, Magrini (1997) divides knowledge into two categories, abstract and tacit, and gives a particular role for growth disparities to the tacit knowledge with regard to within- and between-regions knowledge spillovers. Caniels (2000), on the other hand, assumes that the cross-regional disparities in long-run total factor productivities exist because of the technology gaps across regions, and that technologically lagging regions with appropriate capabilities can close the gap faster and thus grow faster.

In order to empirically test the role of own-region R&D efforts and R&D spillovers across regions, we specify an equation based on the intuition of Romer's (1989) model and in the light of the above discussion of knowledge. We assume that disparate regional growth results from a process such as that specified in such empirical studies as Magrini (1999), Cheshire and Magrini (1999), or Cheshire and Carbonaro (1996) along with the regional adaptation of the Romer-type theoretical model by Magrini (1997). That is to say, own R&D efforts together with particular local fixed characteristics and spatial connections of local economic units to each other over the geography allow regional knowledge accumulation. In addition to the generation of knowledge within locations, knowledge accumulation of spatial economic units results from knowledge spillovers across regions.

Specifically, we test the influences of local employment in R&D activities implemented or funded by private or government sectors on labor productivity growth. Beside own-region resources devoted to R&D activity, growth in labor productivity is expected to be influenced by knowledge spillovers across regions due to the R&D efforts of other regions. We assume that the potential extent of knowledge spillovers hinges positively on its R&D gap with nearby regions of greater R&D intensity or that it depends on the region's exposure to R&D spillovers from all nearby regions, regardless of relative R&D intensity. Nearby regions are defined in three ways. First-order neighbors are all regions adjacent to the region considered. Second-order neighbors are all regions adjacent to the first-order neighbors. When all other regions are considered neighbors, the values are distance weighted as described in Appendix 10A.1

Other factors are likely to have significant influence on a region's growth rate of labor productivity. Among the variables included as controls are industrial mix and its transformation and industrial specialization, as measured by the Herfindahl index, and its change. Further, to control the region's technological and economic characteristics, we use initial-year labor productivity lagged by one year. Finally, productivity growth may be influenced by labor productivity growth in neighboring regions. Thus, we introduce the average labor productivity growth in neighboring regions. The use of this spatial lag variable is particularly important because we use administratively defined regions rather than functional economic regions as our unit of observation.

All variables are defined in Appendix 10A.1, where definitions are detailed for the constructed variables. In addition, Appendix 10A.2 gives the descriptive statistics. The available data were for 57 Nuts 2 regions (France (21 regions), Italy (19 regions), and Spain (17)) for the years 1985–1995.

10.3   ESTIMATES WITH A NEOCLASSICAL FLAVOR

We decided to use panel data estimators to approach the question of the effects of R&D on European regional growth (see Judge et al., 1988, pp. 489–91; and Green, 1997, pp. 613–34). The use of a panel-data specification allows the introduction of a fixed effect for every region, which, in turn, allows the control of idiosyncratic variables that are fixed in time. In particular, geographic features, transportation networks (given the short time period), political and economic institutions, and cultural and language differences are all controlled. This reduces the chances of omitted-variable bias and controls many of the spatial features that spill over from one region to another. We estimated each equation using the two-way random-effects estimator, but the Hausman test rejected random effects in favor of fixed effects for all equations. The F-test for the presence of fixed effects rejected the null of no fixed effects in all cases. Thus, all of the estimates discussed below were generated with the two-way fixed-effects estimator.

The first equation to be estimated expands equation (10.7) by adding the variables discussed in the previous section. The specification is the region's labor productivity growth as a function of the growth of the labor input, the growth in human capital per unit of labor, the investment share, economic growth spillovers from other regions, initial-year labor productivity, growth of industrial specialization and of industrial mix.

Finally, the R&D variables are added in logarithms, making their coefficients the elasticity of regional growth with respect to the relevant R&D variable. Each estimate has the region's own R&D intensity and a variable designed to capture the effects of R&D spillovers. R&D intensity is defined as R&D employment in a region divided by total employment in the region. Two types of spillover variables are used. One such variable captures the idea of an R&D gap and another captures R&D exposure – a two-way spillover. The gap approach assumes that R&D spill-ins come only from regions that have greater R&D intensity. It is a one-way flow of information. We measure this by computing the difference – the gap – between the R&D intensity of every other region and the region under consideration. We then distance weight the positive differences and sum these differences. Alternatively, we compute the gap between the region in question and all neighboring regions with greater R&D intensity. We then average the positive gaps over the number of regions with such differences. R&D exposure sums the distance-weighted R&D intensities for all other regions or it takes the average R&D intensity for neighboring regions.

In examining Table 10.1, we first consider the growth accounting variables and the various control variables. Models 1 and 2 differ from Models 3 and 4 in that the former use a exposure approach to spillovers and the latter use a gap approach. These models differ only with regard to the R&D spillover measures used. Therefore it is not surprising, as inspection of the table reveals, that the coefficients for the remaining variables do not change much from one estimate to another.

Our first concern is with the estimates of the coefficients from the first three variables, which are directly related to the production function. These coefficients are, respectively, the negative of capital's share in the production function, the share of human capital, and the marginal product of capital. Taking Model 1 as representative, we see that capital's share is estimated as 0.29 and human capital's share as 0.60, leaving a share of 0.11 for raw labor. Capital's share is reasonable, and consequently the remaining share of 0.71 for labor is reasonable. The split of labor's share into that for human capital and raw labor, however, may not be as intuitively satisfying. Finally, the third coefficient directly related to the production function, the one for investment share, is 0.29. To understand the implications of this coefficient note that an increase in investment share from 0.18 to 0.28 (from 0.05 below the average to 0.05 above the average) would increase the growth rate by 2.9 basis points.

Badinger and Tondl (2002) and Keilbach (2000) estimate similar values for capital's share for European regions and German kreise, respectively. They find, however, that the human capital share is much smaller (from 0.10 to 0.17) than our estimate of 0.60. This implies a much higher share for raw labor than we find. Romer (1987) suggests that investment share in national studies generally has a coefficient of between 0.10 and 0.20, compared to our estimates of between 0.20 and 0.30 in Tables 10.1 and 10.2. Because our results for the production function parameters are generally reasonable both in terms of what others have found and in terms of our expectations, we can proceed to an examination of the estimated effects of other parameters, including those of R&D intensity and R&D spillovers, with some assurance that the basic model is a reasonable representation of the regional growth process.

10.3.1 Private Sector R&D

Before examining the R&D results we consider the results for some of the other variables. The economic growth spillover variable may pick up both measurement effects (because the administratively defined NUTS regions probably do not correspond with regions defined according to appropriate economic criteria) and the real economic effects of the growth of economic activity in adjacent regions. Its coefficient is positive and has a value of 0.15. We believe that this significant economic growth spillover tells us that we have an appropriate control for numerous influences that go beyond regional boundaries and increases our confidence in the results for the R&D variables. With this variable and the fixed regional effects, the estimates of R&D's effects discussed below are obtained with many potential confounding effects controlled.

The coefficient of initial year labor productivity is negative with a value of about –0.15. This is a reasonable result for this variable, which can be interpreted as a catch-up variable or as indicating the relative efficiency level of the region at the beginning of the period. In either case, a higher value of initial productivity indicates that the region has less scope for growth. (We do not discuss the results for the growth of industrial specialization and the growth of industrial mix; for our purposes these variables serve only as control variables for variations in sectoral economic composition.)

Table 10.1 Estimating knowledge spillovers across regions: the effects of private sector R&D efforts on labor productivity growth: 1985–95 (dependent variable = labor productivity growth)

Independent variables	Spillover: exposure		Spillover: gap	
	Model 1	Model 2	Model 3	Model 4
employment growth	-0.2886^{***}	-0.2822^{***}	-0.2934^{***}	-0.2879^{***}
	(-10.25)	(-9.98)	(-10.24)	(-10.07)
human capital growth	0.5999^{***}	0.6021^{***}	0.5998^{***}	0.6020^{***}
	(27.41)	(27.49)	(26.51)	(27.05)
investment share	0.2880^{***}	0.2861^{***}	0.3119^{***}	0.3158^{***}
	(9.66)	(9.58)	(10.41)	(10.60)
economic growth	0.1523^{***}	0.1509^{***}	0.1742^{***}	0.1738^{***}
spillover	(5.20)	(5.15)	(5.97)	(5.98)
initial-year labor	-0.1579^{***}	-0.1590^{***}	-0.1539^{***}	-0.1573^{***}
productivity	(-9.36)	(-9.43)	(-8.92)	(-9.23)
growth of industrial	-0.1104^{***}	-0.1110^{***}	-0.1223^{***}	-0.1168^{***}
specialization	(-4.87)	(-4.91)	(-5.33)	(-5.12)
growth of industrial mix	0.0245	0.0242	0.0283^{*}	0.0263
	(1.54)	(1.53)	(1.76)	(1.64)
private sector R&D	0.0040^{**}	0.0032^{*}	0.0085^{**}	0.0208^{***}
	(1.93)	(1.54)	(1.74)	(2.82)
private sector R&D	0.0522^{***}		0.0059	
spillover: distance	(3.99)		(0.95)	
weighted				
private sector R&D		0.0175^{***}		0.0231^{**}
spillover: first and		(4.11)		(2.34)
second order neighbors				
m-Value	222.29^{***}	224.19^{***}	188.08^{***}	195.21^{***}
(Pr > m)	(<0.0001)	(<0.0001)	(<0.0001)	(<0.0001)
F-Value	19.88^{***}	19.96^{***}	18.92^{***}	19.33^{***}
(Pr > F)	(<0.0001)	(<0.0001)	(<0.0001)	(<0.0001)
R-Square	0.9082	0.9084	0.9054	0.9063
SSE	0.0515	0.0514	0.0530	0.0526
DFE	495	495	495	495

Notes:
Models 1 and 2 are Two-way R&D Exposure Models and 3 and 4 are One-way R&D Gap Models. The values of the t-statistics are in parenthesis. *** implies significant at 1 percent level, ** at 5 percent level and * at 10 percent level, respectively. Hypotheses regarding the coefficients of all variables are one-tailed except for initial year labor productivity, the growth of industrial mix, and the growth of industrial specialization. All the coefficients estimated are the elasticity of the corresponding variables except for that of *investment share*, which is the marginal product of capital stock. The implied elasticity estimates of *investment share* variable,

which is in non logarithm form, are 0.0663, 0.0659, 0.0718, and 0.0727 in models 1–4, respectively. Hausman m-test statistics reject the null hypothesis of random effects in favor of fixed effects at any ordinary significance level. Further, F-statistic values reject the null hypothesis of no fixed effects and no intercept at any ordinary significance level. The sample size is 570, which consists of 57 cross-section units over 10 years time series observations between 1985 and 1995. SSE and DFE are respectively the sum of squared errors and the degrees of freedom of the model error term.

In the overall specification used for Table 10.1, R&D affects labor productivity growth by a parallel shift in the function. The coefficient of R&D intensity, the region's R&D employees per unit of labor, takes a positive value, and using the appropriate one-tailed test, is significant at 0.10 in one equation, at 0.05 in two, and at 0.01 in one. The coefficients – elasticities – indicate that a doubling of private sector R&D intensity will result in an increase in the growth rate of between 0.3 and 2 percent.

The spillover effects are also large. Models 1 and 2 are two-way exposure models, which assume that knowledge potentially spills in from all regions: from those with greater and those with less research intensity. These models suggest relatively strong spill-ins. A doubling of R&D intensity in all other regions increases the growth rate by 5 percent; using the neighborhood model a doubling of R&D intensity in adjacent regions and second order adjacent regions would increase the growth rate by 1.75 percent. With the two-way exposure models (1 and 2) a doubling of the spillover potential leads to a 1.75 or 5.2 percent increase in the growth rate.

With the gap models (3 and 4) the spillover effects are smaller and the own-region R&D efforts are larger. The own-region coefficients are 0.008 and 0.02 compared to 0.003 and 0.004 for the exposure models. Similarly, the spillover coefficients for the gap models are 0.023 and 0.006 (insignificant) compared to 0.018 and 0.05 for the exposure models. We believe that this finding suggests that spill-ins come from both types of nearby neighbors: those with higher and those with lower research intensity. The former could be called spill-downs and the latter spill-ups. When the gap spillover measure is used, the own region's R&D intensity may pick up effects from the corresponding nearby regions with lower research intensity – a spill-up effect. This implies that there may be an omitted variable in the gap equations. The omitted variable would be the research intensity of the nearby neighbors that have lower research intensity. If so, the spillover coefficient in the exposure model would be a weighted average of the presumably larger spillover coefficient from the more research-intense regions and a smaller spillover coefficient from the less research-intense regions. If this speculation is correct, this could account for the different effects of intensity and spillover in the two types of models.

10.3.2   Government Sector R&D

In Table 10.2 we examine the effects of government R&D activity on the growth of labor productivity. Because the data available for government R&D constrained us to a shorter time period – 1988–1995 – these results could differ from those in Table 10.1 for that reason. Comparison of the two tables, however, suggests that this is not a problem.   Although the coefficients of the production function variables and the control variables for the two time periods differ, the differences are not large. The most notable ones are the smaller effects of investment share and economic spillover and the larger and more precisely estimated industrial mix effect in the second period.   In particular, Model 3 in Table 10.1 and Model 1 in Table 10.2 are the same specification. Note that the estimates of the coefficients of R&D intensity and the spillover due to the R&D gap are larger and estimated more precisely in Table 10.2.

We now ask, does government sponsored R&D have similar own-region and cross-region effects on regional growth similar to those of privately sponsored R&D? To answer note that the first two models in Table 10.2 replace measures of private sector R&D in Models 1 and 3 in Table 10.1 with government sector R&D, using the distance-weighted R&D exposure and gap spillover measures.   The coefficients for the effect of government sector R&D intensity on own-region growth are 0.0037 and 0.0154 compared to 0.004 and 0.0085 for the comparable private sector coefficients in Table 10.1. If we compare Models 2 and 3 in Table 10.2, which have the same data and differ by substituting government for private R&D, we see that the coefficients of R&D intensity are almost identical – 0.0153 and 0.0154 – and precisely estimated.   Clearly, government sector R&D intensity has own-region effects similar to those of private sector R&D.

The spillover effects of government R&D are also similar to those of private R&D. In Table 10.2, which uses distance-weighted spillovers, the spillover coefficients are 0.0249 for the exposure measure and 0.0186 for the gap measure. In Table 10.1, Models 1 and 3, the comparable coefficients are 0.0522 and 0.0059, with the latter not being significant. If we compare the gap coefficients for the two comparable models in Table 10.2, we see that they are 0.0186 and 0.021 and are highly significant. Government sector R&D intensity and spillovers have effects similar to private sector intensity and spillovers. Does this suggest that both government and private measures of research both measure some overall research intensity or overall knowledge accumulation?

Apparently not!   Models 4 and 5 of Table 10.2 include private and government measures of research intensity and spillovers in the same model. Both measures of research intensity have a positive effect on own-region growth and both the government and private spillover measures are positive. These effects are separate and additive. An increase in either type of research intensity in the own-region or nearby regions has a positive effect on own-region growth.

Table 10.2 *Estimated knowledge spillovers across regions: the effects of government sector R&D efforts on gaps labor productivity growth (1988–95; dependent variable = labor productivity growth)*

Independent variables	Model 1	Model 2	Model 3	Model 4	Model 5
employment growth	-0.2709^{***} (−8.49)	-0.2650^{***} (−8.28)	-0.2847^{***} (−8.87)	-0.2734^{***} (−8.62)	-0.2557^{***} (−7.99)
human capital growth	0.6482^{***} (24.62)	0.6420^{***} (24.68)	0.6348^{***} (24.12)	0.6378^{***} (24.71)	0.6456^{***} (24.85)
investment share	0.2402^{***} (6.38)	0.2133^{***} (6.08)	0.1862^{***} (5.45)	0.2143^{***} (6.17)	0.2183^{***} (6.25)
economic growth spillover	0.0949^{***} (3.45)	0.0852^{***} (3.09)	0.0887^{***} (3.21)	0.0819^{***} (3.00)	0.0848^{***} (3.10)
initial-year labor productivity	-0.1464^{***} (−7.73)	-0.1542^{***} (−8.18)	-0.1435^{***} (−7.52)	-0.1493^{***} (−7.96)	-0.1620^{***} (−8.56)
growth of industrial specialization	-0.0936^{***} (−3.96)	-0.0968^{***} (−4.10)	-0.0981^{***} (−4.09)	-0.1056^{***} (−4.47)	-0.0953^{***} (−4.03)
growth of industrial mix	0.0593^{***} (3.24)	0.0573^{***} (3.15)	0.0493^{***} (2.67)	0.0521^{***} (2.88)	0.0523^{***} (2.87)
private sector R&D			0.0153^{***} (2.89)	0.0164^{***} (3.16)	0.0234^{***} (2.81)
private sector R&D gap: distance weighted measure			0.0211^{***} (2.94)	0.0233^{***} (3.30)	
private sector R&D gap:__first and second order neighbors					0.0317^{***} (2.78)
government sector R&D	0037^{**} (1.99)	0.0154^{***} (3.49)		0.0164^{***} (3.75)	0.0163^{***} (3.71)
government sector R&D exposure __distance weighted	0.0249^{**} (2.34)				

Table 10.2 (cont.)

Independent variables	Model 1	Model 2	Model 3	Model 4	Model 5
government sector R&D gap __distance weighted		0.0186*** (2.77)		0.0195*** (2.95)	0.0197*** (2.96)
m-Value	84.81***	87.04***	84.30***	100.58***	97.08***
(Pr > m)	(<0.0001)	(<0.0001)	(<0.0001)	(<0.0001)	(<0.0001)
F-Value	18.75***	18.90***	18.61***	19.41***	19.24***
(Pr > F)	(<.0001)	(<0.0001)	(<0.0001)	(<0.0001)	(<0.0001)
R-Square	0.9431	0.9434	0.9428	0.9453	0.9448
SSE	0.0203	0.0202	0.0204	0.0195	0.0197
DFE	327	327	327	325	325

Notes:
Within parenthesis are t-statistic values. *** implies significance at 1 percent level, ** at 5 percent level and * at 10 percent level, respectively. All the coefficients estimated above represent elasticity of corresponding variables beyond that of investment share, which stands for the marginal product of capital stock. The negative sign of estimated parameter corresponding to the employment growth variable is the elasticity coefficient of capital stock. Hausman m-test statistic values above reject the null hypothesis of random effects in favor of fixed effects at any ordinary significance level. Further, F-statistic values above reject the null hypothesis of no fixed effects and no intercept at any ordinary significance level. The sample size is 399, which consists of 57 cross-section units over 7 years time series observations between 1988 and 1995. SSE and DFE imply respectively sum of squared errors and degrees of freedom of model error term.

10.3.3 Summary

The results in this section are encouraging. They suggest that the growth accounting approach is a useful way to examine regional economic growth. Reasonable production function parameters are estimated and, most importantly, the estimates suggest that R&D intensities and spillovers play an important role in regional economic growth. Moreover, government and private research have independent own and cross effects. In the next section, we estimate a model that follows Romer more closely, which provides an opportunity to test the knowledge accumulation approach.

10.4 ESTIMATES WITH A ROMER FLAVOR

Romer's model implies that knowledge accumulation affects growth in two ways if the time period is too short for full adjustment. Knowledge accumulation increases the growth rate directly, so that a variable such as R&D intensity has a positive elasticity, as we found above. It also increases the marginal productivity of capital, which initiates endogenous growth. Equation (10.7) is modified to include a vector of variables (P) that can have a direct effect on productivity growth $(\alpha_A P)$ and an indirect effect through a change in the marginal product of capital from κ to $[\kappa + \alpha_B P]$. Equation (10.8) results

$$q'' = -\varepsilon_K L'' + \varepsilon_H (H_q/L)'' + [\kappa + \alpha_B P] \, (I/Q) + \alpha_A P. \qquad (10.8)$$

This model includes the same variables as the model reported in Table 10.1. The difference is that four variables in the P vector are interacted with investment share (I/Q), allowing the variables to directly affect the marginal product of capital – $[\kappa + \alpha_B P]$. The four interacted variables are the economic growth spillover, initial-year labor productivity, R&D intensity, and R&D spillover. We expect the coefficient of initial productivity times investment share to be negative, because a higher level of income for a given investment share suggests a greater capital intensity (Romer, 1989) and a lower marginal product of capital. We expect the coefficient of R&D intensity (R&D spillover) times investment share to be positive because the associated knowledge accumulation raises the marginal product of capital. Finally, the interaction of the economic growth spillover with investment share could have a positive or negative coefficient. Rapid economic growth in surrounding regions could attract labor (either through commuting or migration) from the region in question to the surrounding regions. Thus, for a given investment share, capital intensity might be greater, reducing the marginal product of capital. Alternatively, the economic growth spillover might be a proxy for knowledge spillover and accumulation, which would increase the marginal product of capital.

10.4.1 The Effects of Initial Productivity and Economic Growth Spillovers on the Marginal Product of Capital

The estimates in Table 10.3 use the same specification as the estimates in Table 10.1, except that interactions of investment share with these four variables – initial productivity, growth spillover, and the two R&D variables – are included. The effect of each of these variables on economic growth is in two parts. We discuss them in turn, using the following framework for all variables. Suppose growth = α_i * *investment share* + α_p * *initial productivity* + α_{ip} * *investment share* * *initial productivity*. The effect of a higher initial level of productivity on growth would be $\alpha_p + \alpha_{ip}$ * *investment share*, and the effect of a higher investment share would be $\alpha_i + \alpha_{ip}$ * *initial productivity*.

In all of the models in Table 10.3, the coefficient of initial productivity is positive and the coefficient of the interaction term is negative. If investment share is at its average value of 0.23, using the Model 1 results the implied coefficient for initial productivity is –0.16, which is similar to its value in Table 10.1. As investment share goes from its smallest to its largest observed value, the coefficient goes from –0.21 to –0.07.

Similarly, the effect of faster growth in neighboring regions on productivity growth is 0.71 (*economic growth spillover*) – 2.69 (*economic growth spillover * investment share*). (Again we use the coefficients in Model 1 for the economic growth spillover and for the interaction term.) At the average investment share, the implied coefficient for the economic growth spillover is 0.09, and from the smallest to the largest observed investment share, the implied coefficient goes from 0.31 to –0.04. Both initial productivity and economic growth spillovers have a positive effect on productivity growth at very low values of investment share. As investment share increases, its effect on productivity growth diminishes.

Thus, higher levels of initial productivity and of economic growth in neighboring regions are associated with a lower marginal product of capital. For most observed values of investment share, the economic growth spillover has a positive effect on regional growth and the initial productivity level has a negative effect.

10.4.2   The Effects of Research Intensity and Research Spillovers on the Marginal Product of Capital

Analogously with the other interaction variables, the effect of research intensity on regional growth becomes α_r ** R&D variable* + α_{ir} ** investment share * R&D variable*. The effect of an increase in the R&D variable on growth is α_r + α_{ir} ** investment share*. The results in Table 10.3 indicate that the positive effect of R&D on growth comes through its positive effect on the marginal product of capital. This positive effect is consistent with the implications of the Romer model.

In Models 1 and 2 the elasticity of own-region R&D on economic growth is –0.008 + 0.05 investment share. At the average investment share, it is 0.0035, very similar to its value for the exposure models in Table 10.1. In the gap models the elasticities of growth with respect to R&D at the average investment share are 0.012 and 0.019, similar to the corresponding values in Table 10.1. In Model 3, the elasticities range from –0.01 to 0.02, and in Model 4 they range from 0.01 to 0.025, with the variation as usual depending upon investment share.

The interaction of R&D spillovers with investment share are insignificant in three of the four cases. Unlike the own-region research intensity variable, there is little evidence that the R&D spillovers increase the marginal product of capital. Model 3 is the exception.

Table 10.3 Estimating knowledge spillovers across regions: the effects of private sector R&D efforts on labor productivity growth: 1985– 95(dependent variable = labor productivity growth)

Independent variable	Spillover: exposure		Spillover: gap	
	Model 1	Model 2	Model 3	Model 4
employment growth	-0.2468^{***}	-0.2441^{***}	-0.2487^{***}	-0.2438^{***}
	(-9.04)	(-8.91)	(-9.11)	(-8.84)
human capital growth	0.6369^{***}	0.6369^{***}	0.6327^{***}	0.6414^{***}
	$(29.23)^{***}$	$(29.23)^{***}$	(28.80)	(29.38)
investment share	0.6414^{***}	10.3959^{***}	11.0236^{***}	10.9185^{***}
	(29.38)	(7.38)	(7.96)	(7.83)
economic growth	0.7066^{***}	0.7165^{***}	0.7489^{***}	0.7623^{***}
spillover	(2.90)	(2.94)	(3.09)	(3.12)
investment share*	-2.6886^{**}	-2.7247^{**}	-2.8196^{***}	-2.8592^{***}
economic growth	(-2.48)	(-2.51)	(-2.60)	(-2.62)
spillover				
initial-year labor	0.0777^{**}	0.0719^{**}	0.1135^{***}	0.0933^{**}
productivity	(2.16)	(2.00)	(3.17)	(2.45)
investment	-1.0266^{**}	-1.0051^{***}	-1.1952^{***}	-1.0934^{***}
share*initial-year	(-7.11)	(-7.06)	(-8.28)	(-6.96)
labor productivity				
growth of industrial	-0.0785^{***}	-0.0796^{***}	-0.0868^{***}	-0.0821^{***}
specialization	(-3.59)	(-3.63)	(-3.96)	(-3.73)
growth of industrial	0.0147	0.0143	0.0147	0.0153
mix	(0.97)	(0.94)	(0.97)	(1.01)
private sector R&D	-0.0081^{*}	-0.0077^{*}	-0.0383^{***}	-0.0055
	(-1.81)	(-1.71)	(-3.74)	(-0.29)
investment share*	0.0536^{***}	0.0496^{***}	0.2203^{***}	0.1083^{*}
private sector R&D	(2.93)	(2.64)	(4.74)	(1.30)
private sector R&D	0.0424^{***}		-0.0386^{***}	
spillover__distance	(2.80)		(-2.86)	
weighted				
investment share*	0.0055		0.2106^{***}	
private sector R&D	(0.26)		(3.47)	
spillover__distance				
weighted				
private sector R&D		0.0107^{**}		0.0084
spillover:__first		(2.10)		(0.33)
and second order				
neighbors				

Table 10.3 (cont.)

Independent variable	Spillover: exposure		Spillover: gap	
	Model 1	Model 2	Model 3	Model 4
investment share*		0.0063		0.0530
private sector R&D		(0.90)		(0.48)
spillover:__first				
and second order				
neighbors				
m-Value	116.79^{***}	–	148.99^{***}	179.86^{***}
F-Value	22.15^{***}	22.12^{***}	21.94^{***}	21.79^{***}
R-Square	0.9183	0.9180	0.9184	0.9171
SSE	0.0458	0.0460	0.0458	0.0465
DFE	491	491	491	491

Notes:
Models 1 and 2 are Two-way R&D Exposure Models and 3 and 4 are One-way R&D Gap Models.
See notes for Table 10.1. A one-tail test is used for the R&D interactions with investment share and a two-tail test for the other interactions.

10.4.3   The Region's R&D Capability and Its Interaction with Spillovers

The final issue raised in the chapter is whether there is an interaction between a region's research intensity (capability) and its receptiveness to spillovers. The expectation is that a region that has greater research intensity would be better able to capitalize on research spillovers from surrounding regions. Thus, the effect of a given level of spillovers would be enhanced by greater research intensity and the effect of a given level of research intensity would be enhanced by a greater level of spillovers.

To test this expectation, we interacted private sector R&D with the exposure and gap spillover measures used in Tables 10.1 and 10.3. Table 10.4 reports the results of estimating this new specification, which simply adds the interaction variable to the specification of Table 10.3. The effect of R&D on regional growth becomes α_r * R&D variable + α_s * R&D spillover + α_{ir} *investment share * R&D variable + α_{rs} * R&D variable * R&D spillover variable +α_{is} * investment share * R&D spillover variable. The effect of increased R&D intensity is now α_r + α_{ir} * investment share + α_{rs} * R&D spillover variable. We only report the results for R&D variables and their interactions. As one would expect adding this interaction variable to the specification in Table 10.3 has minimal effect on the coefficients and significance of other variables.

Table 10.4 Estimates for testing the impact of two-way R&D spillovers across regions (distance adjusted) on the marginal product of capital and on labor productivity growth (dependent variable = labor productivity growth)

Independent variables	Spillover: exposure		Spillover: gap	
	Model 1	Model 2	Model 3	Model 4
private sector R&D	-0.0292^{***}	-0.0173^{***}	-0.0354^{***}	-0.0023
	(-2.99)	(-3.24)	(-3.38)	(-0.12)
	0.0070	0.0043	0.0130	0.0087
investment share*private sector R&D	0.0573^{***}	0.0589^{***}	0.2050^{***}	0.0815
	(3.18)	(3.17)	(4.42)	(0.99)
private sector R&D spillover__distance weighted	0.0048		-0.0353^{**}	
	(0.25)		(-2.28)	
	0.0248		0.0099	
investment share* private sector R&D spillover__distance weighted	-0.0132		0.1936^{***}	
	(-0.58)		(3.20)	
private sector R&D spillover of first and second order neighbors		-0.0046		0.0147
		(-0.72)		(0.59)
		0.0054		0.0128
investment share* private sector R&D spillover of first and second order neighbors		0.0002		0.0239
		(0.03)		(0.22)
private sector R&D* private sector R&D spillover__distance weighted	0.0031^{**}		0.0001	
	(2.45)		(1.02)	
private sector R&D* private sector R&D spillover with first and second order neighbors		0.0014^{***}		-0.001
		(3.25)		(-0.86)
m-Value	149^{***}	154.63^{***}	94.76^{***}	49.21^{***}
F-Value	22.13^{***}	22.44^{***}	21.46^{***}	21.55^{***}
R-Square	0.9216	0.9223	0.9209	0.9200
SSE	0.0439	0.0436	0.0443	0.0448
DFE	490	490	490	490

Notes:
Models 1 and 2 are Two-way R&D Exposure Models and 3 and 4 are One-way R&D Gap Models.
Within parenthesis are t-statistic values. *** implies significant at 1 percent level, ** at 5 percent level and * at 10 percent level, respectively. Hausman m-test statistic values above reject the null

hypothesis of random effects in favor of fixed effects at any ordinary significance level. Further, F-statistic values above reject the null hypothesis of no fixed effects and no intercept at any ordinary significance level. The sample size is 570, which consists of 57 cross-section units over 10 years time series observations between 1985–95. SSE and DFE imply respectively sum of squared errors and degrees of freedom of model error term. The numbers in bold are elasticities at the average value for investment share and research spillovers.

The interactions (*R&D variable * R&D spillover variables*) of private sector R&D and exposure spillover measures (Models 1 and 2) are significant. The positive interaction indicates that R&D intensity enhances exposure spillovers and vice versa. This final interaction model indicates that in the absence of spillovers, research intensity within the region would be ineffective. This can be seen by noting that α_r is negative in Models 1 and 2. Although α_{ir}, the coefficient of investment share, is significant, it is not large enough to make the research intensity effect positive for observed values of investment share. The positive coefficient on the interaction between research intensity and exposure spillovers combined with a level of spillovers somewhat above the minimum observed level is necessary to make the research effect positive. One could conclude that for an isolated region, attempting to grow through own-region research or own-region knowledge accumulation would be ineffective.

In contrast, the interactions between research intensity and the gap measures are not significant. As previously discussed, the gap models may be misspecified because they ignore spill-ins from lower research intense regions. It is perhaps for this reason that we do not find a capability effect with these models.

10.4.4 Summary

The results in this section suggest that own-region R&D intensity increases the marginal product of capital for both exposure models and one of the two gap models. This finding is consistent with the Romer model. In addition, they suggest that research intensity (capabilities) enhance the effects of spillovers and that spillovers enhance the effect of research intensity.

10.5   CONCLUSION

This study relies on ideas from economic growth theory and regional economics to specify an econometric equation to estimate the determinants of regional growth. The model relies on input growth and knowledge accumulation for this explanation. The focus is on the region's R&D intensity and on the effects of R&D spillovers from other regions. Although we find significant – both quantitative and statistical – effects of R&D intensity and R&D spillovers on regional growth in three European countries, we caution that the results apply only to the 57 regions in France, Italy and Spain for which we had appropriate data. Given that we used the fixed-effects estimator, our results do not support inferences regarding the population.

Nevertheless, these tentative results are suggestive. First, the study supports the knowledge accumulation and spillover approach to regional growth. Second, it finds that both private and government sponsored research has both own-region and cross-region effects. Third, the results suggest that the private and government sponsored research effects are independent and additive. Fourth, the mechanisms suggested by Romer are consistent with these results. Fifth, one set of models suggests a positive interaction between research capabilities and research spillovers. If so, it suggests the importance of regional research clusters.

These results can be refined by developing new specifications to better characterize knowledge accumulation over space. Moreover, the construction of the variables that capture spillover can be improved. One of the issues that we barely touch is the rate at which R&D spillovers decay. Understanding this decay rate is important for using R&D expenditures as a regional development tool. We hope to address some of these issues in future research.

ACKNOWLEDGEMENTS

We thank Cambridge Econometrics (Covent Garden, Cambridge CB1 2HS, UK) and College of Business Administration Associates and the Spears School of Business at Oklahoma State University for providing the resources to obtain the data and to support Dr. Kose's research. The analysis and some of the results reported here are drawn from Dr. Kose's dissertation 'Private and public sector R&D efforts, knowledge spillovers and regional growth in Europe' submitted to the Economics Department at the Spears School of Business, Oklahoma State University, 2002. We also thank Dr. Jürgen von Hagen, Director and Dr. Iulia Traistaru, Center for European Integration Studies, University of Bonn for providing a hospitable environment for working on this paper. An earlier version was presented at 2002 annual meetings of the European Regional Science Association, Dortmund. It was also presented at a ZEI Research Seminar, University of Bonn. We thank Paul Cheshire, Robin Pope, Dan Rickman, and participants at these programs for many helpful comments.

REFERENCES

Badinger, H. and G. Tondl (2002), 'Trade, human capital and innovation: the engine of European regional growth in the 1990s', IEF Working Paper Nr. 42, Vienna: Research Institute for European Affairs, University of Economics and Business Administration.

Caniels, M.C.J. (2000), *Knowledge spillovers and economic growth: Regional growth differentials across Europe*, Cheltenham, UK and Northampton, MA: Edward Elgar.

Cheshire, P. and G. Carbonaro (1996), 'Urban economic growth in Europe: testing theory and policy prescriptions', *Urban Studies*, **33** (7), pp. 1111–28.

Cheshire, P. and S. Magrini (2000), 'Endogenous processes in European regional growth: convergence and policy', *Growth & Change*, **31** (4), pp. 455–80.

Green, W.H. (1997), *Econometric analysis* (3rd edn.), New Jersey: Prentice-Hall, Inc.

Jensen, M.C. and W.H. Meckling (1992), 'Specific and general knowledge, and organizational structure', in L. Werin and H. Wijkander (eds), *Contract Economics*, Oxford: Blackwell, pp. 251–74. Reprinted in *Journal of Applied Corporate Finance* (Fall 1995), and Michael C. Jensen, *Foundations of Organizational Strategy*, Harvard: Harvard University Press (1998).

Judge, G.G., R.C. Hill, W.E. Briffiths, H. Lutkepohl, and Tsoung-Chao Lee (1988), *Introduction to the Theory and Practice of Econometrics* (2nd edn), New York: John Wiley & Sons, Inc.

Keilbach, M. (2000), *Spatial Knowledge Spillovers and the Dynamics of Agglomeration and Regional Growth*, Heidelberg: Physica-Verlag.

Magrini, S. (1997), 'Spatial concentration in research and regional income disparities in a decentralized model of endogenous growth', *Research Papers in Environmental and Spatial Analysis*, No. 43, London School of Economics, pp. 1–36.

Paci, R. and F. Pigliaru (2002), 'Technological diffusion, spatial spillovers and regional convergence in Europe', in J.R. Cuadrado-Roura and M. Parellada (eds), *Regional Convergence in the European Union: Facts, Prospects and Policies*, *Advances in Spatial Science*, New York: Springer, pp. 273–92.

Partridge, M.D. and D.S. Rickman (1999), 'Static and dynamic externalities, industry composition, and state labor productivity: a panel study of states', *Southern Economic Journal*, **66** (2), pp. 319–35.

Romer, M.P. (1989), 'What determines the rate of growth and technological change?', Policy, Planning, and Research Working Papers, No. 279,. Washington, DC: Country Economic Dept., World Bank, pp. 1–46.

Romer, M.P. (1990), 'Endogenous technological change', *Journal of Political Economy*, **98** (5), pp. S71–S102.

Romer, M.P. (1993), 'Idea gaps and object gaps in economic development', *Journal of Monetary Economics*, **32** (3), December, pp. 543–73.

APPENDIX 10A.1 VARIABLE DEFINITIONS AND SOURCES

Cambridge Econometrics (Covent Garden, Cambridge CB1 2HS, UK)

The following variables were computed from data provided by Cambridge Econometrics. Growth rates are approximated by logarithmic differences.

labor productivity growth – annual growth rate of value added per employee.

employment growth – annual growth rate of total employment.

investment share – the share of investment in gross value added

initial-year labor productivity – the natural logarithm of gross value added per employee lagged one year

economic growth spillover from first order neighbors – the average growth rate of valued added per employee in regions bordering the one under consideration (first order neighbors).

economic growth spillover from first and second order neighbors – the average growth rate of valued added per employee for first order neighbors and the regions bordering the first order neighbors (second order neighbors.

growth of industrial specialization – the annual growth rate in a region's Herfindahl Index. The Herfindahl Index is measured by sum of the squares of gross value added shares of the 9 sectors in total regional gross value added. It is used to compare the change in degree of sectoral concentration over time.

growth of industrial mix – the annual growth rate of a region's sectoral mix. The sectoral mix = $\{\Sigma_{j=1}^{9} (GVA_{r\,j} / GVA_r) * (GVA_{EU\,j} / EMP_{EU\,j})\}$ / $\{\Sigma_{j=1}^{9} (GVA_{EU\,j} / GVA_{EU}) * (GVA_{EU\,j} / EMP_{EU\,j})\}$ where GVA is gross value added, EMP is total employment, the r subscripts identifies regions, the j subscript identifies sector, the EU subscript identifies the aggregate of the 57 in the study. It represents the extent to which a region has gross value added per employee over or below the European average due to its industrial composition. The variable was suggested by Partridge and Rickman (1999).

Eurostat

Research and Development employee data are from the Eurostat Region database. The availability of this data constrained our study to 57 Nuts 2 regions in France (21 regions), Italy (19 regions) and Spain (17 regions). One such region from Italy, one from Spain, and five from France were excluded because of missing R&D data. R&D employees per regional employee were computed by combining this data from the Cambridge Econometrics data.

private sector R&D intensity – The natural logarithm of personnel employed in business sector research and development activities per 100 000 total employees in the region. Government sector R&D is analogous.

private sector R&D spillover: two-way: distance weighted – The natural logarithm of R&D personnel per 100 000 total employees in all other regions divided by distance from the region in question is aggregated. The overall aggregation of the distance weights is equalized to one, so that the interaction of distance weight elements with the observations simply affects the variation of the relevant variable rather than its mean value. The geographic distance between regions is measured as a straight line on the map, which defines the centers of European regions (NUTS2), as follows. The distance between urban centers of regions within a national border is measured directly. However, the portion of the distance crossing a national border is doubled. The portion of the distance crossing a second national border is tripled. It assumes that the national borders represent cultural, linguistic, ethnic, institutional, social, and national disparities which are much more diverse across nations than across regions within a nation, so they can be significant obstacles to formal or informal human interactions. Moreover, considering the regions made up an island or a group of islands the portion of the distance corresponding to over sea is doubled. This implies that formal or informal communication with this type of isolated regions is more costly and harder relative to others.

private sector R&D spillover: two-way: first and second order neighbors – the average of the natural logarithm of R&D personnel per employee over all first and second order neighbors. See economic growth spillover for neighbor definitions.

private sector R&D spillover: gap: distance weighted – to compute this variable for region r we first subtract the R&D intensity in r from each other region s. All negative values are assigned the value 0. Each positive value is divided by distance. Then these values are aggregated. As above, the overall aggregation of the distance weights is equalized to one.

private sector R&D spillover: gap: with first and second order neighbors – to compute this variable for region r we first subtract the R&D intensity in r from each neighbor s. All negative values are assigned the value 0. Each positive value is summed and divided by the number of neighbor regions that have a positive value.

OECD

human capital growth: To compute this variable regional enrollment in higher education is computed by allocating national enrollment in higher education from the OECD Education Database to the regions based on the regional proportion of gross national value added. The regional enrollment is divided by total employment to obtain human capital accumulation per unit of labor. The annual growth rate of this variable is our proxy for human capital growth.

APPENDIX 10A.2   DESCRIPTIVE STATISTICS

Table 10A.1

Variables	Mean	Std. Dev.	Min.	Max.
labor productivity growth	0.0181	0.0256	−0.0902	0.1064
employment growth	0.0039	0.0245	−0.1224	0.0959
human capital growth	0.0417	0.04012	−0.0901	0.1603
investment share	0.2303	0.0280	0.1471	0.2817
initial-year labor productivity	10.3893	0.1848	9.7262	10.8757
growth of industrial specialization	0.0029	0.0237	−0.1029	0.0709
growth of industrial mix	−0.0007	0.0298	−0.1492	0.1425
private sector R&D intensity	7.4187	1.3769	2.0852	9.8110
private sector R&D spillover: gap: distance weighted	0.7362	0.8648	0	5.1591
private sector R&D spillover: gap: with first order neighbors	0.7362	0.9050	0	5.1382
private sector R&D spillover: gap with first and second order neighbors	0.7362	0.8893	0	5.0464

Table 10A.1 (cont.)

Variables	Mean	Std. Dev.	Min.	Max.
private sector R&D spillover: two way: distance weighted	7.4187	1.1195	4.2145	9.6163
private sector R&D spillover: two way: first order neighbors	7.6864	4.0324	0	17.0511
private sector R&D spillover: two way: first and second order neighbors	7.7231	3.3428	0	14.4315
economic growth spillover from first order neighbors	0.0180	0.0177	−0.0902	0.1064
economic growth spillover from first and second order neighbors	0.0182	0.0133	−0.0387	0.0591

Note: Total number of observations, N = 570, consist of 57 cross-section units over 10 years of time-series observations between 1985 and 1995.

11. Foreign Direct Investment and Learning Regions in Central and Eastern Europe

Marina van Geenhuizen and Peter Nijkamp

11.1 SETTING THE SCENE

In Central and Eastern Europe investment from abroad is often seen as a catalyst for socio-economic improvement and as an important source of alternative finance for the transformation of former state-owned enterprises, the latter in the absence of large domestic savings and limited access to international capital markets (cf. Svetlicic and Rojec, 1994; Meyer, 1995). In addition, foreign direct investment (FDI) is increasingly considered to be a way of knowledge transfer to enhance the introduction of innovative products, new production processes, and management skills (for example Bell, 1997), but addressing the acquisition of western technology by firms in Central and Eastern Europe as a policy issue at its own right is relatively new. This is particularly true for the regional level and regional policies (for example van Geenhuizen, 2001).

FDI in transition economies has been extensively analysed in the literature with regard to size of flows, number of projects, location-specific barriers and geographical distribution (for example Dunning, 1993; Meyer, 1995; van Geenhuizen and Nijkamp, 1996, 1998). There is now an increased recognition of the need for research on the way regional economies may benefit from investment impacts – through active learning and spillover effects – and become more competitive (for example Svetlicic and Rojec, 1994; Hooley et al., 1996; OECD, 1996a; Pavlínek and Smith, 1998; Smith and Ferenciková, 1998; Radosevic, 1999, van Beers, 2003; Nijkamp et al., 2003). Thus, the key questions are not only concerned with changes in size of investment flows but also with motivations of foreign investors to operate a subsidiary (joint venture) in Central and Eastern Europe, the extent to which the investments create local forward and backward linkages and knowledge transfer to domestic firms, and integrate endogenous knowledge.

Our approach in exploring impacts of FDI on the innovative level of regional economies is the one of learning regions (for example Morgan, 1997; Morgan and Nauwelaers, 1999) or the 'active space' approach (van Geenhuizen and Ratti, 2001). One reason is the strong emphasis in this approach on institutional conditions for learning and innovation, like networks of supportive organisations such as universities, chambers of commerce, R&D institutes and intermediary organisations, and sets of incentives and support. In addition, localised learning mechanisms and learning processes are seen as essential for innovation, underpinned by a mutual understanding and confidence among major stakeholders on problems shared in the regional economy. It is this institutional 'seedbed' that needs to be present to benefit from potential knowledge spillovers from FDI in the regional economy.

The structure of the chapter is as follows. First, in Section 11.2 the size of FDI flow and FDI stock is investigated for each country, with a special focus on the countries that joined the EU in 2004. Attention is also paid to differences in investment on the regional level. Then in Section 11.3 the focus of analysis shifts to factors underlying differences in attraction between countries, particularly their stage of transition and institutional proximity to the EU. In Section 11.4 we outline entrepreneurial motives behind FDI and the broader corporate strategies involved, using various original case studies and studies from the literature. The more general conditions for technology acquisition, learning and innovation, as set by the national systems of innovation, are the next subject we discuss in Section 11.5. Against this background, entrepreneurial motives and strategies of foreign investors are linked to potentials for regional embeddedness of foreign subsidiaries and concomitant knowledge spillovers in the regional economy in Section 11.6. We conclude the chapter with some recommendations for policy action and future research.

11.2   THE GEOGRAPHY OF FDI

There is quite some differentiation in FDI inflow at the country level. With an inflow of almost 15 billion US$ over the past two years FDI is largest in the Czech Republic. Poland holds the second position (almost 10 billion US$), with Slovakia and Russia as third and fourth (between 4 and 5 billion US$) (Table 11.1). The rank order of countries in terms of FDI stock – broadly seen as accumulated flow in the past years – may be slightly different, due to, for example, differences in year of take-off of FDI and in reaching a complete privatisation. For example, Hungary has been the leading recipient country since the lifting of the iron curtain in 1989, but lost this position towards the end of the 1990s due to near completion of the privatisation. In terms of FDI stock in 2002 we find Poland in first place, followed by the Czech Republic, Hungary and Russia. FDI stock in Central and Eastern Europe (CEEC) is heavily concentrated in countries adjacent to Western Europe, that is approximately 80 percent in total. This was true in 1996 (van Geenhuizen, 2001) and remains true in 2002 (see also Resmini and Traistaru, 2003). Poland (29.3 percent), the Czech Republic (25.0 percent), and Hungary (15.9 percent) are largely responsible for this pattern.

Table 11.1 FDI in Central and Eastern Europe (CEEC) and parts of CIS

Country	Inflow *		FDI stock 2002 *	FDI stock 2002 as share in GDP (%)
	2001	2002		
Albania	207	213	988	21.0
Bulgaria	813	479	3 889	24.0
Croatia	1 561	981	6 029	28.4
Czech Rep.	5 639	9 319	38 450	54.8
Estonia	542	307	4 226	65.9
Hungary	2 440	854	24 416	38.2
Latvia	164	396	2 723	32.4
Lithuania	446	732	3 981	31.4
Poland	5 713	4 119	45 150	23.9
Romania	1 157	1 106	8 786	20.5
Slovakia	1 579	4 012	10 225	43.2
Slovenia	503	1 865	5 074	23.1
Total CEEC	*20 764*	*24 383*	*153 937*	
Belarus	96	227	1 602	11.2
Moldova	156	111	717	45.0
Russia	2 469	2 421	22 563	6.5
Ukraine	792	693	5 355	n.a.

Notes: * Million US$. Serbia, Bosnia-Herzogevina, Macedonia, and ex-Soviet republics in Asia excluded.

Source: World Investment Report 2003 (UNCTAD, 2003).

The above-indicated patterns suggest that the first countries to enter the EU in 2004, particularly the larger ones (Poland, Hungary, the Czech Republic and Slovakia), have attracted large amounts of FDI in the past decade. In terms of causality, it remains unknown to what extent this happened just because these countries had already reached advanced stages of transition or because of the attractiveness of future membership of the EU.

If we consider FDI in relative terms, that is as share in gross domestic product (GDP) per country, the picture is different from the one above (Table 11.1). With shares between 65 percent and 40 percent FDI is relatively large for Estonia, the Czech Republic and Slovakia. Remarkably, with a low absolute level of FDI inflow, Moldova also turns out to have a large share of FDI stock in GDP (45 percent). In most economies in Central and Eastern Europe the share of FDI stock in GDP is between 20 percent and 40 percent. Russia, although receiving large amounts of FDI, turns out to be an economy with a small share of FDI in GDP (6.5 percent).

The regional dimension of FDI was often neglected in the first years of the transition because all the attention was attracted to problems of macro-economic stabilisation. Despite a lack of comparable regional data on FDI, there seems sufficient indication for an ongoing trend of reinforcing existing regional disparities. Thus, FDI inflow concentrates in the borderlands with the EU and in the large metropolitan areas (for example Gorzelak, 1996; van Geenhuizen and Nijkamp, 1998; Hardy, 1998; Pavlínek and Smith, 1998; Petrakos, 2000). For example, Warsaw has received 35 percent of all inflow into Poland and Bratislava 60 percent of all inflow into the Slovak Republic. In contrast, many regions – often in the eastern parts – have received limited FDI or none. However, this process is not uniform across economic sectors and over time (Altomonte and Resmini, 2002). This can be illustrated with the car industry in Poland facing investments in almost all parts of the country.

11.3   FACTORS UNDERLYING AGGREGATE FDI PATTERNS

The spatial patterns of FDI partly reflect the influence of the state of transition, that is progress made in the development of a new system for the generation and allocation of resources, with private production and well-functioning markets as corner-stones (Svetlicic and Rojec, 1994; Meyer, 1995; Gorzelak, 1996; Lankes and Venables, 1997; van Geenhuizen, 2001). A major component of this transition is the change and creation of institutions, including enterprises and legal structures (EBRD, 1996).

In considering the influence of the stage of transition on FDI patterns, it is now increasingly realised that transition is *not a linear* process, but a development with ups and downs, spurts and stops, regarding the different dimensions. For example, Bulgaria and Romania suffered serious macro-economic setbacks in 1997, but the crises triggered the emergence of new governments that have begun to implement bold programs of stabilisation and structural reform (EBRD, 1997). In addition, transition does not follow one particular trajectory, but various different ones, dependent upon the interplay of generic macro-economic trends and local specificity. It is, therefore, difficult to make generalisations valid for the entire area of Central and Eastern Europe.

Towards the end of the 1990s the stage of transition is clearly different between countries according to indicators concerning enterprises, markets, financial institutions and the legal system, but all have moved away from the initial stage in which primary emphasis was placed on reforms aimed at establishing markets and private ownership (Table 11.2). The more advanced stages are observed in the Czech Republic, Hungary, Poland, Slovakia and Slovenia, as well as the Baltic States (Estonia, Latvia and Lithuania). In this grouping Croatia is a borderline case. Countries in an advanced stage have pursued comprehensive market-oriented reform since the late 1980s or early 1990s. Gross Domestic Product (GDP) is generated mainly from the private sector, witness a share of 65 percent to 75 percent in most cases. The most extensive privatisation programme has been implemented in the Czech Republic, Estonia and Hungary (EBRD, 1996). Having privatised most of their manufacturing enterprises, the two latter countries are now focusing on privatisation in the banking sector, infrastructure, and public utilities. In Latvia, Poland, Croatia, and Slovenia large-scale privatisation has lagged somewhat behind other areas of reform, although progress has been made now in all four countries. Poland's long-delayed mass privatisation programme is now in implementation for a few years.

The countries at less advanced stages of transition include Albania, Belarus, Bulgaria, Romania, Moldova, Russia and Ukraine (Table 11.2). They have all moved decisively to principles of market competition, but they are less advanced in enterprise restructuring (indicator C) and reform of financial institutions (particularly indicator G). In 1997, Bulgaria and Romania restarted once lagging mass privatisation schemes, as well as direct sales of large enterprises. The private sector share in most of the countries listed below falls between 45 and 60 percent of GDP.

Note that Russia holds a unique position, being alone for its sheer size. Problems of transition are different here from those in Central and Eastern Europe because private trade was eliminated a quarter of a century earlier, meaning that industrialisation took place almost from the beginning under the communist command economy, causing the absence of any roots (experience) in private ownership in manufacturing at the beginning of the transformation. Russia started the implementation of a reform scheme in 1992, involving price and trade liberalisation, small-scale privatisation and unification of the exchange rate, however, fiscal and credit policies remained modest in their impact, and monetary policy was not able to stabilise the exchange rate of the rouble for a number of years.

Table 11.2 Progress in transition in Central and Eastern Europe and parts of CIS based on selected indicators (1997)

Country	Private Sector GDP (%)	Enterprises			Markets (trade)			Financial		
		A	B	C	D	E	F	G	H	I
Albania	75	2	4	2	3	4	2	2	2–	2
Bulgaria	50	3	3	2+	3	4	2	3–	2	3
Croatia	55	3	4+	3–	3	4	2	3–	2+	4
Czech Rep.	75	4	4+	3	3	4+	3	3	3	4
Estonia	70	4	4+	3	3	4	3–	3+	3	4
Hungary	75	4	4+	3	3+	4+	3	4	3	4
Latvia	60	3	4	3–	3	4	3–	3	2+	3
Lithuania	70	3	4	3–	3	4	2+	3	2+	3
Poland	65	3+	4	3	3	4+	3	3	3+	4
Romania	60	3–	3	2	3	4	2	3–	2	3
Slovakia	75	4	4+	3–	3	4	3	3–	2+	3
Slovenia	50	3+	4+	3–	3	4+	2	3	3	3
Belarus	20	1	2	1	3	1	2	1	2	2
Moldova	45	3	3	2	3	4	2	2	2	2
Russia	70	3+	4	2	3	4	2+	2+	3	3
Ukraine	50	2+	3	2	3	3	2	2	2	2

Notes:
Serbia, Bosnia-Herzogevina and Macedonia, and ex-Soviet republics in Asia excluded. Indicators A–I stand for: A = large-scale privatisation; B = small-scale privatisation; C = enterprise restructuring; D = price liberalisation; E = trade and foreign exchange system; F = competition policy; G = banking reform and interest rate liberalisation; H = securities markets and non-bank financial institutions; I = extensiveness and effectiveness of pledge law, bankruptcy and company law. Ratings from 1 to 4+ (with 4+ for most advanced situations).

Source: van Geenhuizen, 2001 (adapted from EBRD, 1997).

Aside from the stage of transition, FDI at the country level also reflects the influence of geographical and cultural proximity to major investing countries, the latter for example based on political ties in history and more recent flows of tourism. In the EU, Germany is by far the largest source of investment while showing a large preference for investing in countries like Hungary, Poland and the Czech Republic, based on short distances and a certain cultural similarity. The same holds for Austria, with important investments in adjacent Hungary, Czech Republic, Slovakia and Slovenia (Alzinger and Winklhofer, 1998; Meyer, 1995; van Geenhuizen and Nijkamp, 1998). Today, this situation has changed somewhat. Already for some years,

Germany has been putting strong efforts into reunification and internal economic problems, at the same time that an important investing country has entered the field, that is the Republic of Korea. In 1996, for example, Korea became the largest investor in Poland, for example with planned investments by Daewoo of 1.1 billion US$.

In the remaining section we try to estimate 'distance impacts' on the inflow of FDI, including both institutional distance (based on the stage of transition) and geographical and cultural distance. In a 'quasi-experimental approach' we compare pairs of recipient countries which are roughly similar in size of the domestic economy, but different in distance. The countries facing a relatively small distance are the ones identified above as the most advanced in transition, that is the Czech Republic, Hungary, Poland, Slovakia, Slovenia, the three Baltic States and Croatia as a border case. These are without exception also countries at close geographical and cultural distance from the EU. We distinguish between two periods, that is 1989–1995 and 1996–2002, since we think that countries that were most advanced in transition and highly attractive for FDI in earlier years might show signs of a completed privatisation later on.

The results based on FDI stocks using 14 pairs of countries are given in Table 11.3. The countries facing a large institutional distance are Bulgaria, Belarus, Romania, Ukraine, Moldova and Albania. The table shows a pair-wise comparison of the absolute size of FDI stocks of similar countries – in terms of size of the economy – and the concomitant reduction levels in FDI. A reduction level of 10.1 percent, for example, means a diminishing influence of institutional distance on cumulative FDI to 10.1 percent. Of course, this is a rough estimate because some more factors may influence the size of FDI flow to a country, like individual policies of recipient countries to attract FDI and the political atmosphere, causing some 'noise' in the outcomes.

We observe a reduction in all cases but there is a large differentiation ranging from a huge reduction (to a level of 0.4 and 0.7 percent) caused by almost absence of FDI to a reduction to approximately half (57.1 percent).. In the first years, reduction is most dramatic for Belarus and Bulgaria, that is a level lower than 10 percent. It is least dramatic in the case of Albania, that is a reduction to a level between 60 percent and 30 percent in most pair-wise comparisons.

If we consider developments over time, various differences become clear. Some countries improve their performance, that is Bulgaria and Belarus, both starting from a very modest level, and Romania. Others, however, show a decreasing performance over time in various comparisons, that is Moldova and Albania. To conclude, our data illustrates a large diminishing influence of institutional distance on the amount of FDI, be it that this impact is differentiated between countries and time periods.

Table 11.3 Reduction in FDI stocks (inwards)

Pairs of countries	1995 FDI stocks (million US$)	Reduction level %	2002 FDI stocks (million US$)	Reduction level %
Czech Rep.–Bulgaria	7 350 – 446	6.1	38 450 – 3 889	10.1
Czech Rep.–Belarus	7 350 – 50	0.7	38 450 – 1 602	4.2
Hungary–Bulgaria	11 919 – 446	3.7	24 416 – 3 889	15.9
Hungary–Belarus	11 919 – 50	0.4	24 416 – 1 602	6.6
Poland–Romania	7 843 – 821	10.5	45 150 – 8 786	19.5
Poland–Ukraine	7 843 – 910	11.6	45 150 – 5 355	11.9
Lithuania–Moldova	352 – 93	26.4	3 981 – 717	18.0
Slovakia–Moldova	810 – 93	11.5	10 225 – 717	7.0
Latvia–Moldova	615 – 93	15.1	2 723 – 717	26.3
Lithuania–Albania	352 – 201	57.1	3 981 – 988	24.8
Slovenia–Albania	1 763 – 201	11.4	5 074 – 988	19.5
Latvia–Albania	615 – 201	32.7	2 723 – 988	36.3
Croatia–Albania	478 – 201	42.1	6 029 – 988	16.4
Croatia–Moldova	478 – 93	19.5	6 029 – 717	11.9

Source: Adapted from UNCTAD World Investment Report 2003.

11.4 FOREIGN INVESTORS AND THEIR STRATEGIES

Foreign direct investment is the transfer by a firm of capital (and other resources) into a business venture abroad, aimed at acquiring control of the venture. Although motivation for FDI in transition economies tends to be mixed, four broad types of FDI can be distinguished according to the dominant motive:

- efficiency or cost-based, aimed at cheap inputs, like low wages, and labour market flexibility;
- market-driven, aimed at the penetration of new markets;
- resource-based, aimed at the exploitation of (cheap) natural resources;
- knowledge-based, aimed at the use of specialist (cheap) knowledge.

To date, market-driven motives and cost-based motives dominate inward FDI in Central and Eastern Europe (EBRD, 1994; Welfens and Jasinski, 1994; Meyer, 1995; Radosevic, 1997). Some authors have seen a gradual increase in the importance of cost-based FDI connected with declining standards of living and consumption in particular countries, and a slower market growth than expected. Accordingly, an increasing factor in investment decisions is access to the relatively low-wage but often medium-skill workforce (for example, Smith and Ferencikova, 1998). This seems particularly true for the current downturn of the global economy.

We can illustrate the above motives using a few case studies from the Netherlands in the mechatronics sector (combined metal, electronics, optics, and so on) in the past years (Table 11.4). In most cases, the major motives are cost-based, namely low wages; sometimes this is related to a high level of skills.

Market motives in this particular manufacturing branch are of minor importance. The latter situation means a danger to the investments in CEEC if another development takes place, that is a gradual increase in wage levels. China is emerging as an attractive alternative with a booming market and significantly lower wages. The only thing that hampers a shift of investments to China to date is lack of skills specific for the sector.

The case studies also indicate that if the investment is done by an original equipment manufacturer (OEM) and the entire product is produced abroad, there is a large chance that local outsourcing takes place and that training by the investor is given to both the main factory and local suppliers. This phenomenon touches upon the regional embeddedness issue to be discussed in Section 11.6. The type of subsidiaries related to the dominant motives, the broader strategic context of FDI decisions and the consequences for learning regions are discussed in the remaining part of this section.

A useful typology of subsidiaries is given by Radosevic (1997) in which investment motives are combined with the technological deepening and type of integration of the factory into the (global) corporate network. Accordingly, a distinction can be made between offshore factories, sourcing factories, focused factories, trading companies, knowledge-based factories, and resource-based factories (extractor and processor type).

Table 11.4 FDI by Dutch mechatronics companies

Case studies	Year, country, (city)	(1) Motives (2) Type of manufacturing (3) Additional comments
Company 1 (main supplier)	1992, Poland	(1) Low salaries. (2) Manufacturing of components. (3) Closed-down in 2002 due to low efficiency and increasing salaries. Already investment in China.
Company 2 (OEM)	1995, Czech Rep. (Brno)	(1) Low salaries, skilled labour force, and flexibility in labour market. (2) Manufacturing of entire product (microscopes).
Company 3 (main supplier)	1993, Czech Rep. (Brno)	(1) Low salaries and skilled labour force. (2) Manufacturing of components.
Company 4 (main supplier)	1997, Czech Rep. (near Brno)	(1) Low salaries. (2) Manufacturing of components.
Company 5 (main supplier)	1993, Poland (Polmor)	(1) Low salaries. (2) Manufacturing of components. (3) Serious plans to invest in China.

Source: Original case studies by the authors.

The most 'primitive' cost-driven FDI is concerned with offshore factories, common in sectors like the clothing industry and electronics. A concentration of this type can be found in the western Czech Republic, on the border with Germany. The firms are export processing and vertically integrated into German subcontracting networks, based upon low-wage and low-skill labour. These investments compare with the US–Mexico maquiliadora type (Pavlínek and Smith, 1998). One step higher on the technology dimension are sourcing factories, very common in the automotive industry and also – as evident from our case studies – in the mechatronics sector. With regard to the automotive industry, General Motors in Hungary is an example within a broader strategy of the mother company to develop lower-cost sources for the supply of components. The same holds for the Daewoo Electronics operation in Poland. Furthermore, there is now an increasing number of focused factories, with VW-Skoda in the Czech Republic, Suzuki Magyar in Hungary and the Polish Fiat factory as examples (Radosevic, 1997). The sourcing here includes a broad range of components or entire products, a situation in which foreign investment may also be attracted by local suppliers. Focused factories are integrated at a relatively high level in global corporate networks.

Regarding market-driven motives, trading companies are certainly the most common type. In practice, trading companies are often coupled with assembly plants to avoid high tariff barriers. Most market-based investments aim at capturing additional new markets in Central and Eastern Europe but there are various examples in which foreign investors have shut down the factories here to stop competition from the latter in Western European markets, eventually only leaving a trade organisation (for example Kiss, 1995; Bernard, 1996; Grayson and Bodily, 1996).

Knowledge-driven investments are still rare, but there are some examples in Russia linked with the military sector working through subcontracting and joint ventures (such as in aerospace and aviation) and there are partly skills-driven investments, like in Slovakia, based on a traditionally high skill level in the weapons industry. Resource-based investments are more common, most of them being of the extractors type. This type is found in Russia with its large reserves of oil and natural gas, and limited processing facilities, and also in Estonia with its vast amount of wood.

To date, it is not possible to assess the relative importance of the above types of foreign subsidiaries in transition economies. In investment studies a micro-perspective on subsidiaries has seldom been used in a systematic and comparative way, and this is the reason why the current evidence is still fragmentary. Moreover, this importance also differs per manufacturing sector, such as between the food industry and electronics industry. The preliminary evidence suggests limited prospects for local learning and innovation, connected with offshore factories, sourcing factories, trading companies and resource based-factories, all without any (autonomous) R&D activity (Rojec, 1994; Bernard, 1996; Radosevic, 1997; Smith and Ferenciková, 1998). Note that there are of course clearly positive aspects on a number of the above investments, that is the introduction of new technology and equipment critical for getting specific production from the ground – such as state-of-the-art equipment at green field oil and gas attraction sites by Shell in Russia (Sharp and Barz, 1996) – and the upgrading of existing facilities to modern best practice standards. In the latter cases the investors provide know-how, manufacturing facilities, tools, components and licences for plant reconstruction, and introduce new corporate and management cultures. In addition, as previously indicated, there is a recent growth of focused factories, mainly in the automotive industry (Radosevic, 1997). Through their larger scope of activities and stronger integration in the global industry, these factories provide relatively good potentials for local dynamic learning both on-site and in local supply networks.

Aside from the type of subsidiary, ownership relations may play a role in learning and enhancing the innovative level of domestic factories. In general, joint ventures offer good opportunities for domestic partners to acquire western technology and derive new skills and management practices; however, there have been some important gradual take-overs of ownership shares of joint ventures by the foreign investor – such as in Slovakia – thereby causing an increased isolation of the joint venture from its domestic partner (Smith and Ferenciková, 1998).

The picture indicated above is certainly not optimistic but it needs to be stressed that it is based on some snapshots. In the medium term, the subsidiaries may face a stronger technological deepening and integration at higher levels, while increasing on-site R&D activity. We now move our attention to the broader context in which important conditions are set for learning and innovation: the national innovation system.

11.5   SYSTEMS OF INNOVATION

In western economies, innovation is a process taking place in companies and between companies in networks, such as with suppliers, customers, and with universities and other knowledge institutes (Lundvall, 1995; OECD, 1996b). In this context, innovation is primarily an interactive and socially embedded process, including both interpersonal relationships dominated by informal communication and formal relationships using codified procedures and scientific language (for example Storper, 1996).

The current systems of innovation in Central and Eastern Europe are still influenced by the features of the communist past (Dyker and Perrin, 1997). First, there were weak links between research institutes and companies, and concomitantly between research and the market. For example, in the former Soviet Union, science and technology were traditionally carried out in branch research institutes, being extensions of the appropriate ministries. These institutes responded to pressures from the hierarchy and were relatively isolated from the users of their findings (Egorov, 1996). In addition, in many countries the Academy system made a large contribution to basic and applied research, similarly in relative isolation from companies causing an almost absence of the essential notion of design (Dyker and Perrin, 1997). By contrast, in western economies large user-firms play a major role in interactively developing and modifying production equipment, as does the network of small specialised suppliers. Secondly, in the communist past the scarce links between research institutes and companies were concerned with different concepts of technological progress compared to the Schumpeterian definition of innovation (cf. Egorov, 1996; Imre and Varszegi, 1996). Progress used to be defined in terms of either increase of unit capacities of existing equipment or re-invention (imitation) of western consumer goods. A third important feature at that time was the absence of notions of interactive technology transfer and innovation processes. Thus, the acquisition of new technology was seen as a one-way process while it was overlooked that the success in acquisition of new technology critically depends on the capacity of the recipient firm to develop its own technology (for example Bell, 1997).

Today, one of the important potential players in future innovation networks, that is the old R&D institutes, is facing a process of deep restructuring. There is a shift from complex, technology-led projects towards simpler, market-oriented R&D and services like testing, quality control and certification (Radosevic, 1995; Egorov, 1996). Thus, R&D institutes develop towards non-R&D and service organisations through privatisation and establishment of new companies (spin-off), or they undertake internal restructuring and attempt to create new relationships with R&D in companies, independent institutes and universities. However, each direction seems to be fraught with difficulties. There is a danger that spin-off companies are launched from aims to compensate for funding shortfalls rather than from planning strategies including a careful selection of competitive products and markets (for example Oakey et al., 1996). Furthermore, an impediment to the transformation of R&D institutes seems to be the brain drain. Low wages and lack of orders (budget cuts) have caused an outflow of research workers to other sectors. More importantly, there is a hidden brain drain involving a combination of formal maintenance of the workplace in a scientific institute and the spending of most working time by R&D workers on alternative activities. Developments like these are likely to erode the base of R&D institutes in some countries.

Accordingly, there is a need for R&D to be carried out by industry or by institutes actively connected with industry. With the collapse of many large industrial conglomerates and the absence of typical western institutions in the public and private sector, attention in policy is increasingly drawn to the development of small and medium-sized enterprises (SMEs) (for example EBRD, 1995; Bernard, 1996; OECD, 1996a). SMEs are seen as important vehicles to introduce innovation and competition in local markets and to provide demonstration effects. They also allow flexibility in uncertain environments and provide re-employment opportunities for displaced employees from the state sector (OECD, 1996a). The numbers of SMEs are now rapidly increasing in most transition economies but there seems to be an emphasis on short-term (temporary) business requiring small capital investment, such as in trade and service activities.

The above circumstances indicate that regional production systems based on innovative products from endogenous forces could develop only in a limited number of cases. Examples of such rare cases are the car industry and weapons industry in former Czechoslovakia. Moreover, the critical institutional conditions for localised learning as identified in specific regions in Western Europe and North America (for example Morgan, 1997) could not develop under communist rule. The self-organisation of regional communities and the development of initiatives aimed at societal progress (different from the official party system) were often discouraged. Vertical structures or fragmentation prohibited the development of horizontal co-operation that allows for open and interactive learning in a frame of planning based on responsibility of local actors and based on flexibility. Although major changes have occurred, it is reasonable to assume that the institutional layer that supports the new developments is still relatively thin. It can be concluded that the creation of conditions that enhance a learning region development is still littered with stumbling blocks.

11.6   REGIONAL EMBEDDEDNESS

Recently, the attention in research has shifted to looking at the regional impact of FDI in terms of market and supplier links, and to analysis of causes of uneven embeddedness (Grabher, 1997; Radosevic, 1997; Hardy, 1998; Pavlínek and Smith, 1998; Smith and Ferenciková, 1998; van Geenhuizen, 2001). The number of case studies dealing with impacts of FDI in terms of regional linkages is now rapidly increasing. Results from these studies point to both positive and negative developments (Kiss, 1995; Sharp and Barz, 1996; Pavlínek and Smith, 1998). Negative developments include the crowding out of traditional linkages with local suppliers of inputs (raw material, ingredients, components), such as found in parts of the Hungarian food industry, with these inputs being replaced by imports (Kiss, 1995).

Positive developments occur if foreign investors act as organisers of a local supply base, make use of knowledge and skills and undertake action to bring these skills to a higher level. For example, FEI, a company (US, NL) producing microscopes in Brno (Czech Republic) works with local suppliers, while providing training to further improve the local skills. On a larger scale, VW-Skoda in and around Mlada Boleslav (Czech Republic) has taken an active role in the establishment of its suppliers' network leading to a majority of VW-Skoda's purchases in the country. Particularly, supply integration –

requiring the suppliers to join the assembly line to install the parts themselves – creates opportunities to increase local learning and innovation. In contrast, the situation in the Slovak VW-Skoda investment (Bratislava) is completely different. Local supplier relationships are relatively few here, causing a factory that is almost entirely disconnected from its regional environment (Pavlínek and Smith, 1998). Similar issues currently play in Trnava close by the Skoda-VW factory, based on large investments by French Peugeot Citroen (*NRC-Handelsblad*, September 23, 2003). Local knowledge and skills are available here due to earlier production facility of ambulances in the city. It remains however, to be seen whether local supplier linkages will be developed based on existing networks, or components will be imported from France or produced locally in Slovakia by French suppliers that have followed their major client.

The difference in embeddedness between the VW-Skoda factory in the Czech Republic and the one in Slovakia can be explained as follows. First of all, the inherited production system was different. The Skoda factory in the Czech Republic had a tradition of skills and independent innovation with an established network of suppliers. In contrast, the Skoda factory in Slovakia was a latecomer and became structured as a branch plant in the old system with limited autonomous production and R&D. Accordingly, the foreign investor has simply built upon an existing structure. Secondly, the existing supply structure matched with the investor's strategy, such as Just-in-Time production schemes. It appears that regional supply structures are usually not created anew by foreign investors whereas existing supply structures are truncated if investors cannot see advantages in using them. In the latter case, regional supply structures are replaced by internationalised systems of supply integration, leading to only modest opportunities for local learning and innovation (Pavlínek and Smith, 1998).

In conclusion, the analysis has revealed two conditions under which a high regional embeddedness develops, that is an existing and innovative supply system and a sufficient match between this system and the specific needs of the investors. Note that circumstances may change in a favourable or unfavourable direction with regard to knowledge spillovers in the region (Pavlínek and Smith, 1998).

11.7 CONCLUDING REMARKS

The analysis of FDI flow into Central and Eastern European countries presented in this study has produced the following results. The three largest countries, EU accession countries in 2004, have attracted the majority of FDI since 1989, that is Poland, the Czech Republic and Hungary. Presently, the

Czech Republic attracts the largest amounts of FDI, with Poland in second position; however, such patterns are subject to change over time. One factor is the near completion of privatisation in particular neighbouring countries (currently in Hungary), another factor is competition from alternative attractive countries in the world. Currently, China is emerging as such an attractive country, driven by large market opportunities and relatively low wages compared with Central and Eastern Europe. Whereas institutional (and geographical) distance to the EU plays a role in the differentiation in FDI flows across Central and Eastern Europe, this factor is apparently not important any more in the case of China.

In this study we also attempted to identify conditions favouring knowledge spillovers from FDI in the regional economies of Central and Eastern Europe. Our preliminary results indicate that to date FDI has a modest impact on the rise of such spillovers and connected processes of learning and innovation. Most investments to date seem to be in offshore factories, sourcing factories and trading companies, all facing low levels of independent technology development and weak linkages in the regional economy. Thus, the acquisition of western knowledge and regional absorption of this knowledge are not automatic by-products of FDI, thereby underlining the need for policy action. Policy action can follow two lines. The first line would focus on a general improvement of conditions to benefit from newly acquired knowledge, whereas the second line would include various targeted policies to attract innovative investments that advance a high level of knowledge spillovers in the regional economy.

We observe important policy tasks for the national governments as follows. In order to benefit from newly acquired knowledge, there is a pressing need to continue to foster processes of domestic knowledge transfer and absorption, such as by establishing liaison offices at higher educational institutes and universities, and technology centres focusing on generic technologies (such as micro-electronics) (for example Imre and Varszegi, 1996). Such centres have been established recently in various countries, partially with the assistance of EU programmes. Attention needs to be given to the operation of these centres and the development of active linkages with regional and national learning networks. In addition, a supporting policy needs to be developed towards R&D institutions in their transformation towards active players in learning networks. An equally important but more difficult task is to train domestic firms in how to innovate and generate new knowledge, because acquisition and absorption of external knowledge is very much dependent on the knowledge level that is available. This covers the entire spectrum of learning mechanisms, from formal R&D to learning-by-doing using tacit knowledge. It involves the learning of new routines but also a further de-learning of traditional routines. In addition, policy attention is necessary to better satisfy specific corporate needs following from the more risky nature of innovative activities. For example, it is important to establish a safe system of intellectual property rights (such as patent protection), a condition that matters in the pharmaceutical and advanced chemicals industry (Sharp and Barz, 1996). Finally, we address the use of generic tools to attract specific innovative industry. For example, the foreign investment agency Czechinvest attempts to attract innovative investments by offering incentives. So far, few national policies are selective in attempting to attract innovative activities.

There are three policy ingredients to be proposed to *regional* governments regarding the attraction of FDI to foster innovative supply structures in the regions. A first policy ingredient would be the improvement of the skills of existing suppliers to satisfy the requirements of multinationals. This is mainly concerned with skills at the workplace level (western best practice) and management skills. A second but more difficult component would be to advance regional self-organisation and regional entrepreneurial initiatives that can interact with foreign investment projects (van Geenhuizen and Nijkamp, 1999). A good example in this respect is found in the region of Hungarian Székesfehérvár with a combination of a forward-looking local government, entrepreneurial initiatives and a skilled labour force (*Business Central Europe*, June 1998). A third, and again difficult, ingredient would be to pursue specific policy action to ensure that knowledge of foreign companies spills over into the local and wider economy. A regulation policy may prevent the cutting of domestic supply chains, but the way of negotiation may be a better one The previously discussed VW-Skoda investment in the Czech Republic seems to be a rare example in which the state was able to negotiate local content agreements (Pavlínek and Smith, 1998). Note that opportunities for negotiation may increase when existing suppliers are already upgraded close to western standards.

With regard to regional (local) policies the following model may be used if adapted to specific local circumstances: the 'free science park'. This is a combination of financial incentives to attract innovative FDI and a knowledge interaction infrastructure connected with regional universities and/or R&D institutes that support expertise to be commercialised. Currently, various initiatives come close to this model. A careful monitoring of their operation is necessary to learn from their development, particularly to learn which knowledge interaction infrastructure is most productive.

The role of the above policies should, however, not be overestimated because some of them have a long lead-time, particularly the ones concerning institution building and upgrading of skills based on endogenous forces. Furthermore, there is still a lack of insight into the ways important processes work. Therefore, there is a need for solid comparative research to better underpin and monitor policy action.

REFERENCES

Altomonte, C. and L. Resmini (2002), 'Multinational corporations as a catalyst for local industrial development: the case of Poland', *Scienze Regionali* **2**, pp. 29–58.

Alzinger, W. and R. Winklhofer (1998), 'General patterns of Austria's FDI in Central and Eastern Europe and a case study', *Journal of International Relations and Development*, **1**, pp. 65–83.

Beers, C. (2003), *The Role of Foreign Direct Investments on Small Countries' Competitive and Technological Position*, Helsinki: Government Institute for Economic Research.

Bell, M. (1997), 'Technology transfer to transition countries: are there lessons from the experience of the post-war industrializing countries?', in D.A. Dyker (ed.), *The Technology of Transition*, Budapest: Central European University Press, pp. 63–94.

Bernard, K.N. (1996), 'Eastern Europe: a source of additional competition or of new opportunities?', in B. Fynes and S. Ennis (eds), *Competing from the Periphery, Core Issues in International Business*, London: The Dryden Press, pp. 439–74.

Business Central Europe, June 1998.

Dunning, J.H. (1993), 'The prospects for foreign investment in Eastern Europe', in P. Artisien, M. Rojec and M. Svetlicic (eds), *Foreign Investment in Central and Eastern Europe*, New York: St. Martin's Press, pp. 16–34.

Dyker, D.A. and J. Perrin (1997), 'Technology policy and industrial objectives in the context of economic transition', in D.A. Dyker (ed.), *The Technology of Transition*, Budapest: Central European University Press, pp. 3–19.

EBRD (European Bank for Reconstruction and Development) (1994), *Transition Report, Foreign Direct Investment*, London: EBRD.

EBRD (European Bank for Reconstruction and Development) (1995), *Transition Report, Investment and Enterprise Development*, London: EBRD.

EBRD (European Bank for Reconstruction and Development) (1996), *Transition Report, Infrastructure and Savings*, London: EBRD.

EBRD (European Bank for Reconstruction and Development) (1997), *Transition Report, Enterprise Performance and Growth*, London: EBRD.

Egorov, I. (1996), 'Trends in transforming R&D potential in Russia and Ukraine in the early 1990s', *Science and Public Policy*, **23** (4), pp. 202–14.

Geenhuizen, M. van (2001) 'Which role for foreign direct investment? Active space development in Central and Eastern Europe', in M. van Geenhuizen and R. Ratti (eds), *Gaining Advantage from Open Borders. An Active Space Approach to Regional Development*, Avebury (UK): Ashgate, pp. 173–91.

Geenhuizen. M. van, and P. Nijkamp (1996), 'Foreign investment and regional development scenarios in Eastern Europe', *Current Politics and Economics of Europe*, **4**, pp. 1–12.

Geenhuizen, M. van and P. Nijkamp (1998), 'Potentials for East–West integration: the case of foreign direct investment', *Environment and Planning C*, **16**, pp. 105–20.

Geenhuizen, M. van and P. Nijkamp (1999), 'Regional policy beyond 2000: learning as device', *European Spatial Research Policy*, **6** (2), pp. 5–20.

Geenhuizen, M. van and R. Ratti (eds) (2001), *Gaining Advantage from Open Borders. An Active Space Approach to Regional Development*, Avebury (UK): Ashgate.

Gorzelak, G. (1996), *The Regional Dimension of Transformation in Central Europe*, London: Jessica Kingsley.

Grabher, G. (1997), 'Adaptation at the cost of adaptability? Restructuring the Eastern German economy', in G. Grabher and D. Stark (eds), *Restructuring Networks in Postsocialism: Legacies, Linkages and Localities*, Oxford: Oxford University Press, pp. 107–34.

Grayson, L.E. and S.E. Bodily (1996), *Integration into the World Economy: Companies in Transition in the Czech Republic, Slovakia, and Hungary*, Laxenburg: IIASA.

Hardy, J. (1998), 'Cathedrals in the desert? Transnationals, corporate strategy and locality in Wroclaw', *Regional Studies*, **32**, pp. 639–52.

Hooley, G., T. Cox, D. Shipley, J. Fahy, J. Beracs and K. Kolos (1996), 'Foreign direct investment in Hungary: Resource acquisition and domestic competitive advantage', *Journal of International Business Studies*, Fourth Quarter, pp. 683–709.

Imre, J. and G. Varszegi (1996), 'The transformation of science and technology in Hungary', in A. Kuklinsky (ed.), *Production of Knowledge and the Dignity of Science*, Warsaw: EUROREG, pp. 231–42.

Kiss, J. (1995), 'Privatization and foreign capital in the Hungarian food industry', *Eastern European Economics*, **33** (4), pp. 24–37.

Lankes, H.-P. and A.J. Venables (1997), 'Foreign direct investment in economic transition: the changing pattern of investments', *The Economics of Transition*, **5**, pp. 331–47.

Lundvall, B.-A., (ed.) (1995), *National Systems of Innovation. Towards a Theory of Innovation and Interactive Learning*, London: Pinter.

Meyer, K.E. (1995), 'Foreign direct investment in the early years of economic transition: a survey', *Economics of Transition*, **3** (3), pp. 301–20.

Morgan, K. (1997), 'The learning region: institutions, innovation and regional renewal', *Regional Studies*, **31**, pp. 491–503.

Morgan, K. and C. Nauwelaers (eds) (1999), *Regional Innovation Strategies. The Challenge for Less–favoured Regions*, London: The Stationary Office.

Nijkamp, P., L. Resmini and I. Traistaru (2003), 'European integration, regional specialization and location of industrial activity: a survey of theoretical and empirical literature', in I. Traistaru, P. Nijkamp and L. Resmini (eds), *The Emerging Economic Geography in EU Accession Countries*, Avebury (UK): Ashgate, pp. 28–45.

NRC-Handelsblad (2003), 'Trnava smokes the pipe of pere Peugeot', Issue of 23 September 2003.

Oakey, R.P., P.G. Hare and K. Balazs (1996), 'Strategies for the exploitation of intelligence capital: evidence from Hungarian research institutes', *R&D Management*, **26** (1), pp. 67–82.

OECD (1996a), *Small Firms as Foreign Investors: Case Studies from Transition Economies*, Paris: OECD.

OECD (1996b), *Science, Technology and Industry Outlook 1996*, Paris: OECD.

Pavlínek, P. and A. Smith (1998), 'Internationalization and embeddedness in East-Central European transition: the contrasting geographies of inward investment in the Czech and Slovak Republics', *Regional Studies*, **32**, pp. 619–38.

Petrakos, G. (2000) 'The spatial impact of East–West integration in Europe', in G. Petrakos, G. Maier and G. Gorzelak (eds), *Integration and Transition in Europe: The Economic Geography of Interaction*, London: Routledge, pp. 38–68.

Radosevic, S. (1995), 'Science and technology capabilities in economies in transition: effects and prospects', *Economics of Transition*, **3** (4), pp. 459–78.

Radosevic, S. (1997), 'Technology transfer in global competition: the case of economies in transition', in D.A. Dyker (ed.), *The Technology of Transition*, Budapest: Central European University Press, pp. 126–58.

Radosevic, S. (1999), *International Technology Transfer and Catch-up in Economic Development*, Cheltenham, UK and Northampton, MA, USA: Edward Elgar.

Resmini, L. and I. Traistaru (2003), 'Spatial implications of economic integration in EU accession countries', in I. Traistaru, P. Nijkamp and L. Resmini (eds), *The Emerging Economic Geography in EU Accession Countries*, Avebury (UK): Ashgate, pp. 3–27.

Rojec, M. (1994), *Foreign Direct Investment in Slovenia*, Ljubljana: University of Ljubljana.

Sharp, M. and M. Barz (1996), 'Multinational companies and the development and diffusion of new technologies in Eastern and Central Europe and the former Soviet Union', in A. Kuklinsky (ed.), *Production of Knowledge and the Dignity of Science*, Warsaw: EUROREG, pp. 191–207.

Smith, A. and S. Ferenciková (1998), 'Inward investment, regional transformations and uneven development in Eastern and Central Europe', *European Urban and Regional Studies*, **5**, pp. 155–73.

Storper, M. (1996), 'Innovation as collective action: conventions, products and technologies', *Industrial and Corporate Change*, **5** (3), pp. 761–90.

Svetlicic, M. and M. Rojec (1994), 'Foreign direct investment and the transformation of Central European economies', *Management International Review*, **34** (4), pp. 293–312.

UNCTAD (2002, 2003), *World Investment Report*, Geneva.

Welfens, P.J.J. and P. Jasinski (1994), *Privatization and Foreign Direct Investments in Transforming Economies*, Brookfield, CT: Dartmouth.

Index